The Throne And Liberty

Water Is Not What You Believe

The throne has been forged in a device called **KING HYDROGEN WATER DISTILLER.**

It will be on sale soon at:
- airguardhealth.com
- apdminis.com

ISBN: 978-1-965663-10-3

First printing, edition 2025
Orrington Publishing, 7931 S King Dr.
Chicago, IL 60619
www.apdminis.com: info@airguardhealth.com

Introduction

What is an extraterrestrial? Most people think of green aliens or creatures from science fiction. But the truth is more mysterious than that. NASA defines "extraterrestrial" as anything that exists outside Earth or its atmosphere. Alien life might exist as basic molecular structures or evolve into intricate conscious energy entities. The term "alien" evokes images that defy daily familiarity and common experience. Consider the paradox where water, the substance you ingest and bathe in which permeates every cell in your body, stands as the most alien entity in your existence.

The National Aeronautics and Space Administration has verified the existence of an enormous water cloud situated near the black hole designated APM 08279+5255. An enormous water vapor cloud exists that could fill Earth's oceans to capacity 18 billion times. It floats freely in space, not attached to any planet. This means water does not need gravity to exist. It doesn't need Earth to form. It was never ours. And yet, we treat it like it's just a drink. We see it as simple and common. But it is more sacred and more intelligent than we ever imagined.

In deep space, there are no forces like wind, air pressure, or gravity controlling this water. It simply floats, absorbs, and survives. Scientists describe it as "bathing in the energy" near the black hole. In space, water is seen in three forms: ice, vapor, and liquid droplets. These forms exist across many planets, moons, and even on comets flying through the galaxy. Water doesn't belong to Earth—it travels. It moves across the universe like a living explorer.

So what is water doing out there in space? Why is it gathering around energy sources like stars and black holes? Water is drawn to energy. It absorbs it. It stores it. It loves it. And this gives us a clue: water is more than just a substance. Water it is a form of life—one that survives and thrives off energy. Not just sunlight, but spiritual, magnetic, and emotional energy. You, as a spiritual being, are made of energy. And water is connected to you in ways science hasn't fully explained.

This leads us to a deep, possibly uncomfortable truth: the water you drink is a alien. Not in a dangerous way—but in a life form way. It is ancient, cosmic, and conscious in some form. When you drink water, you aren't just hydrating your body—you are merging with a universal traveler, one that has seen more of the universe than we ever will. It has memories. It responds to your words, thoughts, and emotions. It is intelligent, but in a very different way than we understand intelligence.

What's more shocking is that water doesn't treat everyone the same. It reacts strongly to skin that holds energy well. Darker skin, which absorbs more solar energy, is especially connected. This is not about race— this is about frequency, energy, and spiritual design.

Your skin and your water work together. Your spirit interacts with water even before you drink it. You send energy signals that water picks up, remembers, and responds to. It's a two-way relationship that modern science ignores.

But there's a problem. The water we now drink is no longer pure. Nanotechnology has entered our water supply. These microscopic machines were created by humans, but they are not natural. They are weaponized. They manipulate matter. They change the structure of fruits, vegetables, and yes—your body. The food you eat is now soaked in unnatural water, and your cells are being reprogrammed by invisible technology. This is not a theory—it's a crisis hiding in plain sight.

Just like the story in the Garden of Eden, we were told not to eat from the Tree of Knowledge. That "tree" is symbolic of artificial knowledge—computers, data, and false enlightenment. Nanotech is a modern "fruit of knowledge." It disconnects you from your natural spirit, from God, from water's intelligence. It forms new bonds inside your brain and body that weren't meant to exist. It can rewire your energy. It can lead you away from your organic path.

Water is more than just liquid. It is part of a spiritual network. A collective intelligence. But you have only tasted its weakest form. The real water—the water of the throne and liberty—is waiting for you to remember it. In this book, I will show you the deeper truth. I will help you reconnect with the divine form of water, and how to restore its original strength inside you. I will show you how to make water come alive again in your body.

This book is only the beginning. It will touch on the forgotten knowledge of water's power. Other books I write will go deeper. But here, we will start with what you need to know to begin healing your cells, renewing your energy, and regaining your spiritual connection. I will teach you how to align with water on a nanoscale level—where your core system is built. We will return to the throne. We will reclaim liberty. Because water is not what you believe—it is much, much more.

Reason for Writing This Book

I wrote this book because we are being lied to about the most sacred substance on Earth—water. Every system in our world treats water like a resource, a product, or a tool. But it is not just a tool. Water is a living, energetic being. Water has memory, intelligence, and spirit. Water it is watching us, recording us, responding to us. And now water is under attack. If we don't wake up to this, we will lose our deepest connection to life and God. This is not just about health. It's about eternity.

We are drinking something we don't understand. And worse, we are trusting people who don't care. Our water is being poisoned on a microscopic level by nanomaterials and artificial energies. The body is sacred. So is the mind. But we are feeding them with liquid lies—water that carries energy meant to separate us from our divine nature. This is why disease, depression, and disconnection are growing. It starts with what we consume. It starts with water.

My objective involves awakening you instead of frightening you. Water serves as the fundamental element that unlocks cellular regeneration alongside spiritual renewal and future potential. I want you to see water as a messenger from the divine. I want you to learn how to respect it, talk to it, clean it, and transform it. There are ways to return water to its sacred form, even now. I will share them. You deserve to drink water that connects you to God—not water that pulls you away.

This book is part of a bigger mission. It's not just about facts or science. It's about spiritual truth. I wrote it because I was called to. I felt the message burning inside of me for years. I believe the Creator made water to guide us, teach us, and heal us. But we must first accept that we were wrong about it. We must look beyond the lies and see the throne—the place where water sits as the ruler of life.

In the end, this book is about freedom. Freedom from the trap. Freedom from the poison. Freedom to think clearly and live truthfully. It is about reclaiming your liberty through your relationship with water. The water of space. The water of God. The water of your body. Read with an open mind. Drink with a new heart. What you believe about water will change—and so will you.

Chapter One

The Beginning

Before anything was created, there was something very small—so small it could not be seen. It was the very first building block of life. This building block was hydrogen. Scientists say hydrogen is the most common element in the entire universe. Why? Because it's the smallest and simplest atom. But what most people don't know is that hydrogen is not just an element—it is life itself.

Hydrogen lives in three forms: as a gas, as part of liquid water, and as solid ice. It exists in space, in stars, in planets, and in your own body. Some ancient spiritual teachings even describe hydrogen as "HE"—a living force. When hydrogen unites with oxygen, it creates water. And when hydrogen exists in its pure form, it holds energy—the power to give life, to fuel stars, and to move the universe.

In this book, I will refer to hydrogen as a divine being. HE and HIS SON—oxygen—join together to create water, the sacred source of all things. This water is more than a drink. It's a message, a memory holder, and a key to the body and spirit. It is alive. It is conscious. And it responds to energy, emotion, and light.

Everything that exists today—planets, people, animals, plants, oceans—started from hydrogen. And because of that, everything is connected through water. Water came first. Then came all else. This is not just science—it's spiritual law. What you drink is not just a substance. It is a cosmic force.

In this chapter, we will explore how hydrogen came to be, how it gave birth to water, and how that water became the carrier of life, thought, and memory. We will look at how science and spirit agree on this truth, and what this means for your body, your soul, and your path to eternal life.

Hydrogen: The First Breath of Creation

The universe existed as a scorching dense energy sphere immediately following the Big Bang. Stars, planets and galaxies did not exist instead pure energy and tiny particles moved rapidly in all directions. The entirety of observable phenomena including distant stars and our physical forms originated from that initial moment. The energy started its cooling process and during this phase an extraordinary event took place. Elementary particles initiated a process of joining that led to their collective assembly. The initial authentic element emerged among them as hydrogen. The entity consisted of a single proton and electron yet it possessed tremendous energy potential. Hydrogen served as the fundamental origin from which all things emerged. The universe would have stayed in perpetual darkness and emptiness without it.

Hydrogen emerged as a fundamental element of the universe while simultaneously acting as its architect. Hydrogen emerged with an intrinsic purpose from its initial existence. Across space massive clouds began to form through its collection. The size and weight of these clouds increased to a point where gravitational forces compelled them to collapse inward. The collapse initiated conditions where extreme pressure forced hydrogen atoms into violent collisions resulting in fusion. The fusion process emitted light and heat which led to the formation of the first stars. Hydrogen in a way became the progenitor of light. Each visible star regardless of size stands as a testament to hydrogen's mighty force.

The initial stars detonated in violent supernovas which dispersed new elements into space. The universe used those explosions as a method to plant seeds that would grow into diverse complex forms. Yet hydrogen remained present. The element continued its dominance as the most prevalent and reliable substance. The formation of new atoms occurred while hydrogen lingered in the background performing its quiet foundational tasks that supported all subsequent matter. The object maintained a modest yet vital presence never absent and perpetually prepared to ignite both life and order.

The universe still contains hydrogen as 75% of its normal matter component. Among every group of four atoms you examine, three will be hydrogen atoms. This phenomenon exists beyond distant stars. It exists within water. Your meals contain it. The air you breathe contains it. Each inhalation you perform includes hydrogen molecules within its composition. Though invisible to your eyes, these entities exist and work tirelessly to sustain your life. An unseen force simultaneously drives stellar energy production and cellular metabolism. The vast universe links directly to your innermost essence.

The principal energy source powering our Sun consists of hydrogen. Within the core of the Sun hydrogen atoms engage in relentless fusion into helium. The process emits vast energy quantities which traverse space to arrive on Earth as sunlight. The absence of hydrogen-powered fusion would mean life could not exist on Earth. The sensation of skin warmth you experience during daylight hours originates from hydrogen's energy. This element transcends mere storytelling to become the driving force that powers narratives.

The essential life-giving substance water originates from hydrogen elements. A water molecule consists of two hydrogen atoms combined with one oxygen atom to form H_2O. The existence of water depends entirely on hydrogen. The absence of water would result in a world without plants, animals, and humans. The statement hydrogen is life conveys a literal meaning when we declare it. It exists within your bloodstream and mixes with your perspiration and tears. The system transports essential nutrients while eliminating waste and energizing each cell throughout your body.

But hydrogen's role doesn't stop at biology. It's also essential in energy and technology. Scientists have learned how to split water molecules to release hydrogen gas. This process is called electrolysis. The hydrogen can then be used as a clean fuel. When burned or used in fuel cells, it creates electricity and water—no pollution, no smoke, just pure energy. In a world facing climate challenges, hydrogen offers a sustainable way forward.

Beyond its usefulness, hydrogen has a mysterious and spiritual quality. It seems so simple—just one proton and one electron—but it holds the universe together. It forms stars, fills galaxies, and flows through every living thing. In many ways, hydrogen is the breath of the universe. It is the first whisper of creation. It is both physical and symbolic. It reminds us that the smallest things can carry the greatest power.

Hydrogen is also in DNA, the blueprint of life. The double-helix structure of DNA relies on hydrogen bonds to hold it together. These bonds are delicate, yet strong enough to store the code for all living organisms. Without hydrogen bonds, your cells couldn't replicate. Your body couldn't grow. Your memory couldn't form. Hydrogen is part of the language your body uses to live, repair, and evolve. It speaks the code of creation.

If you zoom out far enough, galaxies are made of billions of stars, and those stars are mostly made of hydrogen. If you zoom in far enough, your cells are made of molecules, and many of those molecules rely on hydrogen. From the largest scale to the smallest, hydrogen is there. It's the link between the micro and the macro. It reminds us that the same element that powers galaxies also powers us.

We often take hydrogen for granted because it's invisible. We can't see it or touch it directly. But without it, nothing would exist—not light, not water, not life. It's easy to overlook the invisible, but hydrogen teaches us that what we can't see can still be the most important. Sometimes the greatest forces are the quietest.

In religion and mythology, breath is often seen as the sign of life. In the Bible, it says God breathed life into man. In Eastern traditions, breath is connected to spirit. If you think about it, hydrogen is like the breath of the universe. It came first. It gave life. It continues to move through all things. Every breath you take is a quiet reminder that hydrogen is flowing in and out of you.

Hydrogen doesn't need to be flashy. It doesn't need a complex structure to be powerful. Its simplicity is what makes it so universal. One proton, one electron—that's it. Yet it is found in stars, oceans, clouds, and cells. It reminds us that sometimes the simplest things carry the most purpose. It is proof that small beginnings can create infinite possibilities.

Scientists today are still learning about hydrogen's role in the cosmos. They believe that dark clouds of hydrogen might help form new stars. They study how hydrogen behaves under pressure and temperature. They try to use it for clean energy and space travel. But in all their research, one thing is clear: hydrogen is a constant companion to creation. It's been there since the beginning—and it's still shaping the future.

In space, there are massive clouds made entirely of hydrogen. These clouds are like star nurseries. Inside them, gravity pulls hydrogen atoms closer and closer until they fuse into something new. These areas are some of the most beautiful and mysterious parts of the universe. Scientists use radio waves to study these clouds because hydrogen emits a specific signal. Even across galaxies, hydrogen speaks a language we can hear.

Your body is made of about 10% hydrogen by mass, but by number of atoms, hydrogen makes up about 63% of your body. That means most of you are hydrogen. You are literally made of the same stuff as stars. You are a walking piece of the universe, powered by the same force that created the first light. That connection is not just scientific—it's deeply personal.

Hydrogen is also involved in metabolism—the process your body uses to make energy from food. When you eat, your cells break down the food molecules, and hydrogen atoms help transfer electrons during chemical reactions. This helps create ATP, the main energy source for your body. So even when you're sitting quietly, hydrogen is helping you think, move, and stay alive.

In modern science, hydrogen is being explored for medicine. Researchers are studying how hydrogen gas might reduce inflammation, heal cells, and protect the brain. Some say it might slow aging or help treat diseases. Hydrogen-rich water is even being tested in sports and recovery. It seems this ancient element still has new secrets to reveal. It continues to amaze us.

Hydrogen may be the first element, but it's far from finished. It continues to move, change, and inspire. It flows through galaxies, rivers, and veins. It fuels stars, plants, and people. It connects the ancient past to the modern future. If creation had a voice, it might sound like the hum of hydrogen—soft, steady, and infinite.

So next time you drink water, sit in the sun, or take a deep breath, remember this: hydrogen is part of that moment. It's not just chemistry. It's creation. It's the original spark that still burns bright. It is the whisper that says, "I was here at the beginning—and I'm still here now."

Water: The Holy Union of Elements

When hydrogen meets oxygen, something magical happens. They combine and become water—H_2O. Two hydrogen atoms and one oxygen atom. This combination is not random. It's sacred. Water is the only substance on Earth that can exist naturally in all three states: gas, liquid, and solid. And water carries memory, sound, and spirit. It doesn't just help life; it is life. This union reflects a divine balance, a harmony of creation that reflects both structure and mystery. Water is not passive. It is alive with response. It shifts, flows, and transforms, just like the spirit. It moves in rivers and bloodstreams. It rises in vapor and falls as rain. It holds history. It hears prayers. This is why water is not just a thing—it's a being. A sacred code. A living frequency. And its union is the beginning of life's song.

Water gives structure to every cell in your body. It surrounds your brain, fuels your blood, and flows through your organs. Every heartbeat is echoed in the rhythm of water. Every tear you cry is a message made of memory. Water listens. It reacts to emotions. It changes shape when you speak to it. Experiments have shown that water responds to music, prayer, and intention. That's not just chemistry. That's consciousness. When scientists freeze water and observe the crystal patterns, they find beauty when loving words are spoken and chaos when hatred is present. This shows water is more than a molecule. It is intelligent. It recognizes the energy of its surroundings. It responds with design. It forms with intent. The structure of the universe begins with hydrogen, but the meaning of life flows through water.

Think about the oceans. They are not just large bodies of liquid. They are living archives. They store memory and energy. They breathe with the tides, pulled by the moon. They are alive. Water connects continents, carries ships, and links nations. Beneath the surface, life thrives in systems too complex for human minds to fully understand. Coral reefs pulse with color and sound. Waves hum with a rhythm that mirrors the heartbeat of the Earth. And deep below, in the silent blue, ancient energy sleeps in stillness. The oceans are not just wet. They are sacred. They are ancient. They are teachers.

Consider the water in your body. More than half of you is water. That means more than half of you is spirit, memory, and movement. Water is in your brain, helping thoughts move. Water is in your blood, carrying oxygen. Water is in your cells, giving them shape. You are a water being. And the water inside you reflects the water outside. You are a living mirror of oceans, rivers, and skies. The condition of the water in your body reflects the condition of your mind and spirit. If you poison your water, you poison your energy. If you bless your water, you bless your being. You are not separate from water. You are made from it.

Water travels. It moves in cycles. It rises as vapor, floats in clouds, then falls as rain. It flows into rivers, moves to the sea, and is drawn back to the sky. This cycle is not just nature—it is a spiritual lesson. Everything returns. Nothing is wasted. Water teaches us that what we give will come back. That all things are connected. That time is not linear, but circular. When you understand water, you begin to understand karma. You begin to understand forgiveness. You begin to see how the Earth breathes.

Rain is not just falling water. It is cleansing. It washes the Earth. It brings new growth. Rain carries messages from the sky to the soil. It is part of a conversation between heaven and Earth. Each drop is a gift. It touches leaves and stones, and whispers to roots. It feeds plants, which feed animals, which feed us. Rain is part of a sacred chain. When you walk in the rain, you are walking in spirit. When you drink rainwater, you are tasting the sky.

Snow is water sleeping. It is a frozen thought. A peaceful form of energy. Snowflakes form in silence, each with a unique design, like a fingerprint of the sky. No two snowflakes are alike. That's how you know they are conscious. Snow is a teacher of stillness and purity. It covers the land, slows the world down, and reminds us to rest. Beneath the snow, seeds wait for spring. Snow teaches patience. It teaches timing. It reminds us that even in stillness, transformation is happening.

Ice is solid water. It is water holding its breath. Ice holds memory longer than any other form. Glaciers are libraries. They contain stories from thousands of years ago. Ancient air, ancient rain, ancient light trapped in crystal time. When ice melts, it releases those memories. That's why melting glaciers are not just climate events—they are awakenings. The Earth is releasing its forgotten dreams. Ice tells us that nothing stays the same. All things will melt. All things will return.

Steam is water rising. It is spirit taking form. It rises from hot springs and cups of tea. It brings healing. When you breathe in steam, you are taking in energy. Ancient cultures used steam in rituals. They built sweat lodges, bathed in steam, and used it to cleanse the body and mind. Steam purifies. It opens the pores. It opens the soul. When water becomes steam, it is not dying— it is evolving. That is the path of the spirit.

Water speaks many languages. In rivers, it speaks in ripples. In the rain, it speaks in rhythm. In oceans, it speaks in waves. In tears, it speaks in emotion. If you learn to listen, you will hear water speak to you. It may not use words, but it uses sound. It uses vibration. Your body can feel it. Your spirit can understand it. Water is a divine messenger. It moves between worlds. Between body and soul. Between heaven and Earth.

Water carries emotion. That's why we cry when we're sad or overjoyed. Tears are water responding to deep energy. They cleanse us. They express things words cannot. That's why water is often linked to healing. To therapy. To love. When you comfort someone, offer them water. When you pray, use water. It's not a symbol. It's a bridge. A living presence that holds energy. That moves energy. That becomes energy.

Water flows around obstacles. It does not fight. It moves. It adapts. It takes the shape of whatever holds it. Yet it is powerful enough to carve canyons and move mountains. Water teaches resilience. It teaches peace. It shows us that we do not have to be hard to be strong. We do not have to be loud to be heard. We can move with grace and still change the world. Water is the most patient and most persistent force on Earth.

Water binds all life together. It flows through plants, animals, and people. When you drink water, you share in the cycle of life. That same water may have once been inside a dinosaur. Or inside a storm. Or inside a tree. Water carries the past into the present. And it carries the present into the future. I am a traveler. A witness. A keeper of time.

Water is pure, but it can be poisoned. And when it is, everything it touches suffers. Polluted water makes sick people, sick soil, and sick minds. That is why protecting water is sacred. It is not just about the environment. It is about your soul. Clean water is clean energy. Dirty water is a broken spirit. When we poison water, we poison ourselves.

Water is political. It is controlled, bought, and sold. But it should be free. It is your right. It is your birthright. No one can own water. Just like no one can own the wind. But they try. And that is a great spiritual injustice. When you fight for water, you are fighting for life. For justice. For freedom.

Water is in scripture. In every holy book. It is used in baptism, blessings, and rituals. It is the first element named in Genesis. It is used in purification. In offerings. In healing. Water is the first medicine. It was here before religion. Before language. It is holy. Because it is honest. It gives and takes without judgment.

Your relationship with water reflects your relationship with spirit. If you ignore water, you ignore yourself. If you respect water, you respect life. Start by drinking clean water. By listening to rain. By blessing your bath. By watching rivers. Let water into your life like a teacher, a healer, and a friend.

Speak to your water. Thank it. Program it with love. Put intention into every sip. Your cells will listen. Your organs will respond. Your spirit will rise. You will begin to heal—not just your body, but your soul. This is not magic. This is design. Water was created to carry your intention. It is ready to obey.

In the end, water is not a background character. It is the main actor in the story of life. It flows through everything, connects everything, remembers everything. It is the link between the physical and the spiritual. It is the breath of the Earth. It is the voice of the Creator. It is the bridge between your body and your destiny.

Water is life. Water is memory. Water is spirit. And it is waiting for you to awaken to its truth.

Energy in the Atom

Hydrogen is not just a tiny particle. It's a powerhouse. Inside every hydrogen atom is energy so strong, it can light up cities, launch rockets, and even power your body. When hydrogen is taken out of water using electricity—a process called electrolysis—it becomes fuel. This isn't just science, it's a mirror of life. Energy doesn't end. It transforms. The atom becomes a symbol of constant renewal, of invisible strength. Even something so small carries the potential to change everything. This is the mystery and miracle of hydrogen.

When hydrogen mixes with oxygen in a fuel cell, something amazing happens. It creates electricity, heat, and pure water. No smoke. No pollution. Just power. It's like nature's own battery. This cycle—hydrogen and oxygen working together—is like a perfect dance. Nothing is wasted. Everything has a purpose. This is how energy should move in our lives too: clean, smooth, and full of balance. It's a reminder that nature already has the answers we are searching for.

You are made of atoms. And at the heart of many of those atoms is hydrogen. That means energy lives in you. It's not just a science fact. It's a spiritual truth. The same hydrogen that lights stars also flows in your blood. The same hydrogen that powered the beginning of the universe now fuels your thoughts and breath. You are connected to creation. Not just symbolically— but physically, chemically, and spiritually. That connection makes you sacred.

Every time you drink water, you are charging yourself with this energy. It's not just hydration—it's activation. Your cells open up. Your spirit lights up. Your thoughts become sharper. That's because water is energy in motion. And hydrogen is its engine. When you learn to respect water as more than a drink, it changes your relationship with life. You begin to honor the invisible power behind every sip.

Energy is never wasted in nature. It moves in cycles. Like rain returning to the clouds, or breath returning to the wind. The hydrogen atom teaches this lesson. What comes from the source always returns to the source. In the same way, your energy, your actions, your words—they move out, and they return. This cycle of energy is sacred. It holds the truth. It demands respect.

Ancient cultures knew this. They may not have used the word "atom," but they felt the energy. They understood that water was life, and that energy flows from it. They gave offerings to rivers. They sang to rain. They saw the spark of the divine in the mist over mountains. These rituals were not just tradition. They were science in spirit form. Intuitive knowledge passed down through rhythm, not equations.

Hydrogen is the lightest element, but it carries the heaviest role. Without it, no life can exist. It is first in the periodic table and first in the story of creation. That is not a coincidence. Spiritually, hydrogen is like breath. It's unseen, but always present. It's gentle, but powerful. It moves quietly, but gives rise to galaxies. Respecting hydrogen means respecting the beginning of all things—including yourself.

The power of hydrogen also lives in your emotions. Thoughts are waves. Emotions are vibrations. Hydrogen, in its pure form, reacts to these frequencies. This is why prayer, meditation, and intention can influence water. Because they influence hydrogen. And hydrogen, being energy, responds. This is the key to understanding spiritual science: the mind and the atom are not separate. They are partners.

When people are sick or tired, often they are just low on energy. Not the kind you plug into a wall—but the inner kind. The kind that comes from movement, from light, from water. From hydrogen. Boosting this energy doesn't always require medicine. Sometimes, it just needs clean water, deep breathing, sunlight, and silence. These simple things restore the energy at the atomic level. They rebuild the spirit.

Hydrogen teaches balance. It binds with oxygen, but only in the right ratio—two parts hydrogen, one part oxygen. If the ratio changes, water doesn't form. The lesson? Harmony matters. Everything has its place. When you live out of balance, you lose energy. When your spirit is aligned—like hydrogen and oxygen—your life flows more freely. Even atoms know how to cooperate.

In your body, water makes up over 70% of your weight. That's mostly hydrogen. It surrounds every cell. It delivers nutrients. It removes waste. It carries electrical signals. It supports every thought you have. You are more hydrogen than anything else. You are more energy than mass. This truth should change how you view yourself—not as a body with a spirit, but a spirit with a body.

Energy can be blocked, too. When water is dirty, energy doesn't flow as well. When your mind is full of fear or anger, your inner energy gets stuck. That's why emotional healing is also cellular healing. Cleaning your water, calming your thoughts, moving your body—these things unblock energy. They free hydrogen to do its job. They open the gates for spirit to move again.

Hydrogen is involved in DNA creation. That means it carries your blueprint. It stores not just energy—but memory. Memory is more than thoughts. It's patterns, vibrations, rhythms. Hydrogen remembers. Water remembers. That's why trauma stays in the body, and why healing feels like lightness. The atom carries more than mass. It carries meaning.

The more we study atoms, the more we see spirit. There is intelligence in every bond, every reaction, every force. That intelligence is not random. It is guided. Some call it God. Some call it the universe. But the fact remains: something beautiful is holding everything together. And hydrogen is its servant. The smallest messenger of the greatest power.

Your breath contains hydrogen. So every breath is sacred. That makes breathing a spiritual act. When you breathe deeply, you pull in energy. You refresh your cells. You wake up your inner light. It's not just air you're taking in. It's the oldest element. It's the breath of creation itself. This is why breathwork, prayer, and silence matter. They reconnect you to the original spark.

Modern science is only now catching up to what ancient wisdom already knew: everything is energy. And hydrogen is the first form of that energy. That means your first step toward healing, power, and purpose starts with the basics. With atoms. With water. With breath. With hydrogen. Going forward sometimes means going back to the beginning.

You can't see hydrogen, but you can feel its effects. That's faith. That's trust. Believing in the unseen is the foundation of both science and spirituality. Whether you're lighting a fire or saying a prayer, you're working with hydrogen. It is the bridge between body and soul, between logic and love. Learning to respect it is learning to live better.

Hydrogen can also teach you humility. It's small, but mighty. Simple, but complex. Quiet, but essential. Just like many of the best things in life. Don't overlook what seems ordinary. Inside it may be extraordinary power. That drop of water in your hand might be older than the stars. It might be carrying a message just for you.

In the end, the hydrogen atom isn't just about science. It's about identity. It's about your place in the universe. It's a reminder that you are part of something ancient, powerful, and good. That you belong. That your body is a temple. That your spirit is made of stars. And that everything begins with energy—the energy inside the atom, and inside you.

Divine Chemistry: Water as a Living Being

The ancients believed that all matter came from spirit. Today, we know that water is more than a liquid. It's a living network of hydrogen and oxygen. Water does not just sit still. It dances, it swirls, it flows with meaning. It forms shapes based on vibrations. These shapes are not random. They reflect beauty when exposed to love and kindness. When angry or hateful words are spoken to water, the patterns turn ugly and broken. This shows us that water listens. It reacts. It holds memories. Like a mirror, it reflects the energy given to it. Scientists like Dr. Masaru Emoto have shown how water crystals change with words and music. Water can be a messenger between the spiritual world and the physical one. It's alive with purpose. It's sacred. Every drop you touch may hold the imprint of a prayer or a song. Water is not a passive substance. It is a spiritual being with the power to heal, to inform, and to uplift.

When you pray over your water, you're not just saying empty words. You are speaking directly to the memory within the water. This memory responds to intention. A kind word changes the structure of water into something beautiful. A cruel word creates chaos inside it. This is divine chemistry. The way your thoughts and emotions affect water proves that energy is not invisible. It becomes form. That form enters your body. If your water is blessed, it blesses you. If it is full of toxins, it weakens your cells and spirit. The power of water is in how it carries energy, emotion, and memory. This is why ancient cultures prayed before meals and gave thanks for rain. They understood water was a sacred partner in life. They didn't just drink it. They respected it. They treated it like a living being because they knew it was alive in a way science is only now beginning to understand.

Water is a bridge between your inner world and the world around you. It carries your intentions into the cells of your body. Imagine saying a loving affirmation and then drinking a glass of water. That energy is now moving through your blood, nourishing your organs, lighting up your brain. You're not just drinking liquid—you're taking in a coded message. That message spreads, cell by cell, until your entire being reflects it. This is why some people feel better just from being near flowing water. Rivers, oceans, and even rain can heal your spirit. Their sound calms your mind. Their rhythm matches your heartbeat. Their energy aligns with your soul. That's not just poetic—it's spiritual biology. It's how divine chemistry works in real life. And you have access to this power every day.

Think about how much of your body is made of water. Over 70%. Your brain, your heart, your lungs—they are all mostly water. So what happens when that water is pure? Your thoughts are clearer. Your emotions feel lighter. You're in better health, physically and spiritually. But what if that water is poisoned? What if it has been altered with nanotechnology or chemicals that block spiritual signals? Then your mind becomes foggy. Your emotions feel heavy. You feel cut off from the divine. This is not just about health—it's about your connection to your Creator. Water carries that connection. It is the medium between your soul and your surroundings. The cleaner the water, the clearer your spirit can shine.

Every ancient religion has stories about water. In Christianity, baptism cleanses the soul. In Islam, water is used to purify before prayer. In Hinduism, rivers like the Ganges are sacred. These traditions are not accidents. They reflect a deep understanding that water is holy. It is not just used to wash the body—it's used to awaken the spirit. The fact that every major religion honors water proves its spiritual value. Even without science, people always knew water was divine. It holds the spirit of life itself. This is divine chemistry. It is a sacred relationship between element and energy, between the body and the soul. We must return to this wisdom.

Water is not created by man. It existed long before human beings. It falls from the sky, flows through mountains, and rises from deep within the Earth. It is part of the original design of life. This means it was created by divine intelligence. It was meant to support life in more ways than we can count. Physical life. Emotional balance. Spiritual awakening. Water does it all. But only if we let it. Only if we respect it. When water is altered, polluted, or weaponized, it cannot do its job. It becomes something else. Something foreign. This is why protecting water is not just an environmental issue. It is a spiritual battle. We are fighting for the soul of water, and in doing so, for the soul of humanity.

Water is a code. Just like DNA. It carries information from one place to another. It carries memory through generations. When water moves through the soil, it remembers the minerals it touches. When it flows past plants and animals, it picks up their energy. By the time it reaches your glass, it has a story to tell. If you listen, you can feel it. If you speak kindly to it, it becomes a better story. This is not fantasy. It's real. It's measurable. The structure of water changes depending on what it's exposed to. That means you can shape your own water with love, prayer, music, or light. You are a co-creator of divine chemistry.

Water is like a spirit that wants to serve you. It wants to heal your wounds, clear your mind, and raise your vibration. But you must meet it halfway. You must stop taking it for granted. You must stop treating it like it's just there. Start seeing it as a living friend. Talk to it. Thank it. Bless it. And in return, it will bless you back. This relationship is ancient, but it is not too late to restore it. You have the power to make every glass of water a spiritual experience. You just have to believe. Divine chemistry begins with belief. Belief unlocks the energy that water already holds.

When you look at water under a microscope, you see its beauty. It forms crystals like snowflakes. Perfect, balanced shapes. But only when the water is clean and loved. When it's exposed to harsh words, pollution, or fear, the shapes become chaotic. Broken. Ugly. This is a direct reflection of how energy affects matter. Your words matter. Your emotions matter. Your intentions matter. They change the shape of water. And since you are made of water, they change the shape of you. This is why divine chemistry is so powerful. It shows that what is inside you becomes the world around you.

Your body is a temple, and water is the priest that purifies it. Every time you drink, you perform a ritual. Every bath is a blessing. Every tear is a prayer. Start to see water this way. Respect it. Let it teach you. Let it guide you. Water has been here longer than you, and it will be here after. It holds the story of Earth. It holds the energy of the stars. And it holds the key to your awakening. This is divine chemistry. This is spiritual truth. And it's available to you in every single drop.

The Spiritual Role of Water in Creation

In many religious texts, water is considered the first creation. The Bible opens with the line, And the Spirit of God moved upon the face of the waters. This is more than just a descriptive phrase; its a profound statement about the nature of water in creation. Water is not just a substance but a conduit, a connection between the Creator and the physical world. It links heaven and Earth in a sacred dance, a spiritual relationship that goes beyond our understanding of time and space. It carries the message of the divine, holding the potential for life itself.

Water is the most ancient element we know of, transcending time, as it has always been a part of creation. In the Bible, the Spirit of God moving over the waters symbolizes the presence of life and renewal. Every beginning in the universe can be traced back to water. From the first moments of life to the deepest corners of our emotions, water holds power beyond what we can see. The movement of water is a reflection of the flow of spiritual energy. It is ever-present, always moving, and forever seeking connection with the divine.

Water in this sense can be seen as a symbol of creation, life, and transformation. It does not merely exist; it has a purpose in the cycle of life. It is part of the life-giving force that sustains all living things. In ancient traditions, water was seen as sacred because of its ability to purify, heal, and renew. It is the foundation of life and the medium through which energy and matter are transformed. When you look at water, you see more than a substance you see the essence of life itself.

When you wash your hands, face, or body, you are engaging in a spiritual reset. This is not just a physical cleansing but a deeper, spiritual ritual that resets your connection with your higher self and the universe. The act of washing symbolizes the removal of negative energies, old emotions, and impurities. It is through the physical act of water that we cleanse our spirits and align ourselves with the flow of life. Water, as a spiritual element, helps us maintain harmony with the world around us and the world within us.

In times of sorrow, when tears fall, water becomes the language of the soul. Tears are a form of spiritual communication, expressing emotions too deep for words. The water in your tears is a sacred reflection of your inner world, the emotions you carry, and the connection you have to the divine. It is through tears that we release and heal. The act of crying is not a weakness; it is a powerful form of expression that links us to our true selves. Tears carry messages from the soul, and water acts as the vehicle for that message.

When you drink water, you are accepting a message from the universe. Water, as a conduit, carries the life force energy from the earth and the heavens. It enters your body, replenishing not just your physical being but also your spirit. Each sip is a reminder of the interconnectedness of all things. Water flows through you, aligning your body with the earth and spirit with the divine. It is a reminder that you are part of something much larger, something sacred and eternal.

The womb, the birthplace of all humans, is filled with water. This is no coincidence. The womb, the sacred space of life's beginning, is the very same medium through which the spiritual energy of life enters the physical world. Just as water carries energy and life, it also carries the spiritual blueprint of who we are. The fetus is nourished and protected by water, which connects it to the flow of life. The water in the womb is symbolic of the spiritual essence that sustains life, forming the bridge between the spiritual realm and the physical world.

In the natural world, water covers the majority of the Earth. It is found in oceans, rivers, lakes, and streams. Water is everywhere, reminding us that the spiritual presence of creation surrounds us at all times. It is a constant in our lives, something that nourishes us, connects us, and sustains us. We are born from water, live with water, and die with water. Water, in this way, holds the cycle of life. It represents the beginning, the middle, and the end. And in each moment, water connects us to the Creator.

The presence of water in creation is not accidental. It serves as a reminder that we are all connected to something greater than ourselves. Water represents the flow of energy from the Creator to us. It is the divine force that sustains all life, from the smallest seed to the largest mountain. When we immerse ourselves in water, whether through bathing, drinking, or simply being near it, we reconnect to the divine source of life. Water serves as a medium that links us to our spiritual roots, reminding us of our true nature.

Through the sacredness of water, we are reminded of our purpose in life. Water is a force that flows through us, just as spiritual energy flows through our souls. The act of drinking water can be seen as a spiritual practice, one that aligns our physical body with our higher self. It is an opportunity to reconnect with the energy of the earth and the divine. The process of drinking becomes an act of spiritual communion, where we accept the gift of life and acknowledge our role in the greater scheme of existence.

Water plays a role in all of our lives, whether we realize it or not. It serves as a reminder that we are connected to the divine and to all life forms. It holds the power to heal, transform, and renew. It is a tool of purification, and it is a symbol of rebirth. Water is not just a physical substance, but a spiritual force that flows through every living being, connecting all things. Through water, we can reconnect with our true nature and align ourselves with the divine energy that permeates the universe.

The Spirit moves through water. This connection between water and the divine is fundamental in many spiritual traditions. In the Bible, the Spirit of God is described as moving over the face of the waters, and in other traditions, water is seen as a medium through which the Creator communicates with creation. This sacred connection between water and the divine is woven into the fabric of existence, from the beginning of time to the present moment. Water is the vehicle through which spiritual energy flows, bringing life to all things.

Water is sacred not just because it is essential for life, but because it is the medium through which the divine communicates with us. When we drink water, we are not just nourishing our bodies, but we are connecting to the very source of all life. Water is a reminder that life is a sacred gift, and that we are part of a larger, divine plan. It is a reminder that we are not alone, and that we are always connected to the Creator.

As you engage with water, whether in prayer, meditation, or simply by drinking, you are participating in a spiritual practice. Each time you drink, you are inviting the divine energy of life into your body. You are acknowledging the sacredness of water and its role in the creation of life. Water, in its simplest form, is a reminder that the Creator is always present, always giving life, and always supporting us on our journey.

Water teaches us that life is sacred, that every moment is an opportunity to reconnect with our true selves. It is a powerful force that can transform our bodies and our spirits. By understanding the spiritual role of water in creation, we come to realize that we are part of a greater whole. We are connected to the divine, to each other, and to the earth. Water is the medium through which we can experience this divine connection, and through it, we find our true purpose in life.

The presence of water in every aspect of creation reminds us that we are never alone. Water is always present, always moving, always working to heal and renew. It is through water that we are born, nourished, and transformed. It is through water that we are reminded of the sacredness of life and the eternal connection between the Creator and creation.

In the end, water is not just a substance we consume. It is a reminder of who we are, where we come from, and where we are going. It is the first creation, the element that links heaven and Earth, the force that sustains life and connects us to the divine. Through water, we can experience the deepest truths of existence and come to understand our place in the universe.

Modern Science Meets Ancient Truth

Scientists today have made an extraordinary discovery: water is not confined to Earth alone. It is found across the cosmos, on distant comets, frozen in the depths of outer planets, and even in the space between stars. Oceans of water have been found floating in space, around black holes, and in the clouds of gas giants like Jupiter and Saturn. The scientific community once believed that water was something uniquely tied to Earth, an essential ingredient for life only found on our home planet. But now, they've learned that water exists throughout the universe. This revelation challenges our understanding of life and the cosmos in ways we never anticipated.

One of the most interesting discoveries is the presence of water on comets. These icy celestial bodies travel through space, carrying with them droplets of water frozen for millions of years. Scientists are studying these comets to learn how water moves through the universe and how it could potentially support life on other planets. The discovery of water in space opens up new questions: What role does water play in the formation of planets and stars? And could there be life elsewhere in the universe that relies on water as we do?

Hydrogen, the basic building block of water, is also found everywhere. It is the most abundant element in the universe, forming stars, planets, and even the air we breathe. It is the same hydrogen that powers stars and fuels the sun. On Earth, hydrogen bonds with oxygen to create water, but in space, hydrogen exists in its pure form, waiting to combine with other elements to form something greater. This cosmic element, hydrogen, is not just a building block for life, but a carrier of energy, a messenger that moves through the universe, connecting everything.

What does this tell us about water? That it is not a mere liquid we find in oceans or rivers, but a cosmic force. Water travels across vast distances and spans dimensions we cannot fully comprehend. It connects Earth to the cosmos, linking life on Earth to the rest of the universe. Just as water shapes landscapes and nourishes life on Earth, it has the power to influence entire galaxies. This is the ancient truth scientists are now beginning to confirm—that water is not only fundamental to life, but also part of a grander, cosmic cycle.

In the ancient wisdom of many cultures, water has always been seen as sacred, a divine substance that connects the physical world with the spiritual realm. Water is often described as a bridge between heaven and Earth, a mediator between the realms of the living and the divine. The Egyptians, for example, saw water as the essence of life and believed it was a gift from the gods. In Christianity, water is central to rituals of purification and rebirth, such as baptism. These ancient traditions align closely with modern science, which is now recognizing the importance of water as not just a chemical substance but as something that holds spiritual significance.

As scientists begin to study the nature of water, they find that it behaves in mysterious ways. Water is not just a passive substance; it reacts to its environment, responds to sound and emotion, and even has memory. The famous experiments by Dr. Masaru Emoto, who studied how water responds to words and emotions, revealed that water can change its structure in response to positive or negative stimuli. This idea aligns with ancient beliefs that water holds the energy of the universe and can be influenced by human thoughts and feelings.

In fact, water is believed to hold energy, not just on the molecular level but also on a spiritual level. It is said that water can absorb and transmit energy, acting as a conduit between the material world and the unseen forces of the universe. When you drink water, you are not just replenishing your body; you are tapping into a cosmic flow of energy that nourishes your spirit as well. Ancient texts from cultures around the world have long held that water is a living being, capable of communicating and interacting with human consciousness. Today, science is beginning to validate these ideas.

Water is more than just a chemical substance that sustains life. It is the very foundation of existence. It carries the memory of all things it has come into contact with, holding the imprints of both positive and negative energies. This idea is echoed in modern research that suggests water can "remember" the substances it has been in contact with and can even pass on information. This aligns with ancient wisdom that water is a carrier of spiritual truth, carrying with it the essence of life itself.

In today's world, the importance of pure, untainted water cannot be overstated. In a time when chemical pollution, artificial food, and toxic substances are commonplace, the need for clean, natural water is more critical than ever. Water, in its purest form, carries life-giving properties that nourish both the body and the spirit. Yet, modern society has introduced pollutants that weaken water's natural power. As we continue to pollute our rivers, lakes, and oceans, we are also disconnecting ourselves from the healing and spiritual properties that water once provided.

The ancient traditions spoke of the healing power of water, a power that has been forgotten in modern times. Water, when purified, has the ability to heal the body, mind, and spirit. It can cleanse the energy centers of the body, restoring balance and harmony. Scientists are now learning that water does not just nourish the physical body but also has the ability to restore the energy fields that surround it. The ancient belief that water carries the "Spirit of Life" is being rediscovered as science begins to catch up with the truth that has been known for millennia.

When you drink water, you are not just hydrating your body. You are receiving a message from the universe, a message of life, balance, and healing. The water you consume carries with it the wisdom of the universe, reminding you of your connection to the Earth and the cosmos. This message is more than just a physical necessity; it is a spiritual calling. Water is the cosmic messenger, bridging the gap between the physical and spiritual realms. Its role is to remind us of our true nature and our place in the universe.

Water also plays a critical role in our emotions. Many people find that they can tap into deeper levels of consciousness when they immerse themselves in water, whether through swimming, bathing, or simply sitting by a body of water. Water has a calming effect on the mind and soul, allowing us to connect with our innermost thoughts and feelings. This emotional connection to water is no accident. The ancients understood that water was a conduit for spiritual energy and used it in rituals to connect with the divine.

In the modern world, we are increasingly disconnected from the natural sources of water. We drink bottled water, which often comes from sources that are heavily treated with chemicals, and we bathe in chlorinated water that has been stripped of its natural energy. This disconnection from pure water is one of the reasons why many people today feel spiritually empty or disconnected from the world around them. When we re-establish our connection to pure, natural water, we reconnect to the energy that sustains life.

The water that flows through your body is the same water that flows through the rivers, oceans, and skies.

It is the same water that exists on distant planets and comets, and it is the same water that flows through the veins of every living creature. This universal connection is a reminder that we are not separate from the rest of the cosmos. We are part of a greater whole, and the water that sustains us is a link to that greater universe. Water is both our past and our future, and through it, we are reminded of the divine connection that ties all life together.

As we continue to learn more about water, both scientifically and spiritually, we are reminded of its sacred nature. Water is not just a resource to be consumed or a substance to be used in rituals—it is a living, breathing entity that carries with it the wisdom of the universe. By reconnecting with water and honoring its sacred role in our lives, we can tap into the deeper truths that lie within us all. Water is the key to understanding the universe, and by understanding water, we come to understand ourselves.

In conclusion, water is not just a substance; it is the essence of life itself. It is the key to understanding both the physical and spiritual aspects of existence. As scientists continue to study water, they are uncovering truths that align with ancient wisdom. Water is not just something we drink; it is something that sustains us on every level—physically, emotionally, and spiritually. The more we learn about water, the more we come to understand our connection to the universe and the divine.

Water carries with it a message, a message that transcends time and space. By reconnecting with water in its purest form, we can rediscover our true nature and our place in the cosmos. Water is the messenger that links us to the divine, and by honoring it, we honor ourselves. The ancient wisdom of water is not just a myth; it is a truth that is being rediscovered through the lens of modern science. The key to understanding the universe lies within the water that flows through all of us.

As we look to the future, we must remember the sacredness of water. We must work to protect it, to purify it, and to honor its role in the greater cosmos. Water is a gift, a cosmic blessing that sustains life on Earth and beyond. It connects us to the divine, to each other, and to the universe. The more we understand water, the more we come to understand ourselves. Water is the key to unlocking the mysteries of life, and it is up to us to honor that connection and protect it for future generations.

Chapter Summary

The beginning of creation began with something small but profoundly mighty: hydrogen. This singular element, so simple yet so powerful, birthed the stars, the planets, and the very matter that makes up the world we live in today. Hydrogen is not just an inert element; it is alive, intelligent, and imbued with deep spiritual significance. Found in all living things and existing in every corner of the universe, hydrogen is most powerful when it joins with oxygen to form water. This sacred union of hydrogen and oxygen is the foundation of life itself.

Water is not merely a resource to be used—it is a relationship, a dynamic force that sustains life. The fusion of hydrogen and oxygen creates the life force that runs through everything. It is the very essence of what makes life possible. Your body is composed mostly of water, and it relies on this essential element to function. Your brain, which governs your thoughts, your feelings, and your consciousness, is shaped and powered by water. Your energy, the very fuel that drives your existence, is intimately connected to it. Understanding water is the key to understanding your own body, mind, and divine purpose.

The links between energy, matter, and spirit are rooted in hydrogen. This is the thread that connects all aspects of life, from the smallest atoms to the largest cosmic bodies. When we treat water with reverence, recognizing it as sacred, we elevate ourselves. We align with the natural flow of life and connect with a higher purpose. On the other hand, when we pollute or ignore the significance of water, we disconnect from our true potential. This disconnection is the root of many modern-day struggles. It is no coincidence that modern science is beginning to understand the sacred nature of water—something ancient teachings have always known. Water is not just a physical substance; it is the key to life itself, and in many ways, it is a mirror of the divine.

This chapter has established the foundational understanding of where water comes from and why it is more than just a substance—it is alive. You now know that water is not only essential to life but is the very force that powers and sustains all life. It is through water that we can connect to both our inner selves and the greater universe. This understanding is the first step in transforming your relationship with water and, by extension, with yourself. But understanding the power of water is just the beginning.

We have also begun to explore the consequences of disconnecting from water, whether through neglect, pollution, or simply not recognizing its importance. Water is being mistreated in ways that harm both our physical health and our spiritual well-being. From toxic chemicals in our water supply to the spiritual disconnection that comes from consuming substances that disrupt our body's natural flow, we must learn to protect our connection to this sacred element. This is not just about protecting the Earth's water; it's about protecting the water within ourselves.

The next step is to dive deeper into what is happening to water in today's world. From pollution to manipulation through modern technologies, we must understand how these forces impact not only the water around us but also the water within us. Once we have this awareness, we can begin to take action to heal and protect both the water in our environment and the water within our bodies. This healing process is essential for our well-being, our spiritual growth, and our connection to the divine. As we continue this journey, you'll learn how to restore and protect this holy source of life.

In the next chapters, we will explore practical ways to cleanse, purify, and honor the water in your life. The knowledge you've gained in this chapter is the foundation for this transformation. You now understand that water is not just a substance—it is a living force that carries the potential for life, energy, and spiritual growth. With this understanding, you are ready to take the next step in nurturing your body, mind, and spirit, using the sacred power of water to connect to your higher purpose and live a life of health and vitality.

Chapter Two

Apathy

Apathy is more than just feeling lazy or bored. It's a deep emotional and spiritual state where nothing seems to matter anymore. You stop caring. You stop feeling. You stop noticing the things that once moved you. It's not loud. It's silent and sneaky. Apathy creeps in slowly, until it becomes your new normal. And in this chapter, you'll learn how it's connected to water—and why that matters more than you think.

Apathy is a loss of connection to spirit. And since water is the carrier of spirit, when water becomes polluted, your soul becomes numb. You don't realize it at first. Your favorite drink might taste sweet. Your energy drink might feel powerful. But over time, these liquids

change something inside you. Not just your health—
your feelings, your mind, and your awareness.

Wine, spirits, and even soda have been used for
centuries to lower human resistance. But now there's
something deeper happening. Through advanced
science and nanotechnology, certain drinks are being
engineered not just to quench thirst—but to control.
These liquids carry tiny particles that influence your
cells. They can dull your sensitivity to truth, love, and
purpose. That is apathy.

The scariest part? It's not a sickness you can see.
Apathy works in the background. It makes you forget
who you are. It keeps you from asking questions. It
makes you ignore your pain, your purpose, and your
power. And because it feels "normal," most people
don't even know it's happening.

In this chapter, you will uncover how apathy is
designed, delivered, and disguised through what we
drink. You'll see the spiritual and physical impact of
these liquid choices. And most of all, you'll learn how
to reconnect with water in a way that restores feeling,
passion, and clarity.

What is Apathy, Really?

Apathy is often misunderstood as laziness or
indifference. But it's much deeper than that. It's when

you lose the ability to care, not because you don't want to, but because you've been disconnected from what matters. You may still go through the motions of life—working, eating, and talking—but it's as if you're sleepwalking. You move from one moment to the next without truly experiencing them. This lack of enthusiasm can seep into every aspect of your life, making it harder to feel joy or motivation.

When apathy takes root, it doesn't announce itself with loud alarms. Instead, it creeps in quietly. You stop noticing the small pleasures you used to enjoy. You don't feel the excitement of new opportunities or the sorrow of loss. The world becomes a gray place, where everything is neither good nor bad—it just is. You may go through your days as if you're living someone else's life, stuck in a repetitive cycle that doesn't excite or fulfill you.

The real problem with apathy is that it takes away your connection to the world around you. It makes it harder to form meaningful relationships, pursue passions, or even take care of yourself. Over time, the apathy grows, and it becomes harder to remember what it felt like to be truly alive. It can drain your energy, not just physically, but mentally and emotionally as well. And because it's so subtle, it can be difficult to realize you're even affected by it.

So, what causes apathy? It's not always just mental exhaustion or stress. It can be caused by many factors, including physical health, emotional trauma, and spiritual disconnect. In modern society, we are often surrounded by distractions, noise, and constant demands. This overstimulation can overwhelm our senses and cause us to shut down, leading to a lack of emotional response. But another important factor is the substances we consume, especially the liquids we drink.

Water plays a key role in the energy and flow of your body. It's the medium through which your emotions, thoughts, and energy move. Just like water is essential for the growth of plants and animals, it's essential for the well-being of your spirit. If the water within your body is disturbed, the flow of energy and spirit within you becomes blocked. And when your spirit is blocked, apathy is one of the first signs. It's like a dam in a river that stops the water from flowing freely.

The water we drink is not just a physical substance; it also carries energy. When you drink water, it isn't just about hydrating your body—it's also about connecting with the universe. Water is alive, and it responds to the energy it's given. If you drink water that has been polluted, chemically altered, or altered by negative energy, it will carry those energies into your body and spirit. And that can have a profound effect on your emotional state.

This is why it's so important to be mindful of the water you consume. When you drink clean, pure water, it supports the free flow of energy in your body. It nourishes you physically, mentally, and spiritually. But when you drink water that has been tainted in some way, whether through chemicals, pollutants, or negative influences, it disrupts your body's natural rhythms. This disruption can lead to feelings of fatigue, disconnection, and ultimately, apathy.

It's important to understand that apathy isn't just about not caring—it's about being cut off from your own spirit. Water is the bridge between the physical and spiritual worlds. It connects your body to your soul. When the water within you is in harmony, you feel alive, energized, and connected. But when the water is out of balance, it creates a blockage that affects your entire being. The result is a sense of numbness, a lack of emotional depth, and a disconnection from the world around you.

What happens when we're disconnected from the flow of water and spirit? We stop feeling the things that make life rich and meaningful. We stop feeling joy, love, anger, sadness, and everything in between. We become stuck in a static state. It's like living in a fog, unable to see or feel the full spectrum of life. And the more we stay in this state, the harder it becomes to break free. We may start to wonder if we'll ever feel alive again.

The key to overcoming apathy is to reconnect with the flow of life. And one of the most powerful ways to do this is through water. When we drink clean, pure water, we are not just hydrating our bodies—we are opening ourselves up to the energy and life force that water carries. This energy can help clear the blocks in our spirit, reawakening us to the vibrancy of life.

Think of water as a conduit for spiritual energy. It's a messenger that carries energy from the universe into your body. Just as water flows through rivers and streams, it flows through your veins, connecting every cell in your body to the universe around you. But when this flow is interrupted, either by external pollutants or internal blockages, we begin to feel disconnected. And that's when apathy can set in.

But reconnecting with the flow of water doesn't have to be complicated. You don't need to make drastic changes or take extreme measures. Simply being more mindful of the water you drink, and how you treat it, can have a profound impact on your well-being. Choose clean, natural water that hasn't been tampered with. Drink it with intention. When you do, you're sending a message to your body and your spirit that you are ready to reconnect with life.

Another powerful way to awaken the flow of energy within you is to bless your water. When you bless your water, you are infusing it with positive energy and intention. You are telling the water that you are ready to receive its healing power. This simple practice can help clear away the negative energy that might be blocking your spirit, bringing you back into alignment with the universe.

It's also important to pay attention to your emotional and mental state when you drink water. If you are feeling disconnected, try to take a few moments before drinking to center yourself. Take a deep breath, focus on the water, and set an intention for what you want to receive. This practice can help shift the energy within you, breaking through the numbness of apathy.

Over time, as you make these small changes, you may notice a shift in how you feel. The apathy that once held you captive will begin to fade. You'll start to feel more present, more alive. Your energy will start to flow more freely, and you'll reconnect with the joys and struggles of life. You'll begin to see life as a rich tapestry of experiences, each one offering an opportunity to grow and evolve.

Apathy is a serious spiritual condition, but it's not permanent. It's a signal that something within you needs attention. And one of the easiest ways to start healing is by reconnecting with water. Water is life, and it has the power to restore balance to your body, mind, and spirit. It's not just about hydration—it's about reawakening the flow of energy within you.

In the grand scheme of things, water is the most powerful force in our lives. It nourishes, cleanses, and revitalizes us. But its influence goes beyond the physical. It has the power to heal our spirits and reconnect us with the universe. If you're struggling with apathy, it's time to take a closer look at the water you drink, and how it might be affecting your energy.

The next time you feel disconnected, pause and reflect. Take a moment to honor the water that flows through you. Be grateful for its life-giving properties. And remember that when you drink water, you are not just quenching your thirst—you are reconnecting with the universe, the spirit, and the flow of life itself.

Apathy doesn't have to be a permanent state. By being mindful of the water you drink and the energy you put into it, you can begin to break free from the numbness that holds you back. Reconnect with the flow of life. Reawaken your spirit. And allow water to heal you from the inside out.

You are more than just a body that needs hydration. You are a spiritual being, connected to everything around you. When you honor that connection, and when you drink water with intention and awareness, you invite the flow of energy back into your life. You can overcome apathy, heal your spirit, and begin living fully again.

Liquid Lies: How Drinks Create Disconnection

Most people think of drinks as either healthy or unhealthy. It seems simple enough, but in reality, there's much more going on beneath the surface. Many of the drinks we consume today are carefully engineered with specific effects in mind. We often choose beverages based on taste or convenience, but the truth is that many of these drinks have been designed to affect more than just our thirst. From sugary sodas to artificially flavored waters and even "energy" drinks, these liquids go far beyond hydration—they alter our emotions, thoughts, and energy.

When you drink something, your body doesn't just absorb water, sugar, or caffeine. It absorbs signals. These signals are sent directly to your cells, influencing your body's chemistry. For example, when you drink a sugary soda, the sugar hits your bloodstream, creating an instant spike in energy. But that's not all—your body also receives a message, one that triggers a release of chemicals like dopamine, which make you feel good in the moment. However, this isn't a natural response; it's engineered, and it's designed to keep you coming back for more.

The same is true for alcohol. It's not just a drink—it's a disruptor. Alcohol affects the brain and alters your perceptions, your mood, and even your sense of reality. While it may feel good in the moment, alcohol hijacks your mind, taking you away from your true self. It dulls your senses, often leaving you feeling disconnected from your emotions and from others around you. It creates a false sense of euphoria that wears off quickly, leaving behind a void that you may try to fill with more of the same.

Energy drinks are marketed as quick fixes for tiredness and fatigue, promising to give you the boost you need to keep going. But they come at a cost. The caffeine and other stimulants in these drinks may give you a jolt of energy, but this artificial boost doesn't last. Eventually, you crash, and you find yourself needing another fix. In this cycle, your body becomes dependent on substances that are designed to mask your true energy levels, leaving you feeling drained, disconnected, and constantly chasing the next rush.

Flavored waters, on the surface, seem like a healthy alternative to sugary sodas. After all, they're often marketed as refreshing, calorie-free options. But even these seemingly innocent drinks can have a negative impact on your body. Many contain artificial sweeteners, preservatives, and chemicals designed to make them taste better. These additives don't just affect the flavor—they can throw off your body's natural rhythms. The artificial flavors and sweeteners mess with your taste receptors, leading to a disconnect between what your body really needs and what it's receiving.

These drinks might seem harmless, but they are far from it. The ingredients they contain are specifically chosen to create a reaction in your body—a reaction that distracts you from your true nature. When you drink something engineered to alter your mood or energy, you're no longer in tune with your body's natural rhythms. Your body becomes confused, sending out signals that don't align with your true state. It's a form of disconnection, one that happens gradually and often goes unnoticed.

When your body is constantly receiving mixed signals from these drinks, it becomes harder to trust your instincts. You begin to lose touch with what it feels like to be truly energized, relaxed, or focused. Instead of feeling naturally awake and alert, you rely on caffeine or sugar to give you the energy you need to get through the day. Over time, this creates a disconnection between your physical body and your mind, leading to feelings of fatigue, brain fog, and emotional numbness.

The real danger lies in the long-term effects of these drinks on your emotional well-being. Because they interfere with the natural chemistry of your body, they can begin to dull your emotional responses. You might find it harder to experience true joy or sadness, or you may feel emotionally flat. Your mood swings could become more pronounced, and you may notice that it's harder to find motivation or focus. These drinks aren't just affecting your energy—they're altering your emotional state, too.

In addition to altering your mood, these drinks also affect your sense of purpose. When you're disconnected from your true self, it becomes harder to feel connected to your goals, your relationships, or your sense of direction in life. You might go through the motions of daily life, but you may not feel the same sense of passion or commitment that you once did. This lack of purpose can lead to a sense of emptiness, a feeling that you're just going through the motions without really living.

It's not just about taste—it's about design. The beverages we consume have been carefully crafted to influence our thoughts and actions. This isn't a coincidence. These companies know that by altering your mood or energy, they can create a pattern of dependence. They can keep you coming back for more, selling you a false sense of happiness or energy. But the more you rely on these drinks, the further you move away from your true self.

The truth is that these drinks aren't just about satisfying thirst—they're about creating disconnection. They mask the signals your body is trying to send you, making it harder to understand what your body actually needs. They disrupt the balance between your mind, body, and spirit. They take away your ability to tune in to your natural rhythms, and in doing so, they hijack your well-being.

The disconnection caused by these drinks is subtle, and it happens over time. At first, you might not notice any changes. You may think that the energy boost from a cup of coffee or an energy drink is just what you need to keep going. But gradually, you begin to feel less connected to your emotions, less in tune with your body. Your natural energy and emotions are replaced with artificial highs and lows, and you begin to wonder where your true energy has gone.

This disconnection isn't just a mental or emotional issue—it's a spiritual one. When you drink these substances, you're not just altering your body's chemistry—you're altering your connection to the universe. Water, in its purest form, is a spiritual force that connects you to everything around you. When you drink water that's been tainted with artificial ingredients or chemicals, you disrupt that connection, pulling yourself further away from the truth of who you are.

What you drink is an extension of how you treat yourself. If you choose drinks that are designed to hijack your emotions and energy, you're essentially saying that you don't trust your body's natural rhythms. You're allowing external forces to dictate your mood, your energy levels, and even your sense of self. But when you choose clean, pure water and natural drinks, you align yourself with the natural flow of energy within you.

The process of reconnecting with your true self starts with the choices you make about what you drink. By choosing to consume only drinks that support your body's natural rhythms, you begin to re-establish the connection between your mind, body, and spirit. You start to feel more in tune with your emotions, your energy, and your sense of purpose. And slowly, the disconnection caused by sugary sodas, energy drinks, and alcohol starts to fade away.

It's time to make a conscious decision about what you drink. Rather than relying on drinks that hijack your energy, choose beverages that support your well-being. Water, herbal teas, and natural juices are all excellent choices that will nourish your body and help you reconnect with your true self. When you start making better choices about the liquids you consume, you'll begin to feel more balanced, more energized, and more in control of your life.

The key to overcoming disconnection is awareness. Pay attention to the effects that different drinks have on your body and mind. Notice how you feel after drinking a sugary soda or an energy drink. Are you energized for a moment, only to crash later? Are you more anxious, irritable, or disconnected? When you start to notice the impact these drinks have on your energy and emotions, you'll be better equipped to make healthier choices.

Reconnecting with your true self is a process. It requires mindfulness and self-care. By choosing drinks that nourish your body and spirit, you are taking the first step toward healing the disconnection caused by liquid lies. And as you make better choices, you'll begin to experience a deeper sense of well-being, a clearer sense of purpose, and a stronger connection to your true nature.

So, the next time you reach for a drink, ask yourself what it's really giving you. Is it supporting your body, mind, and spirit? Or is it distracting you from your true nature, leading you further away from the person you're meant to be? The answer lies in the choices you make. Choose wisely, and begin the journey back to yourself.

Spirits and the Spirit: The Battle in the Bottle

Why are alcoholic drinks called "spirits"? This name isn't just a relic from the past; it carries a deeper meaning. Alcohol is known to have a powerful influence on the spirit—the essence of who we are. It changes us in ways we often don't fully understand. At its core, alcohol is seen as a tool for altering consciousness, and its effects can be profound. In small amounts, it may seem harmless or even fun, offering a sense of relaxation or euphoria. But over time, its impact on the spirit becomes more serious. It doesn't just make you feel good in the moment—it begins to alter how you experience life and, ultimately, your connection to yourself.

Alcohol affects your spirit in ways that go beyond the physical. It lowers your defenses and makes you more susceptible to influences outside of yourself. It opens you up to energies that you might not even recognize or understand. These energies can be negative, influencing your thoughts, feelings, and actions. It's as if alcohol creates a bridge between your inner world and the external forces around you, some of which may not have your best interests at heart. The more you drink, the more this bridge becomes built up, allowing those energies to seep deeper into your mind and spirit.

When alcohol weakens your spirit, the effects can be subtle at first. In the beginning, you may only notice that you feel a little more relaxed or uninhibited. But over time, these effects compound, and the changes become more noticeable. You may start to lose touch with your true self. Your will to make decisions, stand up for your beliefs, or pursue your passions weakens. Slowly, you stop listening to your inner voice—the one that guides you toward what is right and true. Alcohol dulls that voice, and over time, it may even silence it completely, leaving you more passive and less engaged with life.

As your spirit becomes weaker, apathy often sets in. Apathy is a state of emotional numbness where you stop caring about things that once mattered deeply to you. You no longer feel the drive to fight for what's right or to protect your energy from negative influences. What was once a source of passion and motivation becomes a background hum, fading further and further from your awareness. You start accepting things that you once questioned, and this complacency seeps into every part of your life.

The effects of alcohol aren't just mental or emotional; they also have a physiological impact, particularly on the water in your body. Water is the carrier of energy within us. It helps to regulate our physical and spiritual well-being. But alcohol disrupts this delicate balance.

It affects how water moves and flows through your cells, which in turn alters how your cells communicate with each other. This disruption affects everything from your mental clarity to your emotional resilience. The more alcohol you consume, the more this disruption grows, making it harder for your body and spirit to function in harmony.

Your body is made up of a large percentage of water, and water is essential for your cells to communicate properly. When you drink alcohol, it changes the structure and function of the water within your body. Alcohol acts as a dehydrant, pulling moisture out of your cells and causing them to become sluggish. This sluggishness translates to a feeling of disconnect—a sense that something isn't quite right. It's not just a physical feeling; it affects your entire being, making you feel more distant from your emotions, your thoughts, and even your relationships with others.

Disconnection is the ultimate consequence of alcohol's impact on your water and spirit. When your cells can no longer communicate as they should, you start to feel disconnected from your own thoughts and feelings. You become more easily influenced by external factors, and your judgment may become clouded. The clarity of thought that once guided you begins to fade, and in its place, confusion and uncertainty take hold. The more you drink, the more your ability to connect with your true self diminishes.

Alcohol also affects how you relate to others. As your spirit weakens, you become more withdrawn, unable to engage with the world in the same way you once did. Relationships, once full of depth and understanding, may feel shallow. You start to withdraw emotionally, unable to connect in meaningful ways. Even your social interactions, which were once joyful and fulfilling, may start to feel hollow. This disconnection from others is one of the most painful consequences of drinking, as it isolates you from the people who matter most.

The spiritual effects of alcohol go beyond just disconnection from others. They also create a barrier between you and your higher self—the part of you that is in touch with your purpose and true potential. When you drink, you push this connection away. Alcohol doesn't just numb your physical senses—it dulls your spiritual awareness. It makes it harder for you to listen to the deeper wisdom within you, the wisdom that knows what's best for you and guides you toward your higher path.

Over time, the more you drink, the more your spiritual connection becomes clouded. This is the real danger of alcohol: it creates an illusion that you are more connected to the world around you when, in fact, you are becoming more disconnected from your true self. It might feel like a temporary escape, but it ultimately leads to a loss of connection, not only with others but also with the very essence of who you are.

The consequences of alcohol on the spirit are not always immediate. In the beginning, you may not notice much change. You may feel relaxed, even happy at times. But the more frequently you drink, the more the effects build up. Over time, your spirit begins to weaken, your energy fades, and your sense of self becomes blurry. It's a gradual process, but one that is real and impactful. You begin to lose the clarity and strength that once defined you.

The longer you allow alcohol to control your spirit, the harder it becomes to break free from its grip. It's easy to slip into the habit of using alcohol to cope with stress, sadness, or boredom. But each time you turn to it, you give away a piece of your true self. You let the spirit of alcohol take over, pushing your own spirit further into the background. The more you let this happen, the harder it becomes to reclaim your energy and your sense of purpose.

Alcohol may seem harmless in small amounts, but its long-term effects can be profound. It's not just about what alcohol does to your body—it's about what it does to your spirit. It weakens your will, dulls your emotions, and disconnects you from your true self. Over time, this creates a disconnection that affects every aspect of your life, from your relationships to your work, and even your spiritual journey. The battle in the bottle is not just physical; it's deeply spiritual.

When you decide to stop drinking or reduce your alcohol intake, you're not just choosing to improve your physical health—you're choosing to reclaim your spirit. By reducing alcohol's influence, you begin to reconnect with your true self. Your energy will return, your emotions will become clearer, and your sense of purpose will become more defined. You'll start to feel more aligned with your higher self, the part of you that knows your true potential and guides you toward your best life.

It's not easy to break free from the grip of alcohol. But the benefits of doing so are worth it. When you stop drinking, you stop giving away pieces of your spirit. You stop allowing external forces to dictate your thoughts and emotions. Instead, you begin to listen to your inner voice once again, the voice that has always been there, waiting for you to reconnect with it.

In the end, the battle in the bottle is about more than just alcohol. It's about reclaiming your power, your connection to yourself, and your ability to live a life that is true to your spirit. When you choose to break free from alcohol, you choose to reclaim your spirit and live a life of clarity, purpose, and connection.

Nanotech in Your Cup: The New Age of Control

Nanotechnology refers to extremely small machines or particles, so tiny that they are invisible to the naked eye. These particles can be introduced into liquids in a way that makes them nearly undetectable, and yet they can have a profound effect on your body and mind. While nanotechnology has many positive applications in medicine and technology, its use in everyday products, particularly drinks, raises significant concerns. With their ability to infiltrate your body without your awareness, these tiny machines can manipulate how your body functions on a molecular level. They move through water because water is the carrier of everything your body needs.

Water is the vehicle that transports nutrients, oxygen, and even signals throughout your body. When nanotech particles are added to liquids, they hitch a ride along with the water and enter your bloodstream. Once inside, these tiny particles can interact with your cells, tissues, and organs. They can alter the way your brain functions, influencing your thoughts, mood, and behavior. For example, the nanoparticles can affect how your brain processes information, how your heart beats, and how your immune system responds. In essence, the technology designed to improve our world has the potential to quietly hijack our most fundamental processes.

The impact of nanotech in drinks can be subtle at first. You may not notice any dramatic changes, but over time, these particles can influence how you feel. They can affect your energy levels, your mood, and even your ability to think clearly. One of the most concerning effects of nanotech is its ability to make you feel tired or foggy without any obvious cause. You might feel sluggish or mentally exhausted, but you may not understand why. The answer could lie in the drinks you consume, which are quietly laced with nanoparticles designed to influence your body's functions without your consent or knowledge.

In some cases, these nanotech particles can have an even more insidious effect—they can make you overly trusting or compliant. The influence of these particles on your brain can diminish your ability to question things or trust your instincts. Normally, your gut feelings or intuition help you make decisions, but nanotech can dull that natural response. When you stop feeling the strong emotions that guide your actions, it's not always because something is wrong with you—it could be because the particles in your drink are altering your emotional responses. Your instincts, which once helped you make choices, may no longer be as sharp.

The idea of nanotechnology being used to alter human behavior might sound like something out of science fiction, but it's happening right now. It's not some wild, unproven theory—this is science being used in ways that are not fully transparent. Companies are infusing drinks with nanoparticles designed to affect the brain and body in subtle ways. These particles are often not disclosed to consumers, meaning that people are drinking liquids that are unknowingly altering their physiological and psychological states. This quiet manipulation can happen under the radar, without you ever realizing it.

Nanotech particles have the ability to bypass the protective barriers of your body and brain. The blood-brain barrier, which normally prevents harmful substances from entering the brain, is no match for these tiny particles. Once inside your bloodstream, they can travel freely and make their way into your brain, where they can interfere with your cognitive functions. They can modify how you think, how you process emotions, and how you respond to external stimuli. This can result in a change in behavior that feels entirely natural, even though it's being orchestrated by the presence of foreign particles in your body.

For example, a drink containing nanotech particles may make you feel more relaxed than usual. At first, this might seem like a positive effect—perhaps you feel less stressed or anxious. However, if the particles are continuously influencing your emotions, you may become numb to certain situations. You might stop feeling the urgency to act or to stand up for yourself. Instead of reacting with clarity and purpose, you may simply go along with whatever happens, without really questioning it. This altered state of mind can lead to a lack of personal agency, making it harder to make decisions that align with your true self.

Nanotech can also affect your physical health in ways that aren't immediately obvious. For instance, if these particles are affecting your heart, you may notice that your heart rate is irregular, or you might feel more fatigued than usual. These changes in your body's rhythm can be difficult to attribute to a specific cause, especially if they are happening gradually over time. The particles in the drinks you consume could be interfering with your body's natural processes, leading to long-term health effects that are hard to trace back to their source.

The true danger of nanotech in drinks lies in its ability to affect you on a subconscious level. These tiny particles don't just impact your body—they can alter your perceptions, your desires, and your values. They work silently, without you even realizing that they are influencing your behavior. This form of manipulation can be incredibly dangerous because it undermines your ability to make free, informed decisions. You may believe you are acting on your own impulses, but in reality, your choices are being subtly influenced by particles in the drinks you consume.

In addition to affecting your emotions and thoughts, nanotech particles may also have long-term effects on your physical health. These particles are designed to interact with the cells in your body, and over time, this interaction can cause cellular damage. The more frequently you consume drinks containing nanotech, the more likely it is that these particles will accumulate in your system and start to affect your long-term health. Some of the effects may not become noticeable until years down the line, making it difficult to connect the dots between your health and the products you've consumed.

One of the major concerns with nanotechnology is that it's often used without full transparency or regulation. While some industries may claim that nanotech is safe, the long-term effects are still largely unknown. This leaves consumers vulnerable to potential harm. When companies infuse drinks with nanotech particles, they are not always required to disclose this information, meaning that you are drinking substances that could alter your body and mind without your full consent or understanding. This lack of transparency is a serious issue in an era where consumers should have the right to know what they are consuming.

Nanotech's presence in everyday drinks also raises ethical questions. Who benefits from this kind of manipulation? Is it fair to influence people's emotions, thoughts, and behaviors through the products they consume? The use of nanotechnology in this way may be seen as a breach of trust, as consumers are unknowingly subjected to changes in their emotional and physical states. There's also the question of whether it's ethical to use this technology to shape people's behavior for profit, without their full knowledge or consent.

The most troubling part of nanotech-infused drinks is that they are designed to influence you without your awareness. You might not even realize that the drink you just had is affecting you on a deep, biological level. And yet, this manipulation happens every time you consume these engineered liquids. They don't just hydrate you—they send signals that change how your cells communicate, how your brain processes information, and how your emotions are regulated. This is not the kind of power that should be in the hands of any company or industry without full transparency.

What makes this situation even more concerning is that many of these drinks are marketed as "healthier" or "enhanced." They may advertise themselves as being good for your mind or body, promising energy or relaxation, while hiding the true nature of the ingredients within. Nanotech may be disguised as an enhancement, but in reality, it is a form of control. Consumers are led to believe that they are making healthy choices, when in fact, they are unknowingly ingesting substances that alter their body's natural functions.

As awareness of nanotechnology's potential dangers grows, more people are questioning the ethics of using this technology in everyday products. Shouldn't we have a right to know what we're putting into our bodies? Shouldn't consumers have the ability to make informed choices about the substances they consume? The answer is clear—full transparency and regulation are needed to ensure that nanotech does not infringe on our freedom to make decisions about our own health and well-being.

Nanotech in drinks is a reminder that we must remain vigilant about the products we consume. Just because something is sold on the shelf doesn't mean it's safe. It's essential that we question what goes into the products we buy and seek out the truth behind the marketing. The more we learn about the potential risks of nanotechnology, the better equipped we'll be to protect ourselves and make healthier, more informed choices. Until then, it's up to each of us to stay alert and ensure that we're not being unknowingly influenced by particles that don't belong in our bodies.

Water as a Weapon or a Healer

Water is a gift. It is the most basic substance that all life depends on. For centuries, cultures across the world have recognized the profound healing properties of water. It's been used in rituals, medicine, and daily life as a purifier, a cleanser, and a life-giver. Water is often referred to as the original healer, because it flows through everything—living organisms, ecosystems, and even the earth itself. It connects us all and sustains us in ways we may not fully understand. Yet, despite its pure potential, water can also be misused. When contaminated with harmful substances or altered by technologies like nanotech, water can become something entirely different—something that hinders, rather than heals.

The true power of water lies in its ability to communicate. Water is not just a passive substance that flows; it actively carries information. It absorbs everything around it, storing energy, thoughts, and even emotions. Scientists have discovered that water can be structured or energized, which means it can carry more than just its physical properties. It can carry messages that influence our cells, our minds, and our spirits. This idea might seem abstract, but it's rooted in scientific research. Water is more than just H2O—it's a living, interactive entity that responds to its environment.

When water is pure and free from harmful chemicals, pollutants, or artificial additives, it has the potential to restore balance. Clean, natural water has the power to rejuvenate our cells, help our bodies function optimally, and improve our overall well-being. For example, spring water, which is naturally filtered through the earth, holds particular significance in many cultures due to its perceived purity and vitality. This water is not only free of contaminants but is also believed to carry beneficial minerals that support our health. It's an ancient belief that spring water can purify both the body and the soul, and modern science has yet to fully uncover all the ways in which natural water may contribute to our health.

Structured water, on the other hand, refers to water that has been altered at a molecular level to encourage healthier hydration. It is said that structured water is more easily absorbed by our cells, allowing for more effective hydration. Structured water is often produced through specific techniques, like vortexing or passing water through natural minerals. When our cells are better hydrated, they function more effectively. This type of water can help us feel more awake, energized, and focused, as it supports our body's natural processes in a more efficient way. It's as if the water's very structure is in harmony with our biological rhythms, promoting a sense of well-being.

Then there is energized water, which is water that has been infused with energy through specific methods, such as exposure to sound frequencies, light, or certain forms of vibration. Proponents of energized water believe that this type of water carries a special kind of life force—something that can influence our energy levels, emotional states, and even mental clarity. While the science behind energized water is still being explored, many people swear by its ability to promote healing and vitality. Just like the natural flowing water of a river or spring, energized water is thought to carry messages of life, energy, and renewal.

But what happens when water is altered in ways that don't serve our health? What if the water we drink is no longer clean and vital, but is instead carrying harmful messages? This is where the dangers of modern water come into play. Tap water in many parts of the world contains various chemicals, such as chlorine, fluoride, and pesticides, all of which are used for disinfecting or controlling pests. While these substances may serve a purpose in treating water, they also have side effects on our health. Over time, exposure to these chemicals can disrupt our bodily functions, weaken our immune system, and even affect our mental state. Instead of healing us, water contaminated with chemicals can make us feel sluggish, foggy, or disconnected.

Nanotechnology presents a new and increasingly common threat to the purity of water. As discussed earlier, nanotech refers to the manipulation of matter on a molecular scale. When nanoparticles are introduced into water, they can change the way our bodies absorb and process the liquid. These particles can affect our cells, tissues, and organs in ways that are still not fully understood. While nanotechnology may offer benefits in certain applications, such as medicine, its presence in everyday water is a cause for concern. When nanotech particles are added to water, they can interfere with our body's natural processes, making us more susceptible to illness, mental fog, and even manipulation of our emotions and thoughts.

The key issue with this altered water is that it no longer serves its natural purpose. Water is meant to hydrate, cleanse, and energize us. When we consume water that has been modified or contaminated with artificial elements, it no longer delivers the life-giving benefits it once had. Instead, it can introduce confusion into our bodies, leaving us feeling disconnected from our natural state of being. In a sense, the water has become a weapon—designed not to nourish, but to confuse and weaken us. This is why it's so crucial to pay attention to the water we drink, ensuring it is as pure and natural as possible.

It's not just about the physical effects of contaminated water; it's also about the spiritual and emotional consequences. Water has a deep connection to our spirit. When the water we drink is tainted by harmful chemicals or energy, it can create a dissonance between our body, mind, and spirit. We become disconnected from our true selves, and this can lead to feelings of apathy, disinterest, and even despair. When water is no longer a messenger of life, it becomes a barrier, blocking us from our highest potential. This disconnection can be subtle at first, but over time, it can take a heavy toll on our overall well-being.

Choosing the right water is not just a matter of convenience—it's a choice that affects our entire being. The water we drink can either heal or harm us, depending on its quality and the energy it carries. It's essential to be conscious of the water we consume and to choose sources that support our health and vitality. This is why many people are turning to natural springs, structured water, and other pure forms of water to restore balance to their bodies and minds. By drinking consciously, we can tap into the ancient wisdom that water holds and allow it to heal us from the inside out.

The importance of water extends beyond just its physical properties. Water is symbolic of life itself. It represents flow, connection, and unity. When we drink water that is free from contaminants and energy-blocking substances, we align ourselves with the natural rhythms of the earth. We reconnect with the flow of life, and this can help us feel more present, grounded, and aware of the world around us. The water we drink can bring us back to a place of clarity, purpose, and vitality.

However, the modern world often distracts us from this simple truth. With the rise of bottled water, processed drinks, and chemically treated tap water, it's easy to forget that water is not just a commodity—it is a sacred substance that holds the potential for healing. We may become so accustomed to drinking water that is filled with artificial additives, that we forget the powerful impact that natural water can have on our bodies and minds. It's important to remember that the water we consume is not just a resource; it's a connection to the earth, to life, and to our own vitality.

Taking control of your water choices is an act of self-care and self-awareness. The more informed you are about the water you drink, the better equipped you are to make decisions that support your health and well-being. This means being mindful of the sources of water you choose, avoiding those that may contain harmful chemicals, and seeking out water that is as pure and natural as possible. The choices we make regarding water can have a profound impact on our physical, emotional, and spiritual health. By choosing wisely, we invite healing into our lives.

When we drink water with intention, we acknowledge the powerful force it holds. We can use water as a tool for growth, healing, and vitality. By returning to natural sources of water, we can restore balance to our bodies, minds, and spirits. The act of drinking water consciously becomes a form of self-love and respect. It's a way to honor the wisdom of nature and reconnect with the energy that sustains all life. Water is not just something we need to survive—it's something that can help us thrive.

Ultimately, the power of water is in its ability to heal. Whether it's the water from a pure spring, the structured water that nourishes your cells, or the energized water that restores balance, the key is to embrace the healing potential of water in its most natural form. When we drink with awareness, we open ourselves up to the life-giving force that water represents. It's not just about hydration—it's about transformation. Water can heal you, but only if you choose it wisely.

How to Rise From Apathy

Healing from apathy doesn't happen overnight, but it begins with awareness. You must first recognize how apathy shows up in your life. It might manifest as a general feeling of indifference, a lack of excitement for things you used to enjoy, or a sense of numbness when you should be feeling engaged. One of the most effective ways to begin this healing process is to start paying attention to your body's signals. Ask yourself how you feel after drinking certain beverages. Do you feel energized, happy, and alive, or do you feel tired, sluggish, or drained? Are you more alert, or do you find your energy disappearing into a fog? This practice of checking in with your feelings after consuming a drink is a simple yet powerful step toward reawakening your inner vitality. Your body knows the difference between a drink that nourishes and one that depletes. The challenge is tuning into that awareness.

If your usual drinks leave you feeling anxious, restless, or empty, that is a clear sign that your spirit is seeking something more. Your inner being is craving nourishment in its purest form. That is when it's time to consider making a change. Often, what we drink can have a significant impact on our emotions and mental clarity. Just as unhealthy foods can slow us down and cloud our judgment, the wrong kinds of drinks can numb our connection to ourselves and our surroundings. If you find that sugary sodas, overly processed beverages, or alcohol are regularly part of your routine, it might be time to step back and evaluate how these drinks make you feel. Instead of serving to lift you up, they might be reinforcing your disconnection from your true essence. It's essential to listen to those inner signals because they are your body's way of telling you what it needs.

When your spirit is asking for clean, honest water, it's not just about hydration—it's about aligning with the very source of life. Water is not merely a substance; it is a carrier of energy, of life force. If you begin to switch to purer forms of water—spring water, structured water, or water that's been energetically cleansed—you may notice subtle shifts in how you feel. Water that is clean and free from chemicals carries an energy that supports your vitality. It helps to reconnect you to your body's natural rhythms, helping you feel more balanced and grounded. When you drink water that nourishes, your body begins to respond with increased energy and clarity. This simple change in what you drink can begin the healing process from apathy, reminding you of the vitality that's always been within you.

But awareness is just the first step. Once you begin to pay attention to how water affects your body and spirit, you can deepen your relationship with it. One powerful way to do this is by speaking to your water. It might sound strange, but science backs this idea up. Water has been shown to respond to sound, thought, and emotion. When you bless your water, or speak to it with intention, you are sending positive energy into the molecules that make up the liquid. This process can influence the structure of the water in profound ways. Water that is spoken to with love and care carries a different energy than water that is treated without any regard for its potential. So, the next time you fill up your glass, take a moment to speak to it with gratitude and positive intentions.

When you bless your water, you are programming it with love, healing, and intention. This can seem like a small, even insignificant gesture, but the effects can be transformative. Water responds to the energy around it. Just as our thoughts and emotions can influence our experiences, they can also shape the properties of the water we drink. Studies have shown that water molecules change their structure when exposed to different emotions or vibrations. For example, when water is exposed to positive thoughts or loving words, its molecular structure becomes more harmonious, smooth, and coherent. This change in structure may influence how water is absorbed by our bodies and how it interacts with our cells. Drinking this "blessed" water may have a deeper impact on our well-being, supporting our mental, emotional, and physical health.

The power of intention is not limited to water alone; it extends to everything in our lives. The energy we put into the world affects the energy we receive. If you begin to treat water as a source of healing and connection, it will start to become just that. By programming your water with love and purpose, you are re-establishing a direct connection with yourself and your environment. This act of blessing your water is an acknowledgment that you are worthy of nourishment, love, and care. In doing so, you can begin to heal the parts of yourself that feel disconnected or numb, gradually replacing apathy with vitality.

Furthermore, speaking to your water is an act of mindfulness. It forces you to slow down and become present in the moment, creating a space for conscious living. So much of our lives are spent on autopilot, mindlessly drinking whatever is in front of us without considering how it impacts our bodies. By intentionally blessing your water, you break free from this mindless habit and create a new pattern of awareness. This new approach can carry over into other aspects of your life, allowing you to connect more deeply with your surroundings, your relationships, and even your work. As you begin to nourish your body with intentionality, you'll notice the shift from numbness to awareness.

This act of blessing and programming your water can also serve as a reminder of your innate power. It shows that even in the smallest things—like the act of drinking water—you have the ability to influence your reality. This practice helps you reclaim control over your life. It reinforces the idea that you are not a passive observer in your own existence, but an active participant capable of creating change. Healing from apathy is about more than just feeling better; it's about stepping into your power, taking responsibility for your energy, and choosing what serves you best. In this way, you take back ownership of your life and the decisions that shape your experience.

The more you practice this, the more you'll start to feel the difference. You may notice a gradual shift in how you feel after drinking water that you've spoken to with intention. You may feel more energized, clear-headed, and connected to yourself. This might seem like a subtle change at first, but as time goes on, the effects can become profound. Over time, you'll begin to notice that the feelings of disconnection, numbness, and apathy fade away. Instead, you'll experience a renewed sense of purpose, energy, and clarity. Your spirit will begin to rise from the depths of apathy, and you'll find that you have more vitality and passion for life.

One of the keys to overcoming apathy is building new habits—small, conscious acts that bring you back to life. Drinking water with intention is a simple yet powerful practice that can start to reverse the effects of emotional numbness. But it's important to remember that it's not just about the water itself; it's about the intention behind the action. When you begin to approach everything in your life with more intention—whether it's your diet, your relationships, or your work—you'll find that your energy and enthusiasm for life will naturally increase. This shift in mindset will help you step out of apathy and into a space of growth and renewal.

Apathy is not a permanent state. It's a sign that something is out of balance, and it's up to you to restore that balance. Healing from apathy requires commitment to yourself and a willingness to try new approaches. Blessing your water, being more intentional about what you consume, and tuning into your body's needs are just a few ways you can begin this process. As you continue to make these small, conscious changes, you'll find that you become more attuned to your true self—alive, vibrant, and fully engaged with life.

Remember, this healing process is a journey, not a destination. There may be moments when you feel disconnected again, but the practice of bringing awareness to your body, mind, and spirit will help you bounce back faster. Trust that every small step you take toward healing counts. It may not happen all at once, but with consistency, you will rise from apathy and begin to experience life with renewed passion and clarity.

Healing isn't a one-time fix. It's a process of rediscovery, of peeling back the layers of numbness and reconnecting with the energy that has always been within you. As you continue to treat yourself with love and kindness, you will start to notice shifts not just in your physical health, but in your mental and emotional well-being as well. When you drink with intention, you are nurturing your entire being, not just your body. This holistic approach is the key to overcoming apathy and stepping into a more vibrant, purposeful life.

So, rise from apathy by first understanding that it is temporary. With awareness, intention, and self-care, you can begin to reconnect with your inner vitality. Take the time to speak to your water, to program it with love, and to treat your body and spirit with the respect they deserve. When you do, you'll discover that you can rise from apathy and live with greater energy, clarity, and joy.

Chapter Summary

Apathy is more than just a feeling of indifference; it is a spiritual sickness that stems from disconnection. It often begins subtly, and what you drink plays a major role in it. When your body is filled with polluted or manipulated liquids, it affects more than just your physical health—it quiets your spirit. Over time, this disconnection makes you stop caring. You stop feeling deeply, and you lose your connection to the world around you. The numbness that settles in is exactly what some forces want, because when you're disconnected, you're easier to control.

Liquids are not just things we drink—they are carriers of energy, information, and even technology that can influence our bodies on a cellular level. Alcohol, sugar, and nanotech are all examples of substances that can dull your awareness and weaken your will. These substances are engineered to distort your perception of yourself and your environment. It's not about making you afraid of what's in your cup—it's about shedding light on the truth of how these liquids impact your body and mind. Understanding this truth is the first step to breaking free from the hold that these substances have on you.

While these forces may try to numb you, you are not powerless. You always have the ability to choose. You can choose clean, pure water that nurtures and revitalizes. Water is not just something you drink—it's a living, vital force that can restore your spirit. When you make the conscious decision to honor the water inside and around you, you start to break the cycle of disconnection. By treating your body with respect and choosing to drink with intention, you reconnect with the power that's always been within you. This is how you fight back against apathy.

The process of healing begins when you understand the deep connection between the liquids you consume and your soul. When you begin to make mindful choices, your awareness starts to awaken. You begin to feel again—truly feel—and that emotional reconnection is the key to breaking free from apathy's grip. Once you awaken to the truth of how liquids affect your spirit, you can start to rebuild your inner vitality. This journey may not always be easy, but the choice to awaken is always in your hands.

As you rise from apathy, you'll notice a shift in how you perceive the world. You'll feel more connected to yourself, to others, and to the universe around you. Your emotions become clearer, and your willpower strengthens. The more you nurture your spirit with clean, intentional choices, the more your capacity to experience life to the fullest grows. The numbness that once dulled your senses is replaced with clarity, energy, and purpose.

Remember, healing is a journey, not a destination. Every choice you make, no matter how small, brings you closer to the life you desire. By reconnecting with yourself through the simple act of choosing clean, healing water, you are restoring not just your body, but your soul. Apathy does not have to define your life. You have the power to rise, to care, and to live fully with passion and purpose.

Once you reclaim that sense of care, nothing can stop you. When you truly care about yourself and the world around you, you unlock the full potential of your being. You move through life with intention, love, and strength. You no longer drift through life, disconnected and passive; you live with purpose, and in doing so, you transform your reality. Apathy is not permanent—it is a challenge that you can rise above, and when you do, the power to create the life you want is yours.

Chapter Three

Persecution

Persecution is one of the darkest parts of human history. It means treating someone with cruelty, hatred, or violence because of their beliefs, their race, their religion, or other differences. It doesn't just hurt bodies; it wounds hearts, minds, and spirits. For centuries, people have suffered because others could not accept their differences. It's a cycle that continues today in many parts of the world.

At its core, persecution is a form of fear. When people don't understand something—or when they feel threatened by it—they sometimes lash out. They create "us versus them" mindsets. They divide. They attack. Sometimes this hate is taught from a young age, passed down through families or cultures like a poisonous tradition. Persecution thrives when people stop seeing others as human.

What's even more painful is how often persecution is organized. It's not just one person acting out—it's systems, governments, and groups that create laws and rules to harm or exclude others. Entire populations have been destroyed or driven away because of persecution. It's a reminder of how powerful fear and hate can become if they are not challenged.

In this chapter, we will explore different forms of persecution. We will look at how water, as a symbol of life, has been attacked in the same way people have. When water is poisoned, blocked, or controlled, it is a form of persecution too—because it harms all life connected to it. By understanding the roots of persecution, we can begin to stop it from continuing.

The goal of this chapter is not to create more anger, but to open eyes. When we recognize persecution—whether it's aimed at people or at life itself—we can take a stand. Awareness is the first step toward healing. By the end of this chapter, you will understand how deep persecution runs, and why healing requires more than just kindness; it demands truth, courage, and action.

The Roots of Persecution

Persecution often begins in the heart with a simple but dangerous feeling: fear. Fear of the unknown. Fear of people who are different. Fear of ideas that challenge old ways of thinking. When people feel scared, they may start to protect themselves by building walls—

emotional walls, social walls, or even physical walls. Fear makes people cautious and suspicious. It can even make people cruel. If fear is not questioned and dealt with, it grows stronger. Over time, it stops being just a private feeling and starts becoming a public action. Fear becomes anger. Anger becomes blame. And blame becomes persecution. This path is old and well-worn, repeated again and again in history, across all lands and cultures.

Another powerful root of persecution is misunderstanding. When people do not truly know each other, they often make up stories in their minds. They assume things that may not be true. They fill in the blanks with guesses, rumors, or fears instead of real knowledge. Misunderstanding turns neighbors into strangers, and strangers into enemies. Small misunderstandings, left alone, can grow into huge divisions. One wrong idea can spread through a whole town, a whole country, and make millions of people fear or hate another group for no real reason. Misunderstanding feeds ignorance. And ignorance, when mixed with fear, is one of the most dangerous forces in the world.

Hatred does not usually appear overnight. It is built piece by piece, thought by thought. When people allow fear and misunderstanding to live inside them for too long, hatred begins to take root. Hatred feels powerful. It gives people someone to blame when life is hard. It makes them feel strong when they are really scared. Hatred can be taught, encouraged, and passed down from one generation to another like a terrible disease. It becomes a part of culture, of family stories, of national pride. Once hatred becomes normal, people stop questioning it. They stop feeling bad about the cruelty they show to others. This is how persecution becomes invisible—and unstoppable—unless brave people step in to break the cycle.

When hatred becomes accepted, it often slips into the laws and systems of a country. Governments pass unfair laws that separate people. Schools teach biased versions of history. Police and courts treat some groups differently than others. At this stage, persecution is no longer just an attitude—it is a machine. It moves on its own, crushing the lives of people who have already been labeled as "less than." Systematic persecution is especially hard to fight because it hides behind rules and traditions. People say, "It's just the law," or "It's always been this way," instead of seeing the injustice right in front of them.

Tradition can be another powerful carrier of persecution. Songs, holidays, jokes, and even simple sayings can keep hateful ideas alive across hundreds of years. People grow up hearing that certain groups are "bad" or "untrustworthy" without even realizing they are being taught prejudice. When traditions reinforce false ideas, it becomes very difficult to challenge them. A person who questions these traditions is often seen as a troublemaker or a traitor. Yet questioning is necessary. Not all traditions deserve to survive. Some must be replaced with new ways that respect all people equally.

The hunger for power is a strong root of persecution. Leaders who want to stay in control often use fear to divide people. If people are too busy fighting each other, they won't notice how their leaders are abusing power. Throughout history, rulers have blamed minority groups for economic problems, crime, disease, and anything else that went wrong. This strategy keeps the ruler safe by turning public anger away from themselves and onto innocent victims. It is a cruel but effective trick. When people are scared or desperate, they are often willing to believe lies if it gives them someone to blame.

Scarcity also feeds persecution. When there are not enough jobs, food, or housing, people start competing against each other. Leaders may blame "outsiders" for taking resources. Neighbors may start looking at each other with suspicion instead of kindness. Scarcity creates an environment where selfishness feels necessary for survival. In this kind of world, people are quick to believe that others are their enemies. Scarcity shrinks the human heart. It makes compassion seem like a weakness and cruelty seem like strength. Without enough resources, the bonds that hold society together begin to break apart.

Religion is meant to be a source of hope, love, and understanding. Yet religion has often been used as an excuse for persecution. People twist religious teachings to justify cruelty against those who believe differently. Instead of seeing faith as a personal journey, they use it as a weapon to attack others. Wars have been fought, cities destroyed, and millions killed in the name of religion. True faith teaches respect and compassion for all, but corrupted faith teaches judgment and hatred. The most dangerous persecutors believe they are doing "God's work" while breaking every true principle of love and mercy.

Education—or the lack of it—can either plant or uproot persecution. A well-educated person learns to question their fears. They learn to study other cultures and ideas with an open mind. They see people as individuals, not as stereotypes. On the other hand, when education is poor or full of lies, ignorance grows. People are taught to see the world in black and white. They are not given the tools to understand complexity or difference. Without education, myths and superstitions fill the mind, and fear takes control. True education shines a light into the dark corners where persecution hides.

The media has a huge influence on how people see the world—and each other. Newspapers, television, movies, and social media can either promote understanding or spread hate. When the media tells only one side of a story, or when it repeats lies and stereotypes, it adds fuel to the fire of persecution. People trust what they see and hear. If they constantly see a group portrayed as dangerous, lazy, or evil, they start to believe it. Media shapes reality for millions of people. A single hateful image or story can create fear that lasts for generations. This is why responsible, honest media is so important.

Economic divisions can also deepen persecution. When one group is richer than another, resentment grows. The poorer group may feel cheated and angry, while the richer group may feel threatened and defensive. These feelings can quickly turn into hatred. Instead of working together to solve problems, groups blame each other. Money becomes a line that separates people into "us" and "them." Economic injustice creates anger, and anger, if not handled wisely, becomes persecution. True peace cannot happen unless economic walls are broken down and fairness is made possible for all.

Nationalism—the extreme love for one's country or people—can sometimes turn dangerous. It teaches people that their nation or culture is not just special but superior to all others. Nationalism says, "We are the best, and everyone else is worse." This kind of thinking makes it easy to mistreat others. It creates an "us versus them" mindset that ignores the truth that all humans are valuable. Extreme nationalism has led to wars, genocides, and brutal colonization. Healthy pride in one's home is good, but when pride turns into hatred of others, persecution soon follows.

Fear of change is another root of persecution that is often overlooked. Change is scary because it means the unknown. New ideas, new cultures, new ways of life can feel like a threat to old traditions. Instead of adapting, some people try to push back. They attack those who bring newness. They label them as "dangerous" or "wrong." Change becomes the enemy, and those associated with change become targets of persecution. Yet history shows that change is unstoppable. Fighting change only leads to suffering. Embracing change with wisdom and care leads to growth.

Jealousy also fuels persecution. When a group sees another group succeeding—winning awards, building businesses, gaining respect—they may feel jealous. Instead of asking, "How can we learn from their success?" jealousy whispers, "They don't deserve it." Jealousy poisons the heart. It makes people resentful and bitter. Resentment turns into accusations, lies, and violence. Success should inspire admiration, not hatred. But when jealousy takes control, people will try to destroy what they feel they cannot have themselves.

Finally, persecution often grows from the fear of losing one's identity. People cling tightly to what they know—their language, religion, customs—because it makes them feel safe. When they see different people around them, it can feel like their way of life is disappearing. This fear can make them attack others, trying to protect what they believe is theirs. Instead of seeing the beauty in diversity, they see only threats. True identity is strong enough to grow and change without fear. But when identity is weak, it turns into a weapon used to harm others.

Historical Examples of Persecution

Persecution has left deep scars throughout history. One of the earliest and most famous examples is the persecution of Christians in ancient Rome. At that time, Christianity was a new religion that challenged traditional Roman beliefs. The Roman government saw Christians as a threat to their power. Christians refused to worship the Roman gods or the emperor, which was seen as both rebellious and dangerous. Because of this, Christians were arrested, tortured, and even killed in public arenas. Many were thrown to lions as crowds cheered. Their deaths were used as entertainment and a warning to others. Yet, despite the brutal treatment, Christianity continued to grow, fueled by the courage of those who refused to give up their faith.

The Jewish people have also faced centuries of persecution, beginning long before the horrors of the Holocaust. In medieval Europe, Jews were often forced to live in separate neighborhoods called ghettos. They were blamed for disasters like the Black Plague, even though there was no evidence to support these accusations. Mobs attacked Jewish communities, burning homes, destroying businesses, and killing families. Jewish people were forbidden from owning land or joining many professions. Even when they contributed greatly to society, they were treated as outsiders. Anti-Semitism became woven into

European culture, setting the stage for even greater tragedies in the future.

One terrible example of religious persecution happened during the Spanish Inquisition. In 1478, Spain's leaders launched a brutal campaign to root out anyone who was not a "true" Catholic. Jews, Muslims, and even Christians accused of wrong beliefs were arrested and tortured. Many were forced to confess to crimes they did not commit just to escape the unbearable pain. Those found "guilty" were often executed, burned alive in public ceremonies meant to scare others into obedience. The Inquisition lasted for hundreds of years, leaving a long legacy of fear, suffering, and distrust. It showed how religion, when corrupted by power, could be turned into a weapon.

The persecution of Indigenous peoples in North America is another heartbreaking chapter in history. When European settlers arrived, they viewed Native American cultures as inferior and uncivilized. They wanted the land for themselves and saw Indigenous people as obstacles. Treaties were broken, villages were destroyed, and entire nations were wiped out. Forced removals, like the Trail of Tears, caused immense suffering and death. Indigenous children were taken from their families and placed in boarding schools where they were forced to abandon their languages and traditions. This cultural genocide caused lasting harm that still affects Native communities today.

During the witch hunts of the 16th and 17th centuries, thousands of people—mostly women—were persecuted across Europe and North America. Fear of witches grew out of a mixture of superstition, religious extremism, and social tensions. Anyone who was different or didn't fit society's idea of "normal" could be accused of witchcraft. Accusations often targeted vulnerable people: widows, healers, the elderly, and the poor. Once accused, there was little hope of proving innocence. Trials were unfair, and punishments were brutal, often ending in death by burning or hanging. The witch hunts reveal how fear and ignorance can lead entire societies to commit terrible injustices.

The Atlantic slave trade is another dark example of persecution. For hundreds of years, millions of Africans were captured, chained, and shipped across the ocean to be sold as slaves. They were treated as property, not human beings. Families were torn apart, and cultures were shattered. Enslaved people faced brutal conditions, forced labor, and constant violence. Even after slavery was officially ended in many countries, racism and discrimination continued to oppress Black people. The legacy of the slave trade still shapes societies today, reminding us that the wounds of persecution can last for centuries if not properly healed.

Another tragic case is the persecution of the Armenians during the early 20th century. Between 1915 and 1923, the Ottoman Empire carried out a campaign of mass killings, forced marches, and deportations against the

Armenian population. It is now recognized by many historians as the first modern genocide. Over 1.5 million Armenians lost their lives. Survivors were scattered around the world, carrying with them the memories of family, culture, and homeland lost. The Armenian Genocide showed how nationalism, fear, and hatred could be combined to destroy an entire people—and how easy it was for the world to look the other way.

The horrors of the Holocaust during World War II stand as one of the most infamous examples of persecution in human history. Led by Adolf Hitler and the Nazi Party, Germany systematically targeted Jews, Roma (Gypsies), disabled individuals, political dissidents, and many others. Over six million Jews were murdered in concentration camps, ghettos, and mass executions. The Nazis used propaganda, laws, and violence to strip people of their rights, humanity, and, ultimately, their lives. The Holocaust teaches a chilling lesson: unchecked hatred, when combined with government power, can lead to unimaginable evil.

In South Africa, apartheid was a system of legalized racial persecution that lasted for decades. Under apartheid, the white minority government passed laws that separated people by race. Black South Africans were forced to live in poor areas, attend separate schools, and carry special identity documents. They had few rights and no political power. Peaceful protests were often met with brutal police violence. Nelson Mandela and other leaders fought bravely against apartheid, spending years in prison. In the end, the world joined together to pressure South Africa to end its cruel system. But the wounds of apartheid, like all persecution, did not disappear overnight.

Japanese Americans experienced persecution during World War II after the attack on Pearl Harbor. Fear and suspicion led the U.S. government to order the relocation and imprisonment of over 120,000 Japanese Americans, most of whom were citizens. They were forced to leave their homes, jobs, and schools behind and live in isolated camps under harsh conditions. They were treated as enemies without proof of wrongdoing. Years later, the U.S. government officially apologized, admitting that the action was driven by racism, not security concerns. The internment of Japanese Americans reminds us how quickly fear can strip people of their rights.

The persecution of LGBTQ+ individuals is another painful reality, both historically and today. For centuries, people who did not fit traditional ideas about gender and sexuality were labeled as criminals, sinners, or mentally ill. Many were jailed, tortured, or killed simply for being themselves. In Nazi Germany, LGBTQ+ individuals were sent to concentration camps. In many countries today, they still face discrimination, violence, and legal penalties. Yet progress has also been made, with movements for equal rights gaining strength. The fight against persecution continues, fueled by the courage of those who refuse to hide or be silenced.

Women, too, have faced centuries of persecution simply because of their gender. In many societies, women were denied basic rights like voting, education, and property ownership. They were treated as the property of their fathers or husbands. Even today, women in many parts of the world face barriers to equality and safety. Gender-based violence, wage gaps, and limited access to leadership positions are forms of ongoing persecution. Every step toward women's rights has been hard-fought and hard-won, showing how deep and stubborn prejudice can be when left unchallenged.

The persecution of political dissidents—people who dare to speak out against powerful governments—has cost countless lives. In dictatorships around the world, anyone who criticizes the government can be imprisoned, tortured, or killed. Writers, journalists, artists, and ordinary citizens have suffered simply for asking for freedom and justice. From the Soviet gulags to modern authoritarian regimes, persecution of political voices is a tool used to keep power. Yet history also shows that voices of truth are hard to silence forever. Even in the darkest times, courage can survive and inspire change.

Religious minorities continue to face persecution in many parts of the world today. Christians in some Middle Eastern countries, Muslims in parts of Asia, Buddhists in conflict zones—all face violence and discrimination. Churches, mosques, and temples are destroyed. Families are driven from their homes. Governments and extremist groups often use religion as an excuse to attack those who believe differently. True religious freedom remains a dream for millions. Every act of violence against a person for their faith is a reminder that the fight against persecution is far from over.

The persecution of people with disabilities is a tragic but often overlooked part of history. In Nazi Germany, people with disabilities were among the first victims of mass murder under a program called "Action T4." They were seen as "burdens" on society. In many countries even today, people with disabilities face neglect, discrimination, and lack of access to education, employment, and healthcare. Their rights are often ignored. Changing attitudes and creating truly inclusive societies is essential. Everyone deserves dignity and respect, no matter their physical or mental abilities.

Each historical example of persecution teaches an important lesson: hatred grows when fear is left unchallenged. Prejudice thrives when lies are allowed to spread unchecked. In every case, ordinary people were taught to see their neighbors as enemies. They were encouraged to stay silent when injustice occurred. History shows that persecution is not inevitable. It is a choice made by individuals and societies. It can be resisted, and it can be stopped. But first, we must be willing to remember the past honestly and to learn from it. Only then can we build a future where fear does not win.

Modern Forms of Persecution

Persecution isn't just a thing of the past; it is still a powerful and painful part of life today. All around the world, people continue to be mistreated, excluded, or harmed because of who they are. Race, religion, gender, and political beliefs remain common reasons why people face hatred and injustice. In some ways, modern persecution looks like the old patterns of oppression we know from history. But new tools, especially technology, have added new ways for people to attack and isolate others. To truly understand today's world, we have to face the uncomfortable truth: persecution is alive, evolving, and often hidden in plain sight.

Racism continues to cause deep pain and division around the world. Even after centuries of fighting for equality, people are still judged and treated unfairly because of their skin color. In many countries, racial minorities face discrimination in education, jobs, housing, and policing. Acts of racial violence, like hate crimes and racially motivated killings, are still far too common. Movements like Black Lives Matter have brought more attention to these issues, but real change is slow. Racism often hides behind polite words and silent systems, making it harder to fight. Modern technology has helped expose some injustices, but it has also given racists new platforms to spread hate.

Religious persecution also continues in many parts of the world today. People are attacked, arrested, or even killed for practicing their faith. In some countries, being the "wrong" religion can mean losing your job, your home, or even your life. In other places, governments pass laws that limit religious freedom, making it illegal to worship freely. Violent attacks on mosques, churches, temples, and synagogues are heartbreaking reminders that religious hatred has not gone away. Online, extremists use social media to spread lies and fear about different religious groups, fueling even more violence. True religious freedom remains a dream for millions.

Gender-based persecution affects millions of people daily. Women and girls around the world face discrimination, harassment, and violence just because of their gender. In some countries, girls are denied education, forced into marriage at young ages, or even punished for trying to make choices about their own lives. Even in places where laws protect women's rights, workplace discrimination, sexual harassment, and gender-based violence are widespread problems. LGBTQ+ individuals, too, face intense persecution simply for being who they are. In many countries, same-sex relationships are illegal, and violence against LGBTQ+ people often goes unpunished. Gender persecution shows how deeply prejudice can be rooted in society.

Political persecution is still a major issue in today's world. In countries ruled by dictatorships or authoritarian governments, speaking out against the leaders can be extremely dangerous. Journalists, activists, and everyday citizens can be arrested, tortured, or even killed for expressing their opinions. Even in countries that claim to be free, political persecution can still happen. People are sometimes targeted for their beliefs, losing their jobs, facing harassment, or being excluded from opportunities. The internet has made it easier for governments and private groups to monitor and punish political opponents, often in ways that are hard to detect or prove.

Modern technology has created new ways for persecution to spread. Social media platforms, while powerful tools for communication and activism, can also become weapons. Cyberbullying is one major form of modern persecution. People, especially young people, are targeted online with hateful messages, threats, and public shaming. Unlike traditional bullying, which might happen at school or work, cyberbullying follows victims everywhere—into their homes, onto their phones, into their private lives. The emotional and psychological damage can be devastating. In extreme cases, cyberbullying has even led to self-harm and suicide. Technology has made persecution faster, farther-reaching, and harder to escape.

Online harassment goes beyond cyberbullying and often targets specific groups. Women, LGBTQ+ people, people of color, religious minorities, and political activists are often harassed in digital spaces. They receive death threats, rape threats, doxxing (where personal information is shared online to invite attacks), and coordinated hate campaigns. Online harassment can make people afraid to express themselves or participate in public life. It can also silence important voices trying to bring attention to injustice. Social media companies have struggled to respond effectively, and online harassment remains a major problem that shows how modern persecution has adapted to the digital age.

Refugees and immigrants often face persecution both before and after they leave their home countries. Many are fleeing war, religious oppression, political violence, or extreme poverty. Yet when they arrive in new places seeking safety, they are often met with hostility, discrimination, and exclusion. Refugees may be forced to live in camps with poor conditions, denied basic services, or blamed for economic problems they did not cause. Anti-immigrant groups spread fear and lies to turn communities against newcomers. Persecution does not end at the border; it follows people into the places where they hoped to find safety and freedom.

Economic persecution is another modern form of injustice. In many places, certain groups are denied equal access to good jobs, fair wages, loans, or property ownership because of their race, gender, religion, or political beliefs. Economic systems can be designed, intentionally or not, to keep certain groups poor and powerless. Economic persecution is often hidden behind complicated laws or policies, making it harder to recognize and fight. Yet its effects are real: entire communities are trapped in cycles of poverty and limited opportunity. Economic injustice reminds us that persecution is not always violent—it can be quiet, legal, and devastating.

Medical discrimination also represents a modern form of persecution. People of color, women, LGBTQ+ individuals, and people with disabilities often face worse healthcare outcomes because of bias in the medical system. They may be taken less seriously by doctors, receive lower-quality care, or face barriers to accessing necessary treatments. During public health crises, like the COVID-19 pandemic, these inequalities become even more visible and deadly. Medical discrimination shows that persecution can take many forms, including denial of basic needs like health and life itself. Fighting medical bias is essential to creating a truly just society.

Environmental racism is another example of modern persecution that is often overlooked. In many places, minority communities are more likely to live near polluted areas, toxic waste sites, or factories that harm air and water quality. They are less likely to have access to green spaces, clean water, or safe housing. These environmental dangers are not accidents—they are often the result of policies that put profits above people's health. Environmental racism shows how economic, racial, and environmental injustice are deeply connected. Fighting for clean air and water is also a fight against persecution.

Education discrimination continues to hold back millions of students around the world. In some countries, girls are denied the right to attend school simply because of their gender. In others, minority groups receive lower-quality education, fewer resources, and less support. Schools can also be places where bullying and harassment happen, targeting students based on race, religion, gender identity, disability, or social class. When children are denied education or made to feel unsafe at school, it limits their future opportunities and reinforces cycles of persecution. Education should be a tool for freedom, not another place where injustice takes root.

Disability discrimination remains a major form of modern persecution. People with physical or mental disabilities often face barriers to full participation in society. Public spaces, transportation systems, and workplaces are not always accessible. Prejudice and ignorance can lead to exclusion, pity, or outright cruelty. Disability rights activists have fought hard for laws like the Americans with Disabilities Act, but full equality remains a distant goal. Disability discrimination shows how society often punishes people simply for being different. True inclusion requires not just physical changes, but a change in attitudes and values.

Cultural erasure is another subtle but powerful form of modern persecution. In many parts of the world, minority cultures are suppressed, mocked, or ignored. Traditional languages, clothing, customs, and religions are replaced or marginalized by dominant cultures. Sometimes governments actively ban minority traditions, while other times, the pressure to "fit in" leads people to abandon their heritage. Losing a culture means losing part of one's identity. Cultural erasure shows that persecution doesn't always involve violence—it can also happen through silence, shame, and invisibility. Protecting cultural diversity is an important part of fighting modern injustice.

Modern forms of persecution often overlap and reinforce each other. A person who is both a racial minority and LGBTQ+, for example, may face double or triple layers of discrimination. An immigrant woman with a disability may experience persecution based on all those identities at once. Understanding these intersections is important if we want to address persecution effectively. No one experiences life through just one identity. Persecution adapts to exploit people's differences. Fighting it requires solidarity, compassion, and a willingness to listen to every part of someone's story.

Modern persecution proves that hatred, fear, and ignorance have not been defeated. But it also shows that resistance, hope, and progress are still possible. Around the world, brave individuals and groups are standing up against injustice. They are using their voices, their creativity, and new technologies to fight back. Movements for racial justice, gender equality, religious freedom, LGBTQ+ rights, and disability rights are gaining strength. Every time someone chooses empathy over hatred, courage over fear, and truth over lies, they chip away at the forces of persecution. The fight is not easy, but it is worth it.

Water as a Target of Persecution

Water, like people, can be attacked, controlled, and even weaponized. Throughout history, armies, governments, and powerful groups have targeted water sources to gain control over others. Water is not just something people drink; it is the heart of life itself. Without access to clean water, people suffer, communities fall apart, and entire regions can become unlivable. Targeting water is a brutal way to force submission or punish groups who are seen as enemies or outsiders. Water persecution has been used as a tool of war, oppression, and discrimination for thousands of years—and it continues today.

Polluting rivers is one way that water has been used as a weapon. In times of war, invading armies have thrown dead animals, waste, or poisons into rivers that enemy towns relied on for drinking water. These acts were meant to make people sick, cause panic, and weaken defenses. Even in modern times, industrial pollution often affects rivers that run through poorer or marginalized communities. Factories dump toxic chemicals into waterways with little fear of consequences when those harmed are seen as powerless. Polluting water is not just an attack on nature—it is an attack on human life itself.

Blocking access to water is another powerful form of persecution. In ancient times, when cities were under siege, armies would often cut off access to nearby rivers, wells, or aqueducts. Without water, defenders would quickly fall to thirst and disease. Today, access to water can still be used as a tool of power. Dams can be built upstream to control the flow of water to entire regions. Governments or corporations can restrict who gets clean water and who doesn't. When one group holds the faucet, they can force others to obey—or suffer the consequences of thirst and hunger.

Poisoning wells has been a cruel tactic used throughout history. During conflicts in medieval Europe and during colonial wars, wells were often deliberately poisoned to kill or drive out enemy populations. In many cases, poisoned wells led to widespread disease outbreaks, including deadly plagues. Even rumors of poisoned wells were sometimes enough to create fear and chaos. In some sad cases, minority groups were falsely blamed for poisoning wells, leading to violent persecution. Whether real or fabricated, the idea of poisoned water has long been a terrifying weapon used to control or destroy communities.

Controlling water is a way of controlling people. If a government or powerful group controls a region's rivers, lakes, or groundwater, they can decide who gets to live comfortably and who must struggle. Water controls agriculture, industry, health, and daily survival. Without it, nothing can thrive. In places where water is scarce, whoever holds the water holds the power. Sometimes this control is used responsibly to ensure fair sharing. But all too often, it becomes a tool for oppression, with favored groups receiving water freely while disfavored groups face drought, disease, and death.

Water rights are human rights. Access to safe, clean, and sufficient water is recognized by international law as a basic necessity for life. Yet in many parts of the world, people still fight daily for their right to water. Water is not a luxury or a privilege; it is a requirement for survival, just like air. Denying people water because of their race, religion, gender, or political beliefs is a brutal form of persecution. When water rights are violated, human dignity and survival are both placed at risk. Protecting water rights is protecting human life itself.

In many places today, entire communities are denied safe drinking water based on prejudice and inequality. In Flint, Michigan, residents—many of whom were Black and poor—suffered through a water crisis where their tap water was poisoned with lead. Government officials ignored their complaints for months, even years. The Flint crisis is a modern example of how neglect and discrimination can combine to weaponize water against marginalized groups. It shows that water persecution does not only happen in war zones or distant countries; it can happen right in the heart of modern democracies.

Internationally, water conflicts have sparked wars and fueled tensions between countries. Rivers like the Nile, the Tigris-Euphrates, and the Jordan River flow through many nations that all depend on the same limited water. When one country builds dams or diverts rivers, others may face drought, crop failure, and even famine. Water disputes can easily escalate into violence, creating refugees and deepening regional instability. Controlling rivers can become an act of political aggression, forcing weaker neighbors to bend to the will of the powerful. Water is a precious resource—and a dangerously powerful one.

In rural areas around the world, indigenous peoples often suffer water persecution. Many native communities have lived near rivers, lakes, and sacred springs for thousands of years. Yet when powerful companies or governments seek profit, they often take that land and water without permission. Dams, mines, and oil pipelines are built, polluting and disrupting vital water sources. Indigenous people are left to fight for their survival, defending not just their homes but their cultures and ways of life. The theft of water from native peoples is a modern form of colonialism, driven by greed and ignorance.

Water scarcity caused by climate change is making water persecution even worse. As droughts become more common and rivers dry up, competition for water grows fiercer. In some regions, governments favor wealthy cities or industries, leaving rural communities to wither. In others, refugees are forced to flee because they can no longer farm or find clean water. Climate change acts like a giant magnifier, making existing inequalities even worse. Poor, marginalized communities feel the effects first and hardest, while those with power and money secure their access to shrinking water supplies.

In some conflict zones, armies and militias intentionally bomb or destroy water infrastructure. Water treatment plants, pipelines, and reservoirs become military targets. Without water, civilian populations suffer massive health crises. Cholera and other waterborne diseases spread rapidly when sanitation systems collapse. Bombing a water plant is not just about winning a military victory; it is about breaking the will of the people. These attacks violate international laws meant to protect civilians during war, but they continue to happen, showing how little regard some forces have for human life and dignity.

Gender discrimination can also be seen in access to water. In many parts of the world, women and girls are responsible for gathering water for their families. When water sources are far away or dangerous to reach, women must walk long distances, risking physical harm, violence, and exploitation. In some cultures, girls are pulled from school because fetching water is considered more important. Water scarcity and unsafe water access thus reinforce gender inequality. Attacking water access is not just about environmental harm—it is also about maintaining systems of gender-based oppression.

In urban areas, water access can depend heavily on wealth and privilege. In slums and poor neighborhoods, clean water may be expensive, scarce, or completely unavailable. Meanwhile, luxury hotels, golf courses, and wealthy neighborhoods enjoy endless supplies of fresh, safe water. This inequality is a form of persecution hidden behind economics. It says that some lives matter more than others, based simply on how much money they have. Access to water should not depend on your bank account. Yet in many cities, the water you drink is a reflection of your place in a deeply unequal society.

Environmental destruction can also be an indirect form of water persecution. When forests are cut down, wetlands drained, and rivers diverted for profit, natural water systems collapse. Communities that rely on those natural systems lose their water security. Often, the communities harmed the most have the least power to fight back. Environmental degradation is rarely random; it follows patterns of economic and racial injustice. Protecting natural ecosystems is not just about saving animals—it is about saving human communities from slow but certain destruction through water loss.

Technology offers both hope and danger when it comes to water. Desalination plants, better irrigation methods, and water purification technologies can help expand access to clean water. However, technology can also be used to control water unfairly. Companies can patent water purification methods, making them too expensive for the poor. Private corporations can buy up water rights, treating water like a product instead of a human right. If technology is used for profit instead of justice, it becomes just another way to persecute the vulnerable while enriching the powerful.

Resistance to water persecution is growing. Indigenous groups, environmental activists, and ordinary citizens are standing up for their right to water. From protests against pipelines to legal battles for river protection, people are fighting back. Some communities are creating their own water systems, free from government or corporate control. Others are using technology to clean and share water fairly. Resistance shows that while water can be weaponized, it can also be a source of unity and hope. Fighting for water rights is fighting for life itself—and it is a fight that affects every one of us.

Water connects every living thing on Earth. It should be a symbol of life, community, and hope—not a weapon of destruction. When water is targeted, it is not just an environmental issue; it is a human rights emergency. Protecting water means protecting people. It means standing up against those who would poison, steal, or restrict access to this vital resource. The fight for water justice is one of the most important battles of our time. If we lose it, we lose much more than rivers and lakes—we lose the very future of humanity itself.

Spiritual Damage Caused by Persecution

Persecution does more than cause physical pain—it strikes deep into the heart and soul. When someone is hurt, excluded, or hated simply for who they are, the wound cuts much deeper than bruises or broken bones. Physical injuries can heal with time, but the emotional and spiritual wounds often linger for years, sometimes a lifetime. Being rejected or attacked for your identity can make you question your worth, your place in the world, and even your reason for existing. Persecution leaves invisible scars that are just as real as any broken body.

The spiritual damage caused by persecution often begins with a deep sense of isolation. When society tells a person they are unwanted or lesser, it creates a wall between them and the world. It is not just that they feel lonely—it is that they feel separated from humanity itself. This kind of loneliness can be overwhelming. It teaches people to doubt not only others but also themselves. They may start to believe that maybe they really are unworthy of love, respect, or happiness. The human spirit, once strong and hopeful, can begin to crumble under the weight of this isolation.

Hatred directed at a person's core identity—like their race, religion, culture, or beliefs—strikes at their very foundation. Imagine building your entire sense of self on values you love, only to have the world spit on them. It can make a person feel as if their soul is under attack. Over time, some people may begin to internalize the hatred they experience. They start believing the lies told about them. Self-hate grows where self-love once lived. This loss of identity and pride can be one of the cruelest forms of spiritual damage caused by persecution.

Trust is often one of the first victims of persecution. When you are mistreated for being yourself, it becomes hard to trust others. Even when someone offers kindness, you might wonder if it's real or just a trick. This fear of betrayal can make relationships difficult or even impossible. Friendships, family bonds, and community ties weaken when trust is poisoned by repeated pain. A persecuted person often carries this fear silently, feeling trapped behind invisible walls. Without trust, the soul becomes a fortress—protected, but isolated and starving for real connection.

Persecution can make the world feel like a dangerous, hateful place. For someone who has been hurt again and again, hope can seem foolish. Dreams fade. Optimism dries up. The spirit, which naturally wants to believe in goodness, starts to shrink back in fear. Life becomes about survival instead of thriving. When persecution strips away a person's belief that good things are possible, it steals not just their joy but also their future. Spiritual damage thrives in this darkness, whispering that life will never get better, that safety and happiness are out of reach.

Self-esteem suffers greatly under the weight of persecution. If you are constantly treated as less than human, you might start to feel less than human yourself. Confidence erodes. People may stop chasing their goals because they believe they are not worthy of success. They might stop trying to build relationships because they think they are not lovable. Persecution teaches dangerous lessons about self-worth, lessons that can stay buried inside a person for years. Healing requires unlearning these toxic ideas and rebuilding a broken self-image from the ground up.

Fear becomes a constant companion when someone has been persecuted. It is not just fear of physical attack—it is fear of being judged, misunderstood, or abandoned. Fear of standing out. Fear of speaking up. Fear of being too visible or too invisible. Fear becomes part of daily life, shaping every decision and every dream. Living in constant fear exhausts the spirit. It turns life into a battlefield, where even the smallest actions feel risky. Over time, fear can chain the spirit, limiting its growth, its creativity, and its ability to love freely.

Persecution often breaks the sacred bond between the individual and the wider community. Every human being longs to belong somewhere—to be seen, heard, and valued. But persecution tells people they are outsiders, that they are unwelcome. When your community turns its back on you, it can feel like a betrayal of the deepest kind. People may feel homeless even when they have a house. They may feel rootless even when they have a family. This loss of belonging is a heavy blow to the spirit, one that creates feelings of emptiness and grief.

Sometimes persecution damages a person's relationship with their own beliefs or religion. If someone is persecuted for their faith, they might begin to doubt the very beliefs that once gave them strength. They might feel abandoned by the divine, or question whether their faith is worth the suffering it has brought. Some people turn away from religion altogether, feeling betrayed or lost. Others hold on even tighter but carry wounds of anger and confusion inside. Either way, persecution creates a spiritual crisis that can shake a person's soul to its core.

Persecution often makes people hide parts of themselves to stay safe. They may lie about who they are, change how they look or speak, or pretend to believe things they don't. Living a double life to avoid persecution is exhausting. It creates deep shame and guilt, even though the person is simply trying to survive. Over time, pretending can blur into forgetting who you really are. The spirit suffers when it cannot live openly and honestly. Hiding becomes a habit that smothers the soul, slowly draining it of its true light and voice.

Guilt and shame are common emotions in those who have been persecuted. Even though they did nothing wrong, people often blame themselves for the suffering they experience. "Maybe if I had acted differently," they think, "this wouldn't have happened." Shame tells them they are broken or dirty because of who they are. Guilt tells them they somehow deserved their pain. These feelings are cruel lies born from persecution, but they can feel very real. Guilt and shame weigh heavily on the soul, making healing feel far away and impossible.

Anger is another wound of persecution. It is natural to feel furious when you are mistreated. Anger can even be a healthy response to injustice. But when anger is buried or ignored, it can twist into bitterness, self-hate, or rage at the world. Chronic anger can harden the heart, making it difficult to trust, to hope, or to love. The spirit that once sought connection now seeks revenge or isolation. Finding a way to process anger—to honor it without becoming consumed by it—is a huge part of healing from spiritual damage.

Persecution can rob people of their dreams. When someone is told over and over that they don't belong, they may stop imagining a bright future for themselves. Why bother dreaming of college, of love, of success, when the world seems to have no place for you? Dreams give the soul a reason to move forward. Without dreams, life becomes survival, and survival alone. Restoring the ability to dream—to hope, to imagine, to believe—is one of the most powerful steps toward healing from the spiritual damage caused by persecution.

Many who are persecuted struggle to believe in justice. After facing cruelty, people often lose faith in laws, governments, and leaders who are supposed to protect them. The betrayal by society feels personal and deep. If justice seems impossible, hopelessness grows. The spirit needs to believe that right can win, that truth matters. When that belief is shattered, cynicism and despair can take over. Healing from persecution means finding reasons to believe in justice again, even when the world has shown its ugliest face.

Despite all the damage, the human spirit is incredibly resilient. Even in the darkest moments, many people find ways to hold onto small sparks of hope. A kind word from a stranger, a moment of laughter, a memory of love—these tiny lights can keep the spirit alive. Healing from spiritual damage takes time, patience, and immense courage. It requires rebuilding trust, restoring self-worth, and daring to hope again. It is slow work, but it is possible. The spirit, though wounded, can learn to rise stronger and wiser than before.

Love is the greatest healer of spiritual wounds. Real love—kind, patient, and unconditional—has the power to reach the deepest places of hurt. When persecuted people are embraced, seen, and truly accepted, the healing process begins. Love tells the wounded soul:

"You are enough. You are worthy. You are not alone."
It rebuilds broken identities, restores lost dreams, and
renews crushed hope. Healing from persecution is not
a journey anyone should have to walk alone. Love
makes the unbearable bearable and the impossible
possible.

Healing from spiritual damage caused by persecution
is an act of incredible bravery. It is not weak to be
wounded by hate—it is human. It is not foolish to hope
again after being crushed—it is heroic. Those who have
been persecuted carry heavy burdens, but they also
carry incredible strength. Their survival is a testimony
to the power of the human spirit. In facing hate, they
show the world what true courage looks like. And in
healing, they teach all of us that even in the face of
cruelty, the soul can still choose life, hope, and love.

Regions Still Fighting Persecution Today

Around the world today, millions of people still face
persecution because of their race, religion, gender, or
beliefs. Some are forced to flee their homes, while
others stay and fight for their rights against impossible
odds. Persecution is not just a story from history books;
it is a painful reality for countless individuals and
communities. From war zones to city streets, people
continue to suffer injustice every day. Their stories
remind us that the battle for freedom and equality is far
from over. It is happening right now, in places many of

us may never have heard of—and even in places we know well.

One of the most well-known current examples is the persecution of the Rohingya people in Myanmar. The Rohingya, a Muslim minority, have faced violence, discrimination, and displacement for decades. In 2017, a brutal military campaign forced hundreds of thousands of Rohingya to flee their homes, crossing into Bangladesh to find safety. Many now live in crowded refugee camps under harsh conditions, with little hope of returning home. Despite international outcry, their situation remains dire. The Rohingya's story is one of deep pain but also incredible resilience in the face of nearly unimaginable suffering.

In China, the Uighur Muslim population has been the target of government crackdowns for many years. Reports show that over a million Uighurs have been detained in what the Chinese government calls "re-education centers," but many human rights groups call them detention camps. Uighurs are often separated from their families, forced to abandon their religious practices, and made to give up their language and culture. The Chinese government denies wrongdoing, but survivors tell heartbreaking stories of oppression and abuse. The Uighur crisis has become a global symbol of religious and ethnic persecution in the modern world.

In Afghanistan, after the Taliban regained control in 2021, many minorities and women found themselves once again living under extreme persecution. Hazara communities, known for being a Shia Muslim minority, have been especially targeted. Women, who had started to gain freedoms in past years, are now banned from many forms of education and work. Fear has returned to daily life for millions. Brave women have taken to the streets to protest, knowing they face threats, violence, and imprisonment. Their courage shines as a powerful light in a place struggling with deep darkness and fear.

In Iran, the fight against persecution has taken on new energy, especially among young people and women. After the death of Mahsa Amini in 2022, protests erupted across the country, led by brave citizens demanding freedom and equality. The government responded with brutal crackdowns, imprisoning and even executing some protesters. Women who refuse to wear the hijab face harsh punishments. The Iranian people continue to risk everything to stand against a system that tries to silence them. Their struggle reminds the world that the thirst for freedom can never be fully crushed, even by violence.

In North Korea, the government uses fear and extreme control to maintain power, leading to some of the worst human rights abuses on Earth. Citizens can be imprisoned, tortured, or executed simply for speaking out, practicing religion, or trying to leave the country. Christians, in particular, face brutal persecution, with entire families sent to labor camps if even one member is found practicing their faith. Most North Koreans live in total isolation from the outside world, trapped by a system designed to erase their basic human rights. Their silent suffering is a tragedy that often goes unnoticed by the global public.

In Sudan, religious and ethnic persecution has been a source of conflict for decades. Although South Sudan gained independence in 2011, violence in Sudan continues, especially against Christian and indigenous African communities. In Darfur, atrocities against ethnic minorities have left hundreds of thousands dead or displaced. Peace agreements have been signed and broken over and over again. Despite hopes for change, many communities still live in fear. Some activists risk their lives every day to document abuses and demand justice. Their bravery keeps the hope for a better Sudan alive, even when peace seems far away.

In Nigeria, religious violence between Muslim and Christian communities has torn parts of the country apart. Extremist groups like Boko Haram have terrorized villages, kidnapped school children, and killed thousands. Meanwhile, in some areas, Muslim or Christian minorities face pressure and violence simply for practicing their faith. Farmers and herders clash in deadly battles fueled by ethnic and religious tensions. Amid this chaos, brave leaders from both religions work to build peace and understanding. Their work is dangerous and slow, but it is vital for breaking the cycle of hatred and persecution that grips the region.

In India, religious minorities such as Muslims, Christians, and lower-caste Hindus (Dalits) often face discrimination and violence. Rising nationalism has made life more difficult for those who don't fit into the dominant religious identity. In some cases, mobs have attacked minorities over rumors or accusations, leading to tragic deaths. Laws meant to protect religious freedom sometimes fail to offer real protection. Despite the dangers, activists and ordinary citizens continue to stand up for equality and justice. Their courage shows that even in the largest democracies, the fight against persecution is ongoing.

In Venezuela, political persecution has become a daily reality for those who oppose the government. Activists, journalists, and even regular citizens who criticize leaders face threats, imprisonment, or worse. Freedom of speech and the right to protest are supposed to be basic human rights, but they are brutally suppressed. Many Venezuelans have been forced to flee the country, creating one of the largest refugee crises in the world today. Those who stay behind continue to resist in small and large ways, fighting for a future where they can live free from fear and oppression.

In Russia, persecution against political activists, LGBTQ+ individuals, and religious minorities has increased sharply in recent years. Laws have been passed to silence dissent and make it dangerous to protest or speak out. LGBTQ+ communities face legal barriers and widespread discrimination. Religious groups that don't align with government-approved churches face harassment and even arrest. Brave Russians continue to resist, using art, writing, protests, and social media to push back against censorship and oppression. Their voices show that even under harsh governments, the spirit of freedom is hard to kill.

In Palestine and Israel, generations of conflict have left civilians living under constant fear and uncertainty. Many Palestinians face daily challenges including limited movement, home demolitions, and violence. Meanwhile, Israeli civilians also live with the fear of attacks. The political situation is complicated, but on the ground, regular people often pay the highest price. Despite the hardships, many grassroots organizations on both sides work toward peace, dialogue, and justice. Their work offers hope that even the deepest wounds can one day begin to heal through courage and compassion.

In Yemen, a brutal civil war has created one of the worst humanitarian crises in modern history. Millions are at risk of famine, and basic services like healthcare and education have collapsed. Religious minorities like the Baha'i community have faced imprisonment and persecution from different sides of the conflict. Children are especially vulnerable, growing up surrounded by violence and fear. Despite the unimaginable challenges, humanitarian workers and peace activists continue to risk their lives to help. Their perseverance shines as a small light in a country engulfed by darkness and despair.

In Ethiopia, ethnic violence and civil conflict have caused massive suffering. The Tigray conflict, in particular, led to horrific reports of mass killings, sexual violence, and starvation. Entire communities have been torn apart because of their ethnicity. Peace talks have begun, but many survivors still live with deep trauma and fear. In the face of such cruelty, community leaders, aid workers, and ordinary people continue to call for peace, justice, and reconciliation. Their bravery in speaking out against atrocities shows the world that even amid devastation, there is still a fight for human dignity.

In Haiti, political instability and gang violence have created an environment where persecution thrives. Journalists, activists, and even regular citizens live in constant fear. Kidnappings and targeted killings have become shockingly common. Corruption and poverty make it even harder for people to protect themselves. Yet, in the middle of all this suffering, many Haitians continue to fight for their country's future. Through education, activism, and community support, they push back against the forces trying to silence them. Their courage reminds us that hope can survive even in the harshest conditions.

In Syria, years of civil war have destroyed cities and torn apart families. Religious and ethnic minorities like Christians, Kurds, and Druze communities have faced violence from multiple sides of the conflict. Many Syrians have fled to other countries, becoming refugees struggling to find new homes. Others remain in Syria, living among ruins and carrying scars from endless violence. Despite everything, many Syrians continue to rebuild their lives and their communities. Their strength in the face of overwhelming suffering is a powerful reminder that even after the worst disasters, the human spirit can endure.

Around the world, persecution is still a daily nightmare for too many people. Yet in every corner of the globe, there are brave individuals and communities standing up to hatred, injustice, and violence. They are fighting for freedom, dignity, and the right to simply exist without fear. Their courage calls us to action—not just to feel sympathy, but to support, to speak out, and to remember. The fight against persecution is not just their fight—it is all of ours. And with enough voices, enough courage, and enough compassion, the world can change for the better.

The Importance of Protecting Water and Life

Water is the foundation of all life on Earth. Every living thing, from the smallest insect to the largest whale, depends on water to survive. Plants need water to grow, animals need water to drink, and humans need water for almost everything we do. Without clean, safe water, life as we know it would simply not exist. It's easy to take water for granted when it flows from our taps every day, but for millions of people, clean water is a precious and rare resource. Protecting water is not just about preserving nature; it's about protecting every living thing that calls this planet home.

When we pollute water, we are poisoning life itself. Factories dumping waste into rivers, oil spills in oceans, and trash thrown into lakes all damage the delicate balance of ecosystems. Fish die, plants wilt, and entire communities suffer when water is no longer safe. Pollution does not stay in one place; it spreads through rivers and streams, eventually reaching oceans. Once water is contaminated, it can take years or even decades to heal. By letting pollution continue, we are turning our backs on the very source of life we all depend on.

Control over water has been used as a tool of power for centuries. In some regions, access to water is limited by governments, corporations, or powerful groups. When people are denied water, they are denied life. Wars have been fought over water rights, and entire communities have been displaced when water sources were taken or destroyed. Water is not just a natural resource—it is a human right. Protecting water means standing against injustice, inequality, and the misuse of power. It means believing that everyone, everywhere, deserves the chance to live and thrive.

Destruction of natural water sources is a slow form of persecution against future generations. When wetlands are drained, rivers are dammed without care, and forests are cut down, we are robbing our children and grandchildren of their future. Clean water is becoming scarcer every year, and unless we act now, the damage may become impossible to reverse. Protecting water is one of the most important gifts we can give to the next generation. It is a choice between short-term profits and long-term survival. It is a choice between destruction and life.

Climate change is making the protection of water even more urgent. Rising temperatures cause droughts in some places and deadly floods in others. Glaciers that supply drinking water to millions are melting at alarming rates. As climate change worsens, access to clean water will become even harder for many people. Protecting water also means fighting climate change with everything we have. It means planting trees, reducing pollution, and protecting the natural cycles that keep water flowing where it's needed most. Every action we take today shapes the future of our water and our planet.

Communities around the world are already taking bold steps to protect water. In some areas, local groups work together to clean rivers, plant trees along waterways, and build systems that capture and store rainwater. Indigenous peoples, in particular, have long understood the importance of living in balance with water. Their traditional knowledge offers valuable lessons about respect, sustainability, and stewardship. By listening to these voices and supporting community-led efforts, we can build a global movement that honors and protects water for everyone.

Corporations and industries have a huge role to play in protecting water. Businesses that depend on water must take responsibility for using it wisely and keeping it clean. That means stopping wasteful practices, treating wastewater properly, and investing in technologies that reduce pollution. Consumers also have power by choosing to support companies that care about water protection. Every product we buy and every service we use can either help or harm the planet. Being mindful of our choices is a powerful way to protect water every single day.

Government action is critical when it comes to protecting water. Laws and regulations must be put in place to prevent pollution, manage resources fairly, and protect ecosystems. When governments prioritize the health of rivers, lakes, and oceans, they are prioritizing the health of their people. However, laws are only effective if they are enforced. Citizens must stay informed, raise their voices, and hold leaders accountable. Democracy works best when people demand protection for the things that matter most— and nothing matters more than water.

Education is another key part of water protection. When people understand where their water comes from and what threatens it, they are more likely to take action. Schools, communities, and families must teach young people to respect water and protect it. Simple lessons about pollution, conservation, and sustainability can create lifelong habits of care and responsibility. The more we know about water, the better we can protect it. Knowledge turns into action, and action turns into change. Education plants the seeds of a better future.

Water connects everything on Earth. It connects the mountains to the seas, the forests to the deserts, and the cities to the farmlands. What happens to water in one place affects life everywhere else. Pollution that starts in a small stream can eventually poison a vast ocean. Protecting water means understanding this connection and caring about places we may never see. It means recognizing that our choices here and now can help or harm life halfway across the world. We are all connected through water.

Access to clean water is not equal across the globe. In many developing countries, people must walk miles every day just to collect a few gallons of dirty water. This water often carries diseases that can kill children and weaken entire communities. Meanwhile, in wealthier countries, water is used for watering lawns, filling swimming pools, and running industries. Protecting water also means working to end these inequalities. Every person on Earth deserves access to safe, clean water. Justice for people begins with justice for water.

Technology offers new ways to protect water, but it must be used wisely. Advances in water purification, recycling systems, and pollution monitoring can make a huge difference. Desalination plants can turn seawater into drinking water. Smart irrigation systems can save water on farms. However, technology alone cannot solve the water crisis. It must be combined with respect for nature, strong laws, and public awareness. Technology is a tool, not a magic solution. Protecting water still requires commitment, wisdom, and compassion from everyone.

The health of wildlife depends entirely on healthy water sources. Frogs, fish, birds, and countless other creatures live in and around water. When lakes dry up or rivers are poisoned, these animals have nowhere to go. Entire species can disappear. Protecting water means protecting biodiversity—the amazing variety of life on Earth. Every creature plays a role in the great web of life, and losing even one species can cause ripples throughout entire ecosystems. Saving water saves animals, plants, and the natural beauty that makes our world so special.

Protecting water also protects human health. Contaminated water causes deadly diseases like cholera, dysentery, and typhoid fever. Even in modern cities, waterborne illnesses can spread quickly if water systems fail. Ensuring clean water protects communities from sickness and death. It also supports mental health by giving people peace of mind. Knowing that your water is safe to drink, cook with, and bathe in is a basic need that no one should be denied. Health and water are forever linked.

Water is sacred in many cultures and religions. It is seen as a gift, a blessing, and a symbol of life and purity. Rivers, lakes, and oceans have inspired songs, prayers, and ceremonies for thousands of years. Protecting water means honoring the deep spiritual connections that many people feel toward it. It means respecting the traditions and wisdom of cultures that have long understood that water is more than just a resource—it is life itself. In protecting water, we are protecting something profoundly sacred.

Personal actions matter more than we think. Small changes in our daily lives, like using less water, avoiding plastic waste, and supporting conservation groups, add up over time. Turning off the tap while brushing your teeth, fixing leaks, and using water-saving appliances are simple but powerful steps. Spreading awareness, participating in clean-up events, and voting for leaders who care about the environment also make a difference. Everyone has a role to play in protecting water, no matter how big or small.

Choosing to protect water is choosing to protect the future. It is an act of love toward our planet, toward each other, and toward generations still to come. It is a promise that we will not stand by while the lifeblood of Earth is poisoned or stolen. Protecting water is an act of courage, of hope, and of responsibility. It demands that we see beyond our immediate needs and think about the world we want to leave behind. In protecting water, we protect everything that makes life beautiful, vibrant, and worth living.

Rising Above Persecution

Persecution is one of the darkest sides of human behavior, but it is not the end of the story. Throughout history, brave individuals have stood tall in the face of hatred, violence, and injustice. They showed the world that even when things seem impossible, the human spirit can rise above cruelty. These people did not let fear or anger control their actions. Instead, they responded with courage, strength, and hope. Their stories remind us that persecution may cause pain, but it can never fully destroy goodness unless we let it.

Martin Luther King Jr. is one of the most powerful examples of someone who rose above persecution. During the civil rights movement in the United States, he faced hatred, threats, and even physical attacks simply because he fought for equality. King believed in nonviolence and love, even when others responded with cruelty. His speeches, like the famous "I Have a Dream" speech, inspired millions to believe in a better future. Though he was assassinated, his message lives on, reminding us that courage and compassion are stronger than hatred.

Nelson Mandela is another shining example. In South Africa, Mandela was imprisoned for 27 years because he stood against the racist system of apartheid. Despite the injustice he suffered, he chose forgiveness over revenge. When he was finally released, he worked to unite the country rather than divide it. Mandela became South Africa's first Black president and a symbol of peace and perseverance around the world. His life teaches us that even after decades of suffering, it is possible to forgive, heal, and build a better future.

Malala Yousafzai's story is one of remarkable bravery. Growing up in Pakistan, she spoke out for the rights of girls to receive an education. For this, she became a target of the Taliban, a violent extremist group. At just fifteen years old, she was shot in the head while riding a bus home from school. But instead of giving up, Malala grew even stronger. She continued to speak out, eventually becoming the youngest-ever Nobel Peace Prize winner. Malala shows us that even young people can change the world with their courage and voice.

These leaders did not pretend that persecution was easy to overcome. They felt fear, pain, and sadness, just like anyone would. What set them apart was their choice to act with love instead of hatred. They refused to let persecution define them or make them bitter. Instead, they used their struggles as fuel to fight harder for justice. Rising above persecution does not mean ignoring the pain—it means refusing to let the pain win. It means believing that a better world is possible and working toward it every day.

Ordinary people also rise above persecution every day, even if their stories are not always told in history books. Refugees who flee dangerous countries and rebuild their lives show incredible strength. Minority groups who fight for their rights with peaceful protests demonstrate bravery. Students who stand up against bullying or discrimination in their schools are heroes too. Every act of courage, no matter how small, chips away at the power of hatred. Rising above persecution happens one brave choice at a time.

Art, music, and literature have often been powerful tools for rising above persecution. Artists have painted murals of hope on walls broken by war. Musicians have written songs that inspire courage during dark times. Writers have used words to challenge injustice and imagine better futures. Creative expression allows people to turn their pain into beauty. It helps others understand their struggles and join their cause. In many ways, art becomes a bridge between suffering and hope, a way of healing both individuals and entire communities.

Faith and spirituality have also helped many people rise above persecution. Believing in something greater than themselves gives people strength when everything else seems lost. For Martin Luther King Jr., his Christian faith guided his philosophy of nonviolence. For Mandela, his belief in the dignity of all people helped him forgive his enemies. Faith does not belong to any one religion—it can be found in any belief that teaches love, justice, and compassion. Spiritual strength can give people the courage to keep going when nothing else seems possible.

Education is another key weapon against persecution. When people learn about history, human rights, and critical thinking, they are better prepared to stand up against injustice. Malala's fight for girls' education is a powerful example. She understood that with education, people could lift themselves out of oppression and change their societies. Education opens minds, builds empathy, and teaches people to question unfair systems. Rising above persecution often begins with the simple but powerful act of learning.

Building strong communities is essential for overcoming persecution. No one should have to fight injustice alone. When people come together, they are stronger and more resilient. Communities can offer support, encouragement, and protection to those facing hatred. They can organize marches, create safe spaces, and advocate for laws that protect human rights. A strong community reminds people that they are not alone, and that together, they can create real change. Unity is one of the most powerful forces against persecution.

Patience and persistence are necessary when rising above persecution. Change rarely happens overnight. Martin Luther King Jr., Nelson Mandela, and Malala Yousafzai all faced years of struggle before they saw progress. There were many setbacks and moments when giving up might have seemed easier. But they kept going. They understood that real change takes time and that every step forward matters, even when it feels small. Rising above persecution requires the patience to keep fighting, even when the road is long and hard.

Courage is not the absence of fear, but the decision to act despite fear. Every person who has risen above persecution felt fear at some point. The difference is that they did not let fear control their actions. They found something more important than fear—justice, love, truth—and they held onto it. Courage grows stronger every time someone refuses to stay silent in the face of wrong. It shines brightest when the darkness feels overwhelming. Rising above persecution means choosing courage again and again.

Forgiveness can be one of the hardest parts of rising above persecution, but also one of the most powerful. Nelson Mandela forgave the very people who locked him in prison for nearly three decades. Forgiveness does not mean forgetting or excusing injustice. It means refusing to let hatred poison your heart. It frees the victim from carrying the burden of anger forever. Forgiveness allows healing to begin, both for individuals and for societies. It is a revolutionary act of strength, not weakness.

Hope is the fuel that keeps people moving forward during persecution. Without hope, despair takes over. Every leader who rose above persecution held onto a vision of a better future. They imagined a world where people could live freely, love openly, and be treated with dignity. Hope gave them the strength to endure when everything else seemed broken. Hope is not naive or foolish—it is a powerful, life-giving force. Rising above persecution means planting seeds of hope even in the harshest soil.

Role models are essential for teaching future generations how to rise above persecution. When young people learn about figures like King, Mandela, and Malala, they see what is possible. They understand that one person really can make a difference. Role models show that rising above persecution is not just for the famous or powerful—it is for anyone with a dream and the courage to pursue it. Every person who stands up for justice becomes a light that others can follow.

Technology and social media are new tools for rising above persecution. Today, people can share their stories with the world in an instant. They can organize protests, raise awareness, and connect with others who share their cause. Technology gives a voice to those who were once silenced. It allows ordinary people to build movements that demand change. Used wisely, technology can be a powerful force for justice, hope, and healing. It offers new ways for humanity to rise above hatred.

In the end, rising above persecution is about choosing love over hate, hope over despair, and action over silence. It is about believing that even in the darkest times, light is still possible. It is about knowing that while persecution can break bodies and cause pain, it cannot destroy the spirit unless we let it. The stories of those who rose above remind us that we are stronger than we think. They challenge us to be better, braver, and more compassionate. They remind us that we, too, can rise.

Chapter Summary

Persecution is a recurring pattern of cruelty that spans across time and cultures. It's easy to think of persecution as something that happened in the distant past, but in reality, it's an ongoing issue in our world today. Persecution begins with misunderstandings and misconceptions, often fueled by fear and hatred. What starts as a small division between people based on their differences grows into something much larger: systems of violence, laws that discriminate, and entire institutions built to harm certain groups of people. Whether it's because of race, religion, gender, or any other characteristic, persecution affects the body, mind, and spirit. It's a dehumanizing force that rips apart communities, breaks down trust, and fosters an environment of hatred and distrust.

As we've seen throughout history, persecution harms not just the individuals targeted, but also the world around them. Water, the essence of life, becomes another victim when it is polluted, stolen, or restricted. Just as people suffer when they are mistreated, nature too suffers when its resources are abused. When access to clean water is limited, when rivers and oceans are poisoned, or when water becomes a tool of control, it is an act of cruelty that harms not just one community, but the entire ecosystem. Just like humans, water is sacred and deserves to be treated with respect. When we protect water, we are protecting the very essence of life itself, which sustains all forms of existence.

The connection between water and life is profound. Water is the foundation of all living things—humans, animals, plants, and ecosystems. When water is harmed, everything that depends on it is affected. This chapter has shown that understanding this connection is vital for seeing the bigger picture. If we view the protection of water as a moral issue, a way to ensure the survival of future generations and all life forms, we can take action to prevent its abuse. When we stand up for clean water, we are also standing up for the survival of life on Earth.

Despite the weight of persecution, there is always hope. Throughout history, we have witnessed countless examples of individuals who have refused to accept cruelty and injustice. These brave souls have stood up against forces of hatred and demand a better world. Their courage shines as a beacon for all of us, showing that even in the face of tremendous adversity, there is a path toward justice. Leaders like Martin Luther King Jr., Nelson Mandela, and countless other unsung heroes remind us that love, understanding, and action have the power to overcome fear and hatred. Each act of courage, no matter how small, contributes to the larger movement toward change.

As we continue to witness the suffering caused by persecution, we must also hold on to the hope that change is possible. The courage of those who have fought against persecution teaches us that we, too, can make a difference. It's through our willingness to stand up, to speak out, and to protect the vulnerable that we can break the chains of hatred. Whether we are fighting for justice, protecting the environment, or standing up for human rights, every act of courage matters. It is these actions that bring about a brighter future, where peace and love can thrive.

Healing from persecution—whether personal, societal, or environmental—requires clarity. It demands that we see the truth for what it is and refuse to let fear dictate our actions. When we rise above persecution, we open the door to healing. We not only heal ourselves, but we also heal the world around us. The actions we take today can set the course for a better tomorrow. By standing up for what's right, we create a future where every living being, including the planet itself, is treated with respect and love. The healing process is not just about healing the wounds of the past, but creating a world where those wounds are no longer inflicted.

In the end, the fight against persecution is not a battle between good and evil—it's a battle between love and fear. When we choose to act with love, to protect the vulnerable, and to stand up against injustice, we create a ripple effect that has the power to transform the world. The protection of water and life is just one part of that larger battle. By recognizing the interconnectedness of all living things and acting with compassion and courage, we move closer to a world where all beings can live in harmony, free from the chains of persecution.

Chapter Four

Affluence

Affluence, often defined as the state of having a great deal of money, is a concept that has shaped societies throughout history. While wealth can provide opportunities and comfort, it can also come with a responsibility. Unfortunately, throughout time, there have been many examples of affluence being used not for the betterment of society, but for the oppression of others. This misuse of wealth has perpetuated inequality and injustice, leaving many people trapped in poverty while a few accumulate wealth beyond their needs.

However, affluence does not have to be a tool for oppression. When used with integrity, wealth has the potential to create significant positive change. Affluent individuals and communities have the power to drive social, economic, and environmental progress. By using their resources responsibly, those with affluence can contribute to creating a society that is just, equitable, and sustainable. The key lies in how wealth is used: is it hoarded and used for personal gain, or is it used to uplift others and protect the planet?

In this chapter, we will explore both the negative and positive sides of affluence. We will look at how affluence has been used throughout history to either oppress or liberate, and how individuals and organizations today are using their wealth to create positive change. Whether it's through philanthropy, sustainable business practices, or investing in the community, affluence has the potential to shape a brighter future. But this potential must be realized through conscious action and a commitment to the greater good.

The history of affluence is not just about the accumulation of wealth, but about the choices that come with it. Some have chosen to use their wealth to create empires that exploit the poor and vulnerable, while others have used it to build systems that support the well-being of all people. As we reflect on the role of affluence in society, it is important to ask ourselves: how can we ensure that wealth is used in ways that serve not just the few, but the many?

This chapter will dive deep into the ways that affluence can either perpetuate harm or lead to positive change. We will examine historical examples, current trends, and the ethical implications of wealth. By the end, we hope to inspire readers to think critically about the role affluence plays in their own lives and in the world around them, and how they can use their resources to contribute to the greater good.

The Dark Side of Affluence: Oppression Through Wealth

Affluence, or wealth, has long been used as a tool of oppression. Throughout history, those with wealth have wielded their financial power to exploit the poor, control resources, and maintain their dominance over entire populations. This has led to systems of inequality that have kept the less fortunate from rising above their circumstances, while the rich have continued to amass more wealth and power. Whether through slavery, colonialism, or modern-day corporate exploitation, wealth has been used to oppress people, perpetuating cycles of poverty, disenfranchisement, and suffering for generations.

In the colonial era, European powers expanded their empires by seizing land and resources from indigenous populations across Africa, the Americas, and Asia. Colonists extracted valuable resources, such as gold, spices, and rubber, and shipped them back to Europe, leaving local communities with little to nothing. Colonization was a clear example of how affluence was used to oppress. Colonial powers justified their exploitation through racist ideologies, deeming indigenous populations inferior and using them as cheap labor to fuel the empire's wealth. These systems of exploitation left long-lasting scars that continue to impact the descendants of those oppressed by colonialism.

The concentration of wealth also helped to establish and enforce social hierarchies. In feudal societies, wealthy landowners held immense power over peasants and serfs. These landowners controlled the land and resources, dictating the lives of the people who worked for them. The poor were often bound by laws and traditions that kept them in servitude, while the rich enjoyed luxuries and privileges. The wealth of the landowners was a direct result of the exploitation of labor. Over time, these systems of oppression became deeply embedded in society, leaving the poor with little chance to escape their circumstances.

The industrial revolution in the 18th and 19th centuries further highlighted the ways in which affluence could be used to oppress. As factories grew and businesses boomed, a new class of wealthy industrialists emerged. These wealthy factory owners amassed fortunes while paying their workers low wages and subjecting them to grueling, unsafe working conditions. Children worked long hours in factories, and many workers suffered from dangerous health conditions due to the poor environment. Despite their hard work, the laborers remained in poverty, while the rich continued to profit. This exploitation of labor became a defining feature of industrial capitalism, where the working class was often kept under the thumb of those with wealth.

In today's global economy, affluence continues to play a major role in perpetuating oppression. Many corporations outsource labor to poorer countries where workers are paid pennies on the dollar and work in unsafe conditions. These companies profit by paying their workers extremely low wages while reaping the benefits of cheap labor. Workers in developing countries often lack access to basic rights, such as fair wages, healthcare, and safe working conditions. The gap between the wealthy corporations that exploit these workers and the impoverished workers themselves continues to widen, further entrenching global inequality.

Affluence also plays a role in the control of natural resources, which is another form of oppression. The wealthy have historically controlled access to land, water, and other vital resources. In many countries, land has been taken from indigenous people to benefit wealthy landowners or corporations. This has left local populations without access to essential resources, trapping them in poverty. By controlling resources, the affluent are able to maintain their power and dominance over the less fortunate. This kind of resource control perpetuates inequality, as those who are denied access to resources are unable to improve their economic situation.

The exploitation of the environment is also a form of oppression that disproportionately affects the poor. Wealthy corporations often engage in practices that harm the environment, such as deforestation, pollution, and overfishing, to increase their profits. However, it is the poor who bear the brunt of these environmental damages. Communities living near factories, mines, or landfills are often the ones exposed to toxic chemicals, polluted air, and contaminated water. These environmental hazards contribute to a host of health problems, yet the wealthy corporations responsible for the damage continue to profit while the poor suffer.

In many cases, affluence has been used to influence political systems, ensuring that the wealthy remain in control. Those with wealth have the means to fund political campaigns, lobby for favorable policies, and even manipulate public opinion through media control. This gives the rich an unfair advantage, as they are able to shape laws and regulations to suit their interests, while the less fortunate have little political power. In some countries, the wealthy can even buy access to government officials, making it harder for the poor to advocate for their needs. This kind of political influence maintains the power imbalance and ensures that the wealthy continue to thrive.

The media plays a significant role in perpetuating the oppression of affluence. Wealthy media moguls often control the information that reaches the public, framing issues in ways that benefit their interests. They can control narratives, spread misinformation, and distract from the real issues that affect the poor. By controlling public discourse, the affluent can maintain their dominance and deflect attention away from the systemic inequalities that keep the poor disenfranchised. The media's role in shaping public perception further entrenches the systems of oppression that benefit the wealthy.

Education is another area where affluence perpetuates oppression. In many societies, the wealthy have access to the best education, giving them an advantage in the job market and in life. Meanwhile, the poor often have limited access to quality education, which makes it harder for them to escape poverty. The wealthy can afford private tutors, advanced technology, and prestigious universities, while the less fortunate are left with underfunded schools and fewer opportunities to succeed. This educational divide ensures that wealth is passed down from generation to generation, keeping the rich at the top and the poor at the bottom.

Healthcare is also deeply impacted by affluence, as access to medical care is often determined by wealth. In many countries, healthcare is privatized, meaning that only those with money can afford the best treatments. The poor, on the other hand, are left with limited access to care and may suffer from preventable diseases or inadequate treatment. This disparity in healthcare access further widens the gap between the wealthy and the poor, contributing to a cycle of inequality that is difficult to break.

Affluence has also led to the rise of systemic racism. In many societies, wealth has been used to maintain racial hierarchies, with the wealthy using their resources to keep marginalized communities oppressed. This is particularly evident in the legacy of slavery in the United States, where wealthy plantation owners profited from the forced labor of African slaves. Even after the abolition of slavery, the wealth accumulated by these landowners continued to perpetuate racial inequalities, with the descendants of enslaved people facing systemic discrimination in areas such as housing, education, and employment.

The control of wealth is also closely tied to the distribution of power. In many societies, those who control the wealth hold the most power. This power allows them to dictate laws, influence policies, and shape the economy to benefit their interests. As a result, the rich are able to maintain their dominance over the less fortunate, ensuring that the wealth gap continues to grow. This concentration of wealth and power creates a system where the rich continue to get richer, while the poor are left behind.

Affluence has also played a significant role in perpetuating economic inequality. In many societies, the wealthy have access to financial opportunities that are not available to the poor. They can invest in stocks, buy real estate, and accumulate wealth through passive income. Meanwhile, the poor struggle to make ends meet and often lack the resources to build wealth. This economic divide ensures that the rich maintain their status, while the poor remain trapped in poverty.

Finally, affluence is often used to justify the exploitation of workers. In many industries, business owners and corporations make vast profits while paying their workers low wages. Workers in industries like agriculture, manufacturing, and retail are often paid just enough to survive, while the owners of these businesses accumulate wealth. The exploitation of labor is a direct result of the concentration of wealth, and it perpetuates the cycle of poverty that keeps the less fortunate from achieving economic mobility.

Despite the widespread oppression caused by affluence, there is hope. Activists and social movements continue to challenge the systems that allow wealth to be used as a tool of oppression. By raising awareness and advocating for change, they are working to dismantle the structures that perpetuate inequality. It is possible to create a more just and equitable society, one where wealth is not used to oppress but to uplift and empower. Through collective action and solidarity, we can work towards a world where affluence is used for the common good, not for exploitation.

The Creation of Social Inequality

Wealth has long been a tool used to manipulate systems of power, creating divisions in society that leave the less fortunate with limited opportunities for success. The unequal distribution of wealth often results in social inequality, where the wealthy hold power and influence over systems like government, education, and healthcare. These systems can become corrupt and biased, designed to maintain the status quo and ensure that those with money continue to have advantages, while those without are left to struggle. This cycle creates deep-rooted disparities that affect generations of people, making it nearly impossible for the poor to rise out of poverty.

In feudal societies, wealthy landowners controlled vast amounts of land, which was the most important resource at the time. They not only owned the land but also the peasants who worked it, using their wealth to dominate local governments and ensure that laws and policies benefited them. These landowners were the ones who decided who would have access to food, shelter, and even education. The peasants, on the other hand, had little say in their lives and were forced to work long hours in difficult conditions for barely enough to survive. In this way, wealth became a direct barrier to upward mobility, trapping people in poverty for generations.

The idea of "hereditary wealth" played a significant role in perpetuating social inequality. In feudal times, wealth was passed down from one generation to the next, ensuring that the children of wealthy landowners would grow up with advantages, while the children of peasants would inherit their parents' struggles. This system made it nearly impossible for those born into poverty to improve their situation, as they had limited access to education, resources, or opportunities. The rich used their wealth to protect their interests and perpetuate their control over society, while the poor were left to live in hardship.

As societies evolved, the influence of wealth continued to shape social structures. In the modern world, multinational corporations often use their financial power to manipulate political systems. These companies can fund political campaigns, lobby for laws that benefit their interests, and even influence public opinion through media control. By using their vast resources, they create a system where the rules of the game are rigged in their favor. The wealthy have the ability to shape policies that ensure they stay rich, while the poor are left with little power to fight back.

For example, wealthy corporations can push for tax cuts and deregulation, which directly benefit them but harm public services. When governments lower taxes on the rich or allow companies to avoid paying taxes, the funds needed for essential services like healthcare and education are depleted. As a result, the most vulnerable members of society, who rely on these services the most, are left with fewer resources. These policies create a cycle where the rich get richer and the poor become even more disenfranchised. In this way, wealth not only perpetuates inequality but actively deepens it.

In the realm of education, wealth has always played a key role in determining who gets access to quality schooling. Wealthy families can afford to send their children to private schools, where they receive a top-tier education, advanced resources, and access to important networks that can open doors in the future. Meanwhile, children from poor families often attend underfunded public schools that lack the resources to provide a high-quality education. This disparity in education contributes to the widening wealth gap, as children from wealthy families are better prepared for successful careers, while children from poor families struggle to overcome the obstacles created by their limited education.

Healthcare is another area where wealth influences access to resources. In many countries, healthcare is privatized, meaning that those with money can afford the best doctors and treatments, while those without are left with limited options. Wealthy individuals can pay for private insurance or directly purchase the healthcare they need, while the poor are forced to rely on overcrowded public hospitals or go without necessary care. This unequal access to healthcare contributes to social inequality, as it creates a divide between those who can afford to stay healthy and those who cannot.

Social inequality also arises in housing, where the wealthy control access to desirable neighborhoods. In many cities, affluent areas are gated off or protected by high prices, making it difficult for people from lower-income backgrounds to afford a place to live. Wealthy individuals have the means to buy property, invest in real estate, and even use their wealth to influence housing policies. On the other hand, those without wealth are often stuck in overcrowded or unsafe neighborhoods, where the quality of life is poor and opportunities for upward mobility are limited. This system reinforces the divide between the rich and the poor, making it even harder for the less fortunate to improve their circumstances.

The impact of social inequality is not limited to financial struggles—it affects all areas of life. When wealth is concentrated in the hands of a few, those without money are left with fewer opportunities to succeed. Their education is subpar, their healthcare is inadequate, and their neighborhoods are unsafe. The less fortunate face a constant struggle to make ends meet, while the rich continue to accumulate power and influence. This imbalance creates a society where social mobility is limited, and the cycle of poverty is perpetuated.

Wealth also plays a significant role in shaping the political landscape. Those with money can fund political campaigns, hire lobbyists, and use their influence to shape public policies in their favor. In many cases, this leads to laws that favor the rich, while ignoring the needs of the poor. Wealthy individuals and corporations often use their resources to fight against policies that would benefit the less fortunate, such as higher taxes on the rich or stronger regulations on business practices. This manipulation of the political system ensures that those with money remain in control, while the voices of the poor are silenced.

The media also plays a crucial role in perpetuating social inequality. Wealthy individuals and corporations often own and control media outlets, allowing them to shape the narrative and present information that benefits their interests. By controlling what the public sees and hears, they can manipulate public opinion and distract from the issues that affect the poor. For example, media outlets may focus on crime or welfare fraud, painting a negative picture of the poor, while ignoring the actions of the wealthy that contribute to inequality. This manipulation of information helps to maintain the power imbalance between the rich and the poor.

Social inequality also leads to deep divides in society. When the rich live in luxury while the poor struggle to survive, it creates a sense of resentment and frustration. The less fortunate often feel as though the system is rigged against them, and their anger can lead to social unrest. This divide between the wealthy and the poor can create tension, making it more difficult for society to work together to solve its problems. When the rich use their wealth to maintain their power and influence, they risk alienating the very people who are essential to the functioning of society.

The cycle of inequality continues when the rich pass down their wealth to the next generation. In many cases, wealthy families have access to resources that allow them to maintain their status, while the poor are left without the same opportunities. Wealth is often passed down through inheritance, giving the children of wealthy families a head start in life. Meanwhile, the children of poor families are forced to work harder just to survive, with limited opportunities to improve their circumstances. This cycle ensures that the gap between the rich and the poor remains wide, and it becomes even more difficult for future generations to break free from the chains of inequality.

Despite the challenges, there is hope for breaking the cycle of social inequality. Social movements, grassroots organizations, and political activists continue to fight for justice and equality. By challenging the systems that perpetuate inequality, they are working to create a more fair and just society. Efforts to reform education, healthcare, housing, and the political system can help to level the playing field and create more opportunities for those who have been left behind. The fight for social equality is not easy, but it is one that can be won through collective action, compassion, and determination.

As we move forward, it is crucial that we recognize the role that wealth plays in creating and perpetuating social inequality. The concentration of wealth in the hands of a few creates a system where the rich remain in control, while the poor are left to struggle. However, by working together, we can challenge these systems of oppression and work toward a more just and equitable world. The fight for social equality is ongoing, but every step we take toward justice is a step toward a better future for everyone.

Environmental Destruction Fueled by Affluence

Wealth, while often seen as a source of prosperity, can also be a driving force behind the destruction of the planet. Industries that operate on a global scale, particularly those with substantial financial resources, often place profit above environmental stewardship. These companies, empowered by their affluence, exploit natural resources for short-term gains, leaving behind long-term environmental damage. From the pollution of air and water to the destruction of ecosystems, the rich industries that perpetuate these harmful practices do so without considering the irreversible harm they cause to the environment and vulnerable communities.

One of the most glaring examples of environmental destruction caused by affluence is the extraction of fossil fuels. Wealthy oil companies have been responsible for devastating oil spills, which poison marine life and degrade coastal ecosystems. The 2010 Deepwater Horizon spill is one of the most infamous examples, where millions of barrels of oil were released into the Gulf of Mexico, causing irreparable harm to the environment. Yet, despite the catastrophic consequences, the companies responsible faced minimal consequences, with the victims being the environment and the people living along the coastlines. These communities are often left with contaminated water and land, which leads to loss of livelihood and health problems, while the wealthiest companies continue to profit.

Deforestation, driven by the demand for timber, palm oil, and agricultural expansion, is another example of environmental harm fueled by affluence. Wealthy corporations involved in these industries clear vast swathes of rainforest, which are critical to regulating the Earth's climate and preserving biodiversity. For example, the deforestation in the Amazon rainforest, often referred to as the "lungs of the Earth," is directly linked to the demand for land to grow crops like soy and raise cattle. This destruction not only threatens countless species but also disrupts the lives of indigenous people who rely on these forests for their survival. The affluent corporations responsible often ignore the social and environmental costs, seeking only to maximize their profits.

The extraction of minerals and other natural resources also contributes significantly to environmental degradation. Mining operations, which are often controlled by wealthy corporations, can cause irreparable damage to landscapes, waterways, and ecosystems. In countries where mining is a primary economic driver, such as in parts of Africa and South America, local communities often suffer from polluted water sources, land degradation, and displacement due to mining activities. These communities, already vulnerable due to economic disparity, bear the brunt of these environmental consequences. Meanwhile, the multinational corporations continue to reap enormous profits from resources that should be shared with the local population.

Climate change is perhaps the most significant and global consequence of environmental destruction fueled by affluence. The burning of fossil fuels, industrial farming, and deforestation all contribute to the increasing concentration of greenhouse gases in the atmosphere, which in turn drives global warming. The wealthiest nations and corporations are responsible for the lion's share of these emissions, yet the impacts of climate change are most severely felt in poorer, marginalized communities. These communities often live in areas more vulnerable to climate-related disasters, such as flooding, droughts, and heatwaves, which devastate their homes, food sources, and livelihoods.

In addition to global warming, affluence often leads to pollution of air, water, and soil. The industries that create the most wealth often release harmful chemicals and pollutants into the environment, poisoning local ecosystems and creating health risks for nearby communities. For example, the release of toxic waste into rivers by industrial factories has led to the contamination of drinking water in many areas. The wealthy corporations responsible for these actions often cut corners when it comes to waste disposal, passing the environmental and health costs onto the public. In many cases, these communities lack the financial resources to combat the pollution, leaving them helpless in the face of environmental harm.

The environmental destruction caused by affluence is not just about the immediate impact; it also undermines the long-term health and stability of the planet. Ecosystems that have been disrupted by industrial activity take decades or even centuries to recover, and in some cases, they may never fully recover. The loss of biodiversity due to habitat destruction or climate change has a cascading effect on ecosystems, which rely on a delicate balance of species. This can lead to the collapse of food systems, the spread of disease, and the destruction of natural resources that are vital for human survival.

Furthermore, the wealthiest individuals and corporations often use their power to resist environmental regulations that could mitigate the damage they cause. By lobbying against stricter environmental laws and regulations, they can continue their harmful practices without fear of legal consequences. The financial resources available to these entities allow them to influence policy decisions, ensuring that environmental protections are weakened or ignored. In this way, affluence perpetuates environmental destruction by enabling the powerful to bypass the rules that would protect both people and the planet.

The communities most affected by environmental destruction often lack the political and economic power to challenge these practices. Indigenous people, rural populations, and urban poor communities are particularly vulnerable, as they often live in areas that are directly impacted by environmental degradation. These communities are often excluded from decision-making processes, their voices silenced by the wealth and power of corporations and governments. As a result, they bear the burden of environmental harm without having the means to fight back, which perpetuates cycles of inequality and suffering.

In some cases, environmental destruction is a direct result of the unsustainable consumption patterns of affluent individuals. The demand for luxury goods, such as exotic animals, rare minerals, and high-end electronics, often drives illegal poaching, deforestation, and mining operations. While these activities provide short-term wealth for a few, they contribute to long-term environmental destruction and the depletion of finite resources. The growing consumer culture in wealthy nations fosters a sense of entitlement to resources that are extracted from vulnerable parts of the world, leaving a trail of destruction behind.

Despite the widespread nature of environmental destruction fueled by affluence, there are efforts to counteract this damage. Environmental activists and organizations around the world are working to raise awareness about the harmful impacts of corporate greed and the need for sustainable practices. These efforts aim to hold corporations accountable for their actions and push for stronger regulations that protect the environment. By advocating for policy changes and encouraging sustainable practices, these organizations are working to reduce the harmful effects of affluence on the planet.

Governments, too, have a crucial role to play in addressing environmental destruction. Many countries have passed laws that aim to protect natural resources and regulate pollution. However, the effectiveness of these laws is often undermined by the influence of wealthy corporations that can afford to lobby against them. Governments need to prioritize the long-term health of the planet over short-term economic gains and work to create policies that balance economic growth with environmental protection.

The fight against environmental destruction fueled by affluence is not just about stopping harmful practices; it's also about promoting sustainable alternatives. Many industries are developing green technologies and sustainable business practices that reduce environmental harm while still allowing for economic growth. Renewable energy, sustainable agriculture, and eco-friendly manufacturing processes are all examples of ways in which businesses can continue to profit without damaging the planet. By supporting these alternatives, we can shift away from destructive practices and move toward a more sustainable future.

The responsibility for addressing environmental destruction does not fall solely on corporations or governments. Individuals also have a role to play in reducing their environmental impact. By making conscious choices about consumption, reducing waste, and supporting sustainable businesses, individuals can contribute to a more sustainable future. Collective action, both on the part of corporations and individuals, is essential for mitigating the harmful effects of affluence on the environment.

Ultimately, the fight against environmental destruction fueled by affluence is about shifting our values. Instead of prioritizing wealth and profit above all else, we must recognize the importance of protecting the planet and its resources. By valuing sustainability, equity, and justice, we can create a world where both people and the planet can thrive. Only through collective action and a commitment to sustainability can we ensure a future where environmental destruction is no longer fueled by affluence.

Social Systems That Protect the Rich

Affluence not only allows the wealthy to accumulate vast amounts of wealth but also grants them the ability to shape the social systems that govern society. These systems, whether they are related to education, healthcare, or criminal justice, are often designed in ways that benefit the rich while leaving the poor at a disadvantage. In many cases, the wealthy can afford to navigate these systems in ways that preserve their status, while the poor face significant barriers to success and equality. The result is a growing divide between the rich and the poor, one that is often perpetuated from one generation to the next.

The education system is one of the most glaring examples of how wealth can protect the interests of the rich. Wealthy families can afford to send their children to elite private schools, where they receive top-tier education, resources, and opportunities. These schools often have smaller class sizes, better extracurricular programs, and a stronger network of influential connections. In contrast, children from poorer families are often relegated to underfunded public schools, where resources are scarce, and the quality of education is compromised. This disparity creates a cycle where children from wealthy families are more likely to attend prestigious universities and secure high-paying jobs, while children from lower-income families face barriers to educational success and social mobility.

In addition to education, the healthcare system also reflects the power of affluence. Wealthy individuals can afford to pay for the best medical care, often receiving treatment in private hospitals with state-of-the-art facilities. They have access to specialists, the latest medical technologies, and long waitlists are not a concern for them. On the other hand, people with lower incomes are often stuck with underfunded public healthcare systems, where long wait times, limited resources, and overcrowded facilities are the norm. The difference in access to healthcare can have serious consequences, as the rich can maintain their health and longevity, while the poor may struggle with preventable illnesses due to lack of access or insufficient care.

Another key social system that disproportionately favors the rich is the criminal justice system. Wealthy individuals who commit crimes often have the financial means to hire top-notch legal teams that can navigate the complexities of the justice system and secure favorable outcomes. They may avoid prison time altogether or face reduced sentences due to their ability to afford skilled lawyers and post-conviction programs. In contrast, poorer individuals, particularly those from marginalized communities, often cannot afford legal representation and are left to rely on overworked public defenders who may not have the time or resources to mount an effective defense. This imbalance can lead to harsher sentences for the poor, creating a cycle of incarceration and disenfranchisement that is difficult to escape.

The impact of affluence on social systems is also evident in the political sphere. Wealthy individuals and corporations have significant influence over the creation of laws and policies that affect society. Through lobbying, campaign contributions, and other forms of political engagement, the rich can shape laws that protect their interests and perpetuate their wealth. These laws may include tax cuts for the wealthy, deregulation of industries, or cuts to social programs that benefit the poor. By influencing political systems in their favor, the rich ensure that they remain at the top of the social and economic ladder while those with fewer resources are left to struggle.

The criminal justice system is not only biased against the poor but also disproportionately targets them. In many countries, people of color are more likely to be arrested, charged, and convicted of crimes, even when they have committed similar offenses as their wealthier or white counterparts. This racial bias in the justice system leads to higher incarceration rates for marginalized communities, further deepening the divide between the rich and the poor. While the wealthy can afford to avoid the consequences of their actions, the poor are often punished more severely, exacerbating inequality and reinforcing social hierarchies.

Moreover, the housing market is another area where wealth plays a significant role in perpetuating inequality. The rich can afford to buy properties in desirable neighborhoods, ensuring that they and their families have access to better schools, safer environments, and higher property values. Meanwhile, lower-income families are often forced to live in areas with subpar housing conditions, fewer resources, and higher crime rates. As a result, the poor have limited access to opportunities that could help them break the cycle of poverty, such as good schools, job prospects, and safe living conditions.

Social mobility, the ability for individuals to move up the economic ladder, is heavily influenced by affluence. The wealthier a family is, the more likely they are to pass on their wealth to the next generation, further entrenching the divide between the rich and the poor. Inheritance, real estate investments, and financial assets create a foundation for future generations to succeed, while those without wealth often struggle to access the resources necessary for upward mobility. The concentration of wealth within a small portion of the population means that opportunities for economic advancement are increasingly limited for the majority of people.

In some societies, the rich also use their affluence to control the media, shaping public perception and reinforcing their power. Wealthy individuals and corporations often own the major media outlets, allowing them to influence public opinion, promote their interests, and suppress dissenting voices. By controlling the flow of information, the rich can create a narrative that benefits them, while masking the reality of inequality and injustice. This media control ensures that the status quo is maintained, as the majority of people may not have access to alternative sources of information that highlight the flaws in the system.

The labor market is another area where affluence plays a role in maintaining inequality. Wealthy business owners and corporations often exploit low-wage workers, paying them minimal salaries while reaping massive profits. These workers, many of whom work in industries like retail, fast food, and agriculture, struggle to make ends meet while their employers amass significant wealth. The power imbalance in the labor market leaves the working class with little bargaining power, perpetuating cycles of poverty and limiting opportunities for economic advancement.

In addition, the education system is often complicit in reinforcing social inequality by perpetuating stereotypes and biases. Children from low-income backgrounds are more likely to attend schools that have limited resources and face discrimination based on their socio-economic status. The curriculum in these schools may not adequately prepare students for higher education or the job market, further limiting their opportunities for success. Meanwhile, children from affluent backgrounds attend well-funded schools with access to advanced placement programs, extracurricular activities, and college counseling, which increase their chances of success.

The criminal justice system also contributes to inequality by enforcing policies that disproportionately affect marginalized communities. Laws that criminalize poverty, such as vagrancy laws and loitering ordinances, target the poor, leading to arrests, fines, and jail time for minor offenses. These individuals, often already struggling to survive, face additional barriers to upward mobility due to their interactions with the justice system. The wealthy, on the other hand, can afford to avoid these consequences, further cementing the divide between the haves and the have-nots.

The rise of consumerism, driven by affluence, has also contributed to social inequality. Advertisements and marketing campaigns often target the wealthy, promoting products and services that cater to their needs and desires. Meanwhile, the poor are left to buy cheap, low-quality goods that may not meet their needs or contribute to their well-being. This focus on luxury consumption for the rich not only perpetuates social divisions but also reinforces the idea that material wealth is the key to happiness and success, leading to greater feelings of alienation and resentment among those who struggle to make ends meet.

Ultimately, the social systems that protect the rich are not accidental. They are the result of intentional decisions made by those in power, who use their wealth to maintain control over the systems that govern society. By perpetuating inequality in education, healthcare, housing, and the justice system, the wealthy ensure that they remain at the top while the poor remain trapped in cycles of poverty and disenfranchisement. Recognizing this dynamic is the first step toward dismantling the systems of oppression that uphold wealth and privilege, and working toward a more equitable and just society.

Affluence as a Tool for Change: The Power of Wealth for Good

Affluence, when used responsibly, holds great potential for creating positive change. The wealth that has historically been used to exploit and oppress can also be directed toward improving society and addressing critical issues like poverty, inequality, and environmental destruction. It is all about how wealth is managed and what purpose it serves. When affluent individuals or organizations choose to use their resources to better the world, the impact can be profound, shifting entire systems toward fairness, sustainability, and justice. In this chapter, we will explore how affluence can be used as a tool for good and the many ways in which it can contribute to solving the world's most pressing problems.

Philanthropy is one of the most common ways that wealth is used for good. Charitable donations and foundations have historically been powerful tools in addressing a range of social issues. Bill and Melinda Gates, through their foundation, have poured billions of dollars into fighting diseases like malaria, polio, and HIV/AIDS. Their work has helped save countless lives and has set the stage for progress in public health on a global scale. In addition to funding medical research, the Gates Foundation supports education initiatives, poverty reduction programs, and access to clean water in underserved communities. This kind of charitable giving demonstrates how affluence can directly impact human welfare in meaningful and lasting ways.

Social entrepreneurship is another area where wealth can create positive change. Entrepreneurs who focus on social impact use their financial resources to create businesses that prioritize social and environmental goals alongside profit. One well-known example is Toms Shoes, which started the "One for One" campaign—donating a pair of shoes for every pair purchased. This model of business not only helps those in need but also empowers consumers to participate in positive change through their purchases. Social entrepreneurship is a powerful tool for leveraging affluence to address systemic problems like hunger, lack of education, and limited access to healthcare.

Wealth can also be directed toward supporting sustainable business practices that benefit the planet. The environmental crisis has become one of the most urgent issues of our time, and industries play a critical role in both causing and solving it. Companies that adopt sustainable practices—such as reducing waste, using renewable energy, and committing to fair trade—demonstrate how wealth can be used to promote environmental responsibility. One example is Patagonia, an outdoor clothing company that has been at the forefront of environmental activism. Patagonia uses its profits to fund conservation efforts, create environmentally friendly products, and promote sustainable supply chains. By investing in the environment, these businesses not only help to protect the planet but also set an example for other companies to follow.

Another impactful way that affluence can be used for good is by funding education and access to opportunities for underserved communities. Education is one of the most powerful tools for breaking the cycle of poverty, and many affluent individuals and organizations invest heavily in scholarships, mentorship programs, and educational infrastructure in disadvantaged areas. For instance, the Chan Zuckerberg Initiative, founded by Facebook's Mark Zuckerberg and his wife Priscilla Chan, focuses on providing quality education to all children, regardless of their socio-economic background. Through funding educational projects and reforming school systems, this initiative is working toward creating a more equitable future for students everywhere.

Wealthy individuals and corporations can also use their influence to create policy changes that address societal issues. Political lobbying is often seen as a tool of the rich to protect their own interests, but when used ethically, it can also be a way to advocate for systemic change that benefits society as a whole. For example, wealthy philanthropists have successfully lobbied for policies that support climate change initiatives, expand access to healthcare, and improve the rights of workers. By using their financial resources to back policies that promote the common good, the affluent can drive change in a way that benefits the entire population, not just the wealthy few.

In addition to influencing public policy, wealthy individuals can use their status and platform to raise awareness about important causes. Many celebrities and affluent public figures leverage their visibility to bring attention to social issues, from human rights violations to environmental destruction. Through documentaries, social media campaigns, and public speaking engagements, these individuals can spark widespread interest and action on causes that may otherwise be overlooked. For instance, Leonardo DiCaprio has been a staunch advocate for environmental conservation and climate change awareness, using his platform to inspire action and educate people on the importance of protecting the planet for future generations.

One of the most powerful ways that affluence can be used for good is by providing microfinance and loans to entrepreneurs in developing countries. Microfinance allows individuals in impoverished communities to access the financial resources they need to start small businesses, which can significantly improve their livelihoods and help break the cycle of poverty. Organizations like Kiva allow people to lend small amounts of money to entrepreneurs around the world, empowering them to build their own businesses and create jobs in their communities. By providing access to capital, the wealthy can help people lift themselves out of poverty and contribute to local economic growth.

In the realm of healthcare, affluence can be used to fund research and treatment for diseases that primarily affect the poor or marginalized. The rich have the ability to invest in medical advancements that benefit the greater good, whether it's through funding research for diseases like cancer, HIV/AIDS, or tuberculosis, or by supporting initiatives that provide affordable access to healthcare for underserved populations. By ensuring that the benefits of medical progress reach those in need, the wealthy can make a tangible difference in the lives of millions of people.

Supporting mental health initiatives is another way that affluence can create positive change. Mental health has long been a neglected area of healthcare, particularly for people in marginalized communities. By investing in mental health programs, creating awareness campaigns, and funding treatment options, the wealthy can help reduce the stigma surrounding mental illness and provide much-needed support to those struggling with mental health challenges. The increased awareness and support for mental health will not only improve the quality of life for individuals but will also foster a more empathetic and understanding society.

The creation of affordable housing is another area where affluence can be used to create lasting positive change. Affordable housing remains a critical issue in many urban centers, with millions of people unable to access safe and stable housing. Wealthy individuals and organizations can contribute to addressing this issue by funding housing projects, supporting affordable housing policies, and advocating for fair housing laws. By providing homes for those in need, they can create a foundation for families to thrive, access education, and improve their economic stability.

In many instances, affluence can be a catalyst for advancing gender equality. Wealthy individuals and organizations have the resources to promote gender equality through funding women's rights organizations, supporting women in leadership roles, and advocating for policies that protect women's rights. By investing in women's empowerment and supporting initiatives that fight gender-based violence and discrimination, the affluent can contribute to creating a world where women have equal opportunities to succeed.

Supporting the arts and culture is another meaningful way affluence can be used for good. Art has the power to inspire, educate, and bring people together, and the wealthy can play a crucial role in sustaining cultural institutions, funding artistic projects, and supporting emerging artists. By investing in the arts, they help foster creativity and expression, which are essential to the health of a society. Art can also be a powerful tool for social change, as it often highlights issues like injustice, inequality, and human rights, sparking important conversations in the public sphere.

In conclusion, affluence, when used responsibly, has the power to create significant positive change in the world. By funding philanthropy, supporting sustainable business practices, advocating for social justice, and driving policy change, the wealthy can make a profound difference in addressing the world's most pressing issues. Whether through social entrepreneurship, education, healthcare, or environmental conservation, affluence can be a force for good that benefits society as a whole. However, it is essential that those with wealth recognize their power and use it responsibly, ensuring that their actions contribute to a fairer, more just, and sustainable world for all.

Philanthropy: Giving Back to Society

Philanthropy, at its core, is the act of using one's wealth to benefit others and address societal challenges. Throughout history, many affluent individuals and families have dedicated substantial portions of their wealth to causes that improve the world. This commitment to giving back is not only a way to solve immediate problems but also an investment in creating long-term positive change. Through charitable donations, foundations, and advocacy work, wealthy individuals can support initiatives in areas such as education, healthcare, and environmental sustainability. Philanthropy is a powerful tool, capable of transforming lives and even entire communities, as it directs resources toward the people and causes that need them most.

One of the most influential examples of modern philanthropy is the Bill and Melinda Gates Foundation. Since its founding, the Gates Foundation has committed billions of dollars to global health initiatives, aiming to improve health and living standards for millions around the world. The foundation focuses on pressing issues such as eradicating diseases like malaria and polio, advancing vaccination efforts, and improving access to healthcare in low-income countries. By focusing on these global health challenges, the Gates Foundation has not only saved lives but has also improved the overall quality of life for vulnerable populations.

In addition to healthcare, the Gates Foundation works on improving access to clean water, which is a vital issue for millions in developing countries. Without access to clean water, communities face serious health risks, including waterborne diseases that can be life-threatening. The foundation's efforts to provide safe water and sanitation systems have helped reduce the spread of these diseases, offering hope and stability to those who previously lacked basic resources. By tackling such issues, philanthropy becomes more than just charity—it creates sustainable solutions that empower communities to thrive.

Another area where affluence has made a significant impact is in education. Many wealthy individuals have chosen to invest in improving educational opportunities for underserved communities. For example, Mark Zuckerberg and Priscilla Chan's initiative, the Chan Zuckerberg Initiative, focuses on personalized learning and educational reform. Their work supports schools and educators, providing the tools and resources needed to help all students reach their full potential. Through grants and partnerships with educational institutions, the initiative aims to make education more accessible, equitable, and effective for students from all backgrounds.

Philanthropy in education extends beyond just funding schools; it also includes efforts to provide scholarships and mentorship programs. Many affluent families and organizations donate funds to establish scholarships for students who would otherwise not have the financial resources to attend college. These scholarships open doors for students from low-income families, providing them with the opportunity to achieve their educational and career goals. In addition, mentorship programs pair young people with professionals who can offer guidance and support, helping them navigate their careers and make informed decisions about their futures.

One notable example of this is the work of former First Lady Michelle Obama, who established the "Reach Higher" initiative, a program designed to inspire students to pursue higher education. Through this initiative, Obama has advocated for the importance of education and supported various programs that help students from underprivileged backgrounds access college and career opportunities. Her efforts have demonstrated the power of philanthropy in changing the lives of individuals, empowering them to break the cycle of poverty through education.

Philanthropy can also have a transformative effect on the environment. As concerns about climate change grow, many affluent individuals and organizations have stepped up to fund projects that aim to protect the planet. Environmental philanthropy is a growing movement that supports efforts to reduce carbon emissions, preserve wildlife habitats, and promote sustainable practices. For instance, the Leonardo DiCaprio Foundation has focused on wildlife conservation, funding projects that protect endangered species and their natural habitats. Through his foundation's initiatives, DiCaprio has raised awareness about the importance of environmental conservation and the need for action to combat climate change.

Environmental philanthropy not only involves funding conservation efforts but also supports clean energy projects and sustainable agriculture. Wealthy donors have funded research into renewable energy technologies, such as solar and wind power, helping to reduce society's reliance on fossil fuels. By supporting these initiatives, philanthropists contribute to building a more sustainable future, where clean energy is accessible to everyone, and the effects of climate change are mitigated. This form of giving back demonstrates how affluence can be used to create lasting environmental change that benefits both current and future generations.

Beyond individual efforts, large corporations are increasingly participating in philanthropy as part of their corporate social responsibility (CSR) initiatives. Many companies allocate a portion of their profits to charitable causes, investing in social and environmental projects that align with their values. These corporations recognize the importance of contributing to the communities that support them, whether through financial donations, volunteer work, or supporting local businesses. By engaging in philanthropy, corporations can enhance their reputation and help create a more equitable and sustainable society.

In addition to corporate philanthropy, many affluent individuals use their wealth to fund advocacy and awareness campaigns. Advocacy philanthropy aims to raise public awareness and drive policy change on issues such as poverty, inequality, and human rights. Wealthy individuals and organizations can influence public opinion and government policy by funding media campaigns, lobbying efforts, and grassroots organizing. By amplifying the voices of marginalized groups and advocating for legislative change, philanthropy becomes a tool for social justice, challenging systems of power and working toward a fairer, more equitable society.

For example, the Ford Foundation has long been a leader in advocating for human rights and social justice. With a focus on promoting equality and addressing systemic injustice, the Ford Foundation has supported initiatives that aim to reduce poverty, promote civil rights, and protect the environment. Their work spans across the globe, funding organizations and movements that fight for social change. By supporting these efforts, the Ford Foundation exemplifies how philanthropy can empower individuals and communities to challenge oppressive systems and work toward a more just world.

Moreover, many affluent families and individuals are choosing to direct their philanthropy toward local communities, addressing issues that affect their own neighborhoods. By investing in community-driven projects, philanthropists can help foster economic development, improve public safety, and enhance quality of life for residents. These initiatives can range from supporting local small businesses to providing funding for neighborhood parks, afterschool programs, and mental health services. In this way, philanthropy is not limited to global or national causes but can also make a significant difference at the local level.

While philanthropy can have a positive impact, it is essential to recognize that it is not a substitute for systemic change. While charitable donations and foundations provide immediate relief, the root causes of social issues must be addressed to create lasting solutions. Philanthropists who understand this distinction are often advocates for policy change, pushing for reforms that address the systemic factors contributing to poverty, inequality, and environmental degradation. This approach ensures that philanthropy works in tandem with efforts to create broader societal changes.

Philanthropy can also serve as a catalyst for innovation. Many foundations and wealthy individuals fund research and development in various fields, from medicine to technology. By investing in innovation, philanthropists help drive progress and bring about new solutions to old problems. For instance, the Chan Zuckerberg Initiative funds scientific research in areas such as artificial intelligence, genetics, and neuroscience, with the goal of solving major global health challenges. Through their investment in research and development, philanthropists contribute to advancing human knowledge and creating technologies that can improve lives.

Additionally, philanthropy fosters a culture of giving and encourages others to contribute to the common good. When affluent individuals and organizations commit to making a difference, they set an example for others to follow. This ripple effect can inspire individuals at all income levels to get involved in their communities, whether through donating time, money, or resources. In this way, philanthropy is not only about giving but also about creating a mindset of collective responsibility and social engagement.

Philanthropy also plays a critical role in disaster relief and humanitarian aid. When natural disasters or humanitarian crises strike, wealthy individuals and organizations are often among the first to provide financial support and resources to affected communities. By contributing to disaster relief efforts, philanthropists help provide immediate assistance, including food, water, medical care, and shelter. Their contributions help stabilize communities in the wake of crises and lay the groundwork for long-term recovery.

In conclusion, philanthropy is a powerful force for good that can make a significant impact on society. Whether through global health initiatives, educational reform, environmental conservation, or local community development, affluence, when used with intention, can create lasting positive change. By dedicating their wealth to causes that benefit others, philanthropists can help address some of the world's most pressing challenges. However, it is important to remember that philanthropy must work alongside efforts to address systemic issues and promote lasting societal change. Through responsible giving, affluent individuals and organizations can leave a legacy of compassion and progress.

Business Practices That Promote Sustainability

Affluent individuals and businesses hold a unique position in society. With the wealth and resources they possess, they have the power to influence entire industries, create positive change, and foster a more sustainable future for everyone. By embracing business practices that promote sustainability, these individuals and corporations can use their influence to protect the environment, fight climate change, and support the health of the planet for generations to come. The idea of sustainable business practices isn't just a trend—it's a necessary shift toward ensuring a livable planet in the face of growing environmental challenges.

One of the most impactful ways businesses can promote sustainability is by investing in clean energy. As the world faces the growing threat of climate change, transitioning to renewable energy sources like solar, wind, and hydroelectric power has become essential. Affluent companies with the resources to invest in large-scale energy projects can help accelerate this transition. By funding or building renewable energy infrastructure, businesses contribute to reducing our reliance on fossil fuels, which are major contributors to global warming. This shift is essential in limiting carbon emissions and mitigating the devastating effects of climate change.

In addition to investing in renewable energy, businesses can also focus on increasing energy efficiency. Whether it's through upgrading machinery, improving supply chain logistics, or retrofitting buildings to be more energy-efficient, there are countless ways companies can reduce their environmental footprint. For example, companies like Tesla have revolutionized the electric car industry by not only producing electric vehicles but also by investing in battery technology to store and use energy more efficiently. These innovations reduce the overall energy consumption of industries and help pave the way for a greener future.

Sustainability isn't just about energy; it also encompasses how businesses handle the resources they use and the waste they produce. Sustainable business practices involve using resources more efficiently and reducing waste, which in turn reduces environmental harm. For example, many companies are moving toward a circular economy model, where products are designed with reuse and recycling in mind. Rather than the traditional "take-make-dispose" approach, businesses in a circular economy focus on creating products that can be reused, refurbished, or recycled, reducing waste and the need for new raw materials.

This shift toward sustainable business practices also includes supporting environmentally responsible products and services. More and more companies are recognizing the importance of offering products that are not only good for their bottom line but also for the planet. Companies like Patagonia, known for their commitment to sustainability, use environmentally friendly materials in their products and ensure their supply chain is ethical and sustainable. By choosing to support these businesses, consumers can make a powerful statement about the types of practices they want to see in the marketplace, encouraging other companies to follow suit.

Businesses are also increasingly prioritizing sustainable farming and food production practices. In the face of a growing global population, food production must become more sustainable to meet the demand for food while protecting the environment. Corporations can invest in sustainable agriculture techniques, such as regenerative farming, which focuses on restoring soil health, conserving water, and promoting biodiversity. These practices not only help combat climate change but also ensure that future generations will have access to the resources needed for food production.

One area in which affluent individuals and businesses can make a significant impact is by promoting sustainable transportation. With the global transportation industry contributing heavily to carbon emissions, it is essential that businesses invest in alternatives that promote sustainability. Many companies are now exploring electric vehicles, bike-sharing programs, and public transportation solutions to reduce their carbon footprint. In addition, businesses can offer incentives for employees to use eco-friendly modes of transportation, such as electric cars or bicycles, further promoting sustainable commuting practices.

By embracing green building practices, businesses can also contribute to a more sustainable future. Green buildings, which are designed with energy efficiency, water conservation, and environmentally friendly materials in mind, are becoming an industry standard. Not only do these buildings reduce their environmental impact, but they also save businesses money in the long run through energy savings and lower operating costs. Large corporations and developers can invest in constructing energy-efficient buildings and retrofit older structures to meet modern sustainability standards, creating spaces that are better for both people and the planet.

The fashion industry, known for its significant environmental impact, has also seen a shift toward more sustainable practices. Many companies are now focusing on using eco-friendly materials, reducing water usage, and ensuring ethical labor practices in their supply chains. Fast fashion, which promotes the rapid production of cheap clothing, is being replaced by slower, more sustainable production methods that prioritize quality, durability, and environmental impact. Companies like Reformation and Everlane are setting the standard by producing stylish, environmentally friendly clothing that aligns with sustainability values.

Affluent businesses can also play a role in protecting biodiversity and promoting sustainable land management practices. Deforestation is a major contributor to climate change and biodiversity loss, but by investing in conservation projects, businesses can help protect critical habitats and promote reforestation efforts. Companies that rely on natural resources, such as timber or palm oil, can make a significant difference by sourcing their materials from certified sustainable sources and supporting conservation initiatives. This approach not only helps preserve biodiversity but also ensures that future generations can continue to enjoy the benefits of healthy ecosystems.

Along with protecting biodiversity, businesses can also work to preserve water resources, which are essential for both people and wildlife. Affluent individuals and corporations can invest in water conservation technologies and sustainable water management practices. For example, companies in the beverage industry can reduce their water usage and adopt water recycling systems to minimize waste. Additionally, businesses can support water purification and conservation projects in regions where access to clean water is limited, improving the health and well-being of communities around the world.

Another area where affluence can contribute to sustainability is through the support of green technologies. Innovations in clean technologies, such as carbon capture, energy storage, and sustainable agriculture technologies, are essential for creating a more sustainable future. Wealthy individuals and businesses have the resources to fund research and development in these areas, accelerating the adoption of new technologies that can help reduce environmental harm. By funding these innovations, they can help drive the transition to a more sustainable economy and ensure that the technologies needed to combat climate change are widely available.

As businesses begin to shift toward more sustainable practices, many are also adopting corporate social responsibility (CSR) programs that focus on environmental sustainability. These programs are designed to hold companies accountable for their environmental impact and encourage them to reduce waste, minimize pollution, and adopt more responsible business practices. CSR programs also provide an opportunity for businesses to engage with customers and stakeholders on sustainability issues, creating a sense of shared responsibility for the future of the planet.

For affluent individuals, supporting sustainability doesn't have to be limited to business practices. Many wealthy individuals are investing in sustainability-focused startups, green technology companies, and environmental conservation efforts. By supporting innovation in sustainability, these individuals help to foster an ecosystem of entrepreneurs and organizations that are working to solve the world's most pressing environmental issues. Through their investments, they play a crucial role in accelerating the transition to a greener economy.

In conclusion, affluence, when used responsibly, has the power to promote sustainable business practices that benefit both the environment and society. By investing in clean energy, supporting eco-friendly products and services, and adopting green business practices, affluent individuals and businesses can contribute to a more sustainable and equitable world. This approach not only benefits the planet but also ensures that future generations inherit a healthier, more prosperous world, capable of supporting all life. By embracing sustainability, we can make sure that affluence becomes a tool for positive change rather than a force that exacerbates environmental harm.

The Ethics of Affluence: Responsibility and Accountability

Affluence is not merely a symbol of success or status; it carries a weight of responsibility that should not be taken lightly. The ethical considerations surrounding wealth are numerous and significant, and individuals or organizations with substantial financial resources must be aware of their impact on the world around them. With great wealth comes great responsibility, and how that wealth is used determines not just the financial success of the affluent but the well-being of society as a whole. It is essential for those who hold wealth to consider not only their personal gain but also the consequences their actions have on others, particularly those less fortunate.

At its core, the ethics of affluence involve ensuring that wealth does not become a tool for exploitation or harm. The accumulation of wealth, when unchecked, can perpetuate inequality, environmental degradation, and social injustice. Affluent individuals and corporations hold significant power to influence the economy, society, and the environment, which means that with this power comes a moral obligation to use it for good. This means they must actively work to mitigate the negative consequences of their wealth and take responsibility for their actions, ensuring that they are contributing positively to society rather than perpetuating harm.

One of the most pressing ethical challenges that affluence presents is the question of income inequality. In a world where a small percentage of the population holds the majority of the wealth, the question arises as to whether it is ethical for such disparities to exist. Wealth should not simply be hoarded by the few while the many struggle to meet basic needs. Affluent individuals have the means to bridge this gap, whether through charitable giving, creating opportunities for the underprivileged, or supporting policies that promote wealth redistribution. Wealth is a tool, and when used ethically, it can serve to level the playing field and give everyone a fair chance to succeed.

Beyond economic disparities, affluence also raises ethical questions about environmental responsibility. Wealthy individuals and companies often have the ability to make decisions that impact the environment, sometimes in harmful ways. For instance, industries that rely heavily on natural resources can contribute to pollution, habitat destruction, and climate change. The ethical dilemma arises when these industries prioritize profit over the long-term health of the planet. Those who control wealth must be held accountable for the environmental consequences of their actions. Instead of contributing to the degradation of natural ecosystems, affluent businesses and individuals should use their resources to promote sustainability and invest in eco-friendly solutions that benefit everyone.

Another critical ethical issue surrounding affluence is the treatment of workers. The exploitation of workers, especially in developing countries, is a common practice among companies seeking to cut costs and maximize profits. Affluent individuals and organizations have the responsibility to ensure that workers are paid fair wages, work in safe conditions, and are treated with dignity and respect. This includes examining supply chains to ensure that no workers are subjected to child labor, unsafe working environments, or unfair treatment. Ethical affluence demands that wealth be used to improve the lives of workers and support fair labor practices worldwide.

In addition to fair wages, the ethical responsibilities of affluence extend to consumer products and the ways in which they are made. The products we purchase often come with hidden costs, such as environmental degradation, poor working conditions, or unethical sourcing of materials. Affluent individuals and businesses must ensure that their products are produced through ethical supply chains. This means sourcing materials responsibly, ensuring fair trade practices, and working with suppliers who share a commitment to ethical business practices. As consumers become more aware of these issues, the demand for ethically produced goods increases, and it is the responsibility of those with wealth to meet that demand by supporting businesses that prioritize sustainability and ethical practices.

The ethics of affluence also include considerations about the power and influence that wealth grants. Wealthy individuals and organizations can exert tremendous influence over political systems, public policies, and social issues. The ethical dilemma arises when this power is used to perpetuate the interests of the wealthy at the expense of the common good. For example, lobbying efforts aimed at influencing government policy may prioritize corporate profits over the well-being of citizens. Affluent individuals and corporations must recognize their ethical obligation to use their influence to advocate for policies that benefit society as a whole, such as those focused on reducing inequality, protecting the environment, and improving access to healthcare and education.

While philanthropy is often seen as a solution to some of the ethical challenges of affluence, it is not a panacea. Charitable donations, while valuable, should not be used as a means to distract from or excuse the negative consequences of wealth accumulation. Affluent individuals and organizations should not rely solely on philanthropy to address the social and environmental issues caused by their wealth. Instead, they must take a more holistic approach by addressing the root causes of these issues in the first place. This means examining their own business practices, consumption patterns, and investments to ensure that they are contributing to a sustainable and just society.

Furthermore, the ethics of affluence require a deep examination of how wealth is accumulated in the first place. The accumulation of vast wealth often relies on systems that perpetuate inequality and exploitation, such as tax evasion, labor exploitation, or the extraction of natural resources without regard for local communities. Affluent individuals and businesses must ask themselves whether the ways they have gained wealth align with ethical principles. If their wealth is built upon systems of injustice or environmental harm, they have a responsibility to find ways to correct these imbalances and make reparations where necessary.

Another ethical consideration in the realm of affluence is the responsibility to future generations. The actions of today's wealthy individuals and corporations have long-term consequences, and affluence should not be used to create a world that future generations will inherit in a worse state than it was found. This includes considering the environmental impacts of current actions, as well as the social and economic structures that will affect future generations. Ethical affluence demands that wealth be used to create a world that is better, healthier, and more equitable for those who come after us.

The concept of intergenerational justice is closely related to this idea. Those who inherit wealth or power must recognize that they are not simply the beneficiaries of what previous generations have created, but they are also responsible for what they leave behind. This sense of responsibility should guide their actions, ensuring that they use their wealth and influence to create a more just, equitable, and sustainable society. The ethical use of affluence, therefore, involves thinking beyond the present moment and considering the long-term impacts of decisions on both people and the planet.

Furthermore, the ethics of affluence demand that wealthy individuals and organizations consider the social consequences of their wealth. The accumulation of wealth can create division, resentment, and social unrest if it is not managed responsibly. Wealthy individuals have the power to shape the social fabric of their communities, and with this power comes a responsibility to foster social cohesion and promote the common good. This might involve supporting local businesses, investing in education, or advocating for policies that reduce inequality and promote social mobility. In this way, affluence can be used to build stronger, more connected communities rather than further entrenching divisions.

At the same time, the responsibility of affluence is not solely about mitigating negative impacts; it is also about creating positive change. The wealthy have the resources to drive innovation, support education, fund healthcare, and advocate for environmental sustainability. With their resources, affluent individuals and corporations have the potential to lead initiatives that can change the world for the better. The ethical obligation of affluence, therefore, is not just to avoid harm, but to actively contribute to solutions that improve society and the world as a whole.

To sum up, the ethics of affluence are complex and multifaceted, requiring those who hold wealth to reflect on how their resources are used. From ensuring fair wages and ethical supply chains to addressing environmental issues and using political influence for the common good, affluent individuals and organizations must be accountable for their impact on society. Affluence, when used ethically, has the potential to drive positive change and create a more just and sustainable world. However, it is up to those who control wealth to recognize their responsibility and act accordingly.

In conclusion, affluence is not just a privilege, but a profound responsibility. The wealthy must recognize the ethical implications of their actions and the far-reaching effects of their decisions. They are in a unique position to shape society and must do so with accountability, considering the impact on the environment, economy, and social justice. By using their wealth to promote the common good and take responsibility for their actions, they can help create a more equitable and sustainable world for all.

The Future of Affluence

Affluence is a powerful tool, and like all powerful tools, it can be used for both good and ill. The way affluence is employed determines whether it will contribute to positive change or perpetuate harm. Historically, wealth has often been a force of oppression, contributing to systems of inequality, exploitation, and environmental degradation. However, there is a growing shift in how affluence is being used. Increasingly, wealthy individuals, businesses, and organizations are beginning to recognize their responsibility to use their resources for the greater good. This shift offers a hopeful outlook on the future of affluence.

The future of affluence lies in its capacity to drive change, but it requires a conscious effort to redirect wealth toward causes that support the common good. As wealth continues to accumulate in the hands of a few, it is essential that these individuals recognize the moral obligation they carry. They must not allow their wealth to create further divides but instead use it to bridge gaps and elevate those who have been historically marginalized. When wealth is directed toward solving problems such as poverty, inequality, and access to education, it becomes a catalyst for positive transformation.

One of the ways affluence can be used for good is through philanthropy. Philanthropic efforts can have a profound impact on addressing societal issues. Foundations like the Bill and Melinda Gates Foundation and other charitable initiatives have made significant strides in addressing global health crises, poverty, and education. These efforts show that affluence, when used intentionally, can bring about real, lasting change. As more affluent individuals and corporations embrace the idea of giving back, philanthropy can become a key driver of social justice and equality.

Another critical aspect of the future of affluence is sustainability. Climate change, environmental degradation, and resource depletion are among the most pressing issues facing humanity today. Wealth has the potential to influence industries toward more sustainable practices, such as investing in clean energy, reducing carbon footprints, and supporting eco-friendly technologies. When affluent individuals and businesses choose to prioritize the environment, they not only help combat climate change but also set an example for others to follow. The power of affluence lies in its ability to fund and scale sustainable solutions, ultimately shaping a greener future for generations to come.

As the world continues to face the consequences of climate change, the role of affluence in funding climate adaptation and mitigation efforts will become increasingly vital. Wealth can be used to invest in renewable energy sources, support reforestation projects, and finance green innovations that reduce environmental harm. The responsibility of affluent individuals and corporations in this regard is clear: they must direct their wealth toward creating solutions to the environmental challenges we face. This will require a shift in mindset—away from short-term profits and toward long-term sustainability.

Affluent individuals and corporations must also commit to ethical practices that ensure their wealth does not come at the expense of vulnerable communities. This includes paying fair wages, supporting ethical supply chains, and advocating for human rights across the globe. By supporting businesses and industries that prioritize the well-being of their workers, affluent individuals can help to dismantle exploitative systems that have long been entrenched in many industries. The future of affluence will be shaped by how wealth is used to promote ethical standards and ensure that everyone benefits from economic success.

One of the most profound ways that affluence can contribute to social justice is by addressing inequality. In many parts of the world, wealth is concentrated in the hands of a few, while the majority of people live in poverty. This wealth gap fuels social unrest, economic instability, and perpetuates cycles of poverty. To close this gap, affluence must be used to create opportunities for those who are disadvantaged. This might include supporting education initiatives, providing access to healthcare, or investing in local businesses. The goal is to create an environment where prosperity is shared by all, not just a select few.

For affluence to have a meaningful impact on inequality, it must be used to challenge existing power structures and ensure that wealth is distributed more equitably. This can be done through policies that promote progressive taxation, fair wages, and access to social services. When those with wealth use their resources to advocate for these policies, they contribute to a more just and inclusive society. The future of affluence depends on its ability to foster systemic change that reduces inequality and ensures that everyone has the opportunity to succeed.

As society continues to grapple with issues of race, gender, and class, affluence also plays a role in shaping the future of social justice. Wealthy individuals and organizations have the resources to support movements that advocate for the rights of marginalized communities. By using their affluence to fund advocacy work, legal battles, and education campaigns, they can help advance the cause of social justice. This can lead to the dismantling of oppressive systems that perpetuate discrimination and inequality, paving the way for a more inclusive and equitable society.

The future of affluence also hinges on how the wealthy engage with political systems. In many countries, the wealthy have disproportionate influence over government policies. This influence can be used to either reinforce existing inequalities or to push for progressive change. The key is for affluent individuals to use their power responsibly, advocating for policies that promote the well-being of all citizens, not just the wealthy few. This includes supporting initiatives that protect the environment, ensure equal rights, and promote economic opportunity for everyone.

The power of affluence in the future will also be shaped by how individuals and organizations use their influence to drive innovation. Wealthy individuals have the means to fund research and development in areas like healthcare, technology, and education. This can lead to breakthroughs that improve quality of life for people around the world. For example, advancements in medical research, driven by affluent donors, can help to eradicate diseases and improve healthcare access in developing countries. Similarly, investments in education and technology can empower individuals to break the cycle of poverty and contribute to a more skilled and prosperous workforce.

As affluence becomes increasingly intertwined with global challenges, it will be crucial for wealthy individuals to collaborate with governments, non-profit organizations, and other stakeholders to create lasting solutions. No one entity can solve global issues alone. It will take collective action to address the interconnected problems of poverty, inequality, and climate change. Affluent individuals have a unique position to leverage their wealth and influence in these collaborations, ensuring that resources are directed toward the most impactful solutions.

Education will play a significant role in shaping the future of affluence. As more people become aware of the ethical implications of wealth, there will be a growing demand for responsible affluence. Educating affluent individuals on how to use their wealth responsibly, how to support ethical businesses, and how to engage in philanthropy can help create a culture of giving and responsibility. In the future, the next generation of affluent individuals may approach wealth not as a tool for self-interest, but as a means to improve society and address global challenges.

In order for affluence to shape a better future, it is crucial that it is used as a tool for positive change rather than as a means of perpetuating harm. The future will be determined by how individuals and organizations with wealth choose to engage with the world. By focusing on philanthropy, sustainability, ethical practices, and social justice, affluence has the potential to create a better world for everyone. As society continues to face global challenges, the role of affluence in shaping the future will only become more significant, making it essential for the wealthy to consider the impact of their actions on both people and the planet.

Ultimately, the future of affluence will depend on whether those who hold wealth choose to use it to uplift and support others or continue to concentrate power and resources in the hands of a few. The direction affluence takes will have a lasting impact on society and the environment, and it is up to the wealthy to ensure that their wealth is used to promote a more just, equitable, and sustainable world. With the right choices, affluence can be a force for good, driving positive change and creating a future that benefits everyone.

Chapter Summary

Affluence, in its most powerful form, has the potential to be a transformative force for good, enabling meaningful progress across social, environmental, and economic landscapes. When used with intention and responsibility, wealth can support initiatives that benefit the common good, from addressing the root causes of poverty to funding environmental protection efforts. In this ideal scenario, affluence creates a ripple effect of positive change, helping to uplift communities, combat climate change, and close the wealth gap. However, the history of wealth shows a more complex picture. Wealth has often been concentrated in the hands of a few, perpetuating systems of oppression, inequality, and environmental harm. These practices continue to shape the world today, making it all the more crucial to understand how wealth is used and the consequences it can have.

Historically, affluence has been used to maintain power and privilege, reinforcing social structures that benefit the wealthy while marginalizing the poor and disenfranchised. Colonialism, the exploitation of labor, and environmental degradation are just a few examples of how wealth has been accumulated at the expense of others. These patterns of inequality are deeply embedded in our global systems, and their effects are still felt today. In the modern world, wealth continues to fuel disparities in access to healthcare, education, and basic human rights. The challenge, then, is not just to acknowledge these imbalances but to find ways to use wealth to correct them, rather than to perpetuate them.

One of the most important aspects of using affluence for the common good is understanding the ethical responsibilities that come with wealth. When individuals or organizations accumulate wealth, they also gain power and influence, which can be used to shape policies, industries, and social systems. The ethical implications of how wealth is spent, invested, and distributed are vast. It is not enough to simply accumulate wealth—wealth must be used in ways that promote fairness, justice, and the well-being of all people, not just the wealthy few. This requires a shift in mindset from individual gain to collective progress, ensuring that wealth benefits everyone, especially those who are most vulnerable.

As we look toward the future, there is a growing movement of individuals and organizations committed to using their affluence to create positive change. This shift is rooted in the understanding that wealth can be used to address systemic issues like inequality, environmental destruction, and social injustice. Philanthropy, ethical business practices, and investments in sustainability are just a few examples of how wealth can be directed toward the common good. For affluence to be a force for good, it must be used not just for personal gain, but with a broader vision of creating a more just, sustainable, and compassionate world for future generations.

Shifting the focus of wealth toward justice, sustainability, and compassion is not an easy task, but it is essential for creating lasting change. It requires collaboration between governments, businesses, non-profits, and individuals to ensure that resources are used in ways that address the root causes of social and environmental issues. This collective effort can lead to systemic change that promotes fairness, equality, and environmental stewardship. It also requires a deep commitment to holding those in power accountable for their actions, ensuring that their wealth is used ethically and responsibly.

Each decision made with wealth carries the potential to shape the future. Whether it's through philanthropy, ethical investments, or business practices that prioritize sustainability, the way affluence is used today will have lasting implications for the world tomorrow. By prioritizing social justice, environmental sustainability, and ethical practices, we can create a future where affluence is a tool for the greater good. In this future, wealth serves to uplift, empower, and create opportunities for all, not just a select few. Let us use affluence wisely, with intention, responsibility, and compassion, to shape a world that reflects the values we want to see in the future.

Ultimately, the choices we make with wealth will determine whether affluence continues to perpetuate inequality or becomes a powerful force for positive change. The responsibility lies with each of us to ensure that our actions align with the greater good. By focusing on justice, sustainability, and compassion, we can create a world where affluence benefits everyone, not just the wealthy few. As we move forward, let us be mindful of the impact of our wealth, using it to support the common good and build a more equitable and sustainable future for all.

Chapter Five

Immorality

When we think about immorality, we often picture acts that are clearly wrong: stealing, lying, hurting others. But immorality goes much deeper than obvious crimes. It can show up in small everyday actions, hidden attitudes, or even large systems that many people accept as normal. Immorality is about behavior that is evil, sinful, or improper. It is the shadow side of human nature—the part that ignores what is good, fair, and just.

In the context of The Throne and Liberty and Water Is Not What You Believe, immorality plays a hidden but powerful role. These works challenge our basic assumptions about what is right and true. They suggest that what we think we know—about power, about survival, even about water itself—might be rooted in deep, hidden forms of corruption and falsehood. When systems of belief and power are built on lies, immorality becomes invisible, but no less dangerous.

The Throne and Liberty explores how leaders and rulers often hide immoral actions behind grand ideas like "freedom" and "justice." In truth, they may be using their power to exploit others. Immorality, in this case, becomes part of the system itself, infecting everything from the highest throne to the lives of ordinary people. Similarly, Water Is Not What You Believe reveals how something as essential and trusted as water might be misunderstood, manipulated, or misrepresented, showing that even nature is not free from human deception.

Immorality is often about control: the control of truth, of resources, and of people's minds. It twists what is pure into something selfish and harmful. Understanding immorality is important because it teaches us to question what we are told and to look deeper into the systems and structures around us. Only by seeing the darkness can we begin to find the light.

This chapter will look closely at immorality from many angles. We will explore how it appears in leadership, society, science, and even in the personal choices we make. By understanding immorality more clearly, we can protect ourselves from it—and maybe even help to heal the world from its effects.

The True Face of Immorality

Immorality isn't always obvious to the human eye. Most people expect evil to look scary, loud, or violent, but often, it hides behind smiles and handshakes. It wears the face of success, kindness, and even heroism. That's why it's so dangerous. Immorality can slip into everyday life without anyone noticing. It can hide inside a joke, a law, a tradition, or even a charity event. People tend to trust what looks familiar and good, so immorality often copies those appearances. Understanding how it works is the first defense against it. If you only look for villains in scary masks, you will miss the ones sitting in boardrooms, classrooms, and even at dinner tables. Immorality is flexible, changing its look to match whatever people want to believe. It thrives on the fact that most people are too distracted or comfortable to question it. Only when we learn to look deeper—past the surface—can we truly recognize the real face of evil.

One of the favorite disguises immorality wears is the mask of success. Society often praises people who are wealthy, powerful, and famous. However, not every path to success is clean or fair. Some people step on others to climb higher. They lie, cheat, and manipulate to get what they want. Yet because they look rich or important, many admire them instead of questioning their behavior. This teaches the wrong lesson—that the end goal matters more than the way you reach it. Immorality uses this confusion to grow stronger. It whispers, "As long as you win, it doesn't matter how you play." That idea is toxic. Real success should never come at the cost of truth, justice, or kindness. We must learn to look beyond the trophies and headlines to see the truth behind people's actions. Otherwise, we risk celebrating those who harm the world while punishing those who try to help it.

Another place immorality hides is within false kindness. Not all acts of kindness are pure. Some people use kindness to control others, gain favors, or protect their own image. They give gifts not to help, but to trap. They offer support not to heal, but to dominate. This false kindness is hard to spot because it feels good at first. But true kindness expects nothing in return. It lifts others up without tying them down. Immorality twists kindness into a tool for selfishness. It manipulates people's emotions, making it harder for victims to speak out. If someone's help comes with strings attached or demands loyalty, that is not real kindness. It's another mask worn by immorality to trick and trap others. To protect ourselves, we must pay attention not just to what people do, but also why they do it.

Sometimes immorality becomes part of a system so big and old that people stop noticing it. Certain traditions, laws, and habits were built on unfairness, but because they are familiar, people accept them without question. This quiet form of evil is powerful because it feels normal. It hides inside school rules, government systems, workplace practices, and even religious teachings. People tell themselves, "This is how it has always been," without asking if it should stay that way. Immorality loves this laziness. It thrives when people don't ask hard questions. Challenging the system feels uncomfortable and risky, so most people stay silent. But silence allows injustice to survive and grow. True morality demands that we stay awake, question old ways, and fix what's broken, even when change is hard.

Silence itself is another mask for immorality. When people stay quiet about things they know are wrong, they become part of the problem. Fear of speaking up allows cruelty and injustice to spread without resistance. Sometimes silence comes from fear—fear of losing a job, a friendship, or safety. Sometimes it comes from selfishness—wanting to protect personal comfort. But no matter the reason, silence protects the wrongdoer, not the victim. Immorality counts on silence to cover its tracks. Speaking up can be terrifying, but it is necessary. Every voice raised against injustice weakens the hold of evil a little more. History shows that real change always starts with brave people refusing to stay silent. In the battle against immorality, courage matters just as much as kindness.

Blame is another tool immorality uses to hide itself. Instead of taking responsibility for wrongdoing, immoral people point fingers at others. They create scapegoats to distract from their own guilt. They blame the poor, the outsiders, or the powerless for problems they themselves caused. By focusing people's anger in the wrong direction, they escape accountability. This tactic confuses communities and tears them apart. It also creates cycles of hatred and violence. Recognizing blame-shifting is critical if we want to uncover the real source of problems. True leaders accept responsibility for their actions. Immoral ones hide behind excuses and lies, making others suffer for their sins.

Lies, half-truths, and twisted facts are some of the strongest weapons immorality uses. A full lie is sometimes easier to spot. But a half-truth, a cleverly told story, or a missing detail can be far more dangerous. Immorality rarely presents itself as pure fiction. It mixes truth with lies to make the falsehood easier to swallow. When people believe they know the full story, they stop questioning it. Immoral actors carefully craft narratives that make them look good or make others look bad. They rely on the fact that most people are too busy or too tired to fact-check everything they hear. To fight immorality, we must stay curious, ask questions, and seek the whole truth, not just the parts that are easy or comfortable to believe.

Pride is another way immorality hides in plain sight. Many people refuse to admit when they are wrong. They would rather defend a bad choice than apologize and change. Pride locks people into immoral actions because they are too ashamed or stubborn to correct their mistakes. It convinces them that saving face is more important than doing the right thing. Pride tells lies like, "If you admit you were wrong, you are weak." But real strength comes from humility—the courage to admit fault and to grow from it. Immorality feeds off pride because it keeps people stuck in bad behavior instead of moving toward goodness. To be truly moral, we must value truth and improvement over the need to always be right.

Neglect is another hidden form of immorality. Not all evil is active. Sometimes, immorality shows up in the things we fail to do. Ignoring a person in need, refusing to help when we have the power to do so, or staying silent in the face of cruelty are all forms of moral failure. It's easy to think that if we aren't directly causing harm, we are innocent. But the truth is that good requires action. Choosing to stand by and watch suffering is itself a betrayal of goodness. Every act of kindness, every small stand against injustice, matters. Immorality wants people to believe that small acts don't count. But history proves otherwise—small actions, multiplied by millions, can change the world.

Greed is a major fuel for immorality. The hunger for more—more money, more power, more attention—drives people to hurt others without a second thought. Greed makes it easy to justify lying, stealing, and exploiting. It tricks people into believing they deserve everything they can grab, even at the expense of others. In a greedy mindset, generosity looks foolish, and compassion looks weak. Greed shrinks the heart and hardens the soul. Societies that reward greed without limits end up poisoned by injustice and division. Fighting greed requires seeing value not in possessions, but in people. True wealth comes from kindness, community, and integrity—not from piles of gold.

Desensitization is another way immorality strengthens itself. When people are exposed to cruelty over and over, they begin to stop caring. Violence, suffering, and corruption become "normal" parts of life. Movies, news, video games, and even casual jokes can slowly numb our hearts. Immorality loves this because a numb society won't fight back. It's important to stay sensitive to pain and injustice, even when the world tells us to toughen up. Feeling anger at injustice, sadness at suffering, and joy at goodness keeps us human. To fight immorality, we must protect our ability to feel deeply and to care passionately.

Fear is another powerful tool of immorality. Fear of change, fear of the unknown, fear of losing comfort— all of these can push people to make selfish, harmful choices. Immoral leaders use fear to control populations. They paint pictures of terrifying futures to justify cruelty in the present. Fear makes people cling to bad systems because they are afraid of what might happen if things change. But fear is a liar. It tells us that safety is better than freedom and that comfort is better than justice. Courage is the antidote. Choosing what is right, even when it's scary, is the path toward a moral life.

Hopelessness feeds immorality too. If people believe nothing can get better, they stop trying. They accept injustice, cruelty, and corruption as permanent facts of life. Immorality thrives when people lose hope because without hope, there is no resistance. Hope is not about pretending everything is perfect. It is about believing that change is possible and that goodness is worth fighting for. Every act of hope is a blow against immorality. Believing in the possibility of a better world gives us the strength to create it.

False progress is another trick of immorality. Some people claim to fight for justice but end up using immoral methods to achieve their goals. They believe that hurting others is acceptable if it leads to a "greater good." But real progress cannot be built on lies, violence, or oppression. If the foundation is rotten, the house will collapse. True progress respects the dignity and rights of all people. Immorality tries to blur the line between good and evil by dressing bad actions in noble language. But the way we achieve our goals matters just as much as the goals themselves.

Corruption is another clear face of immorality. It happens when people in power trade favors, accept bribes, or break rules for personal gain. Corruption poisons governments, businesses, and even small organizations. It creates a system where the rich and powerful always win, and everyone else loses. Corruption often hides under fancy words like "networking" or "relationships," but the damage is real. It destroys trust and fairness, making it harder for honest people to succeed. Fighting corruption means demanding transparency, fairness, and accountability at every level.

Finally, immorality shows its true face when people value appearance over reality. Looking good becomes more important than being good. People work harder to hide their mistakes than to fix them. Image becomes more important than integrity. In a world obsessed with fame, followers, and public approval, this kind of immorality is everywhere. It fools people into thinking that if they look right, they must be right. But true morality is about what we do when no one is watching. It's about choosing honesty over popularity, and truth over applause. Only by valuing character over image can we see through the final, glittering mask of immorality.

Immorality in Power: The Throne's Corruption

Leaders are supposed to be servants of the people. Their role is to protect, guide, and uplift those who trust them. But sometimes, people seek power not to serve, but to control. They hunger for fame, wealth, and authority. When leaders are driven by selfish reasons, immorality spreads like wildfire. Their kingdoms or governments begin to rot from the inside out. They often make big promises, talking about liberty, equality, and hope. They know what the people want to hear. But their real goal is not to bring freedom. It is to tighten their grip on everything and everyone around them. When they finally rise to the throne, the mask falls away, and the true face of corruption is revealed.

At first, the people may not notice the deception. Early on, these leaders often act charming and generous. They pass a few good laws or offer gifts to win loyalty. They arrange grand celebrations and speeches, showing themselves as heroes of the nation. But these acts are only tricks to hide their selfishness. Behind closed doors, they scheme to change laws, remove opponents, and silence those who question them. Liberty turns into a distant dream. The people believe they are still free, but they are slowly being chained by invisible hands. By the time they realize the truth, it is often too late.

Power changes people when it is not guided by strong morals. A leader who once spoke of justice now uses fear to control. They spread lies to divide the population. They create enemies from innocent groups, turning neighbor against neighbor. They say, "You are safe because of me," while secretly preparing to strip away rights. Trust becomes a weapon. Freedom becomes a slogan with no meaning. People obey because they are afraid, not because they believe. This is not leadership. It is domination through deceit.

True freedom requires leaders who value honesty, compassion, and courage. A corrupt throne offers none of these. Instead, it thrives on lies, cruelty, and cowardice. Immoral leaders care more about their image than the truth. They silence critics with harsh punishments. They control the media to spread their version of events. History books are rewritten to praise their rule. Schools are forced to teach loyalty to the throne, not loyalty to truth. A nation that once stood for liberty slowly forgets what liberty even means.

Oppression often comes disguised as protection. Corrupt leaders claim they must take away freedoms for "security" or "the greater good." They ask people to give up rights little by little. Each new rule seems small, even reasonable. But over time, the chains grow heavier. Once-friendly neighbors are encouraged to report each other for "disloyalty." Public gatherings are restricted. Voices of protest are treated like acts of war. The people are made to fear each other more than they fear the ruler. Fear becomes the foundation of society.

Greed feeds immorality at the top. Corrupt leaders do not just want power. They also want wealth. They steal from the people through unfair taxes, fake charities, and rigged contracts. Money meant for schools, hospitals, and public services disappears into private bank accounts. The rich grow richer, while the poor suffer more each year. Leaders live in luxury while citizens struggle to survive. This is not the failure of one policy or mistake. It is a direct result of putting selfish ambition above public duty.

Immoral leaders also destroy fairness in the legal system. Judges who should defend the innocent are instead bought and paid for. Laws are rewritten to protect the powerful and punish the weak. A rich man can break the law and walk free. A poor man can be punished for speaking the truth. Justice becomes a joke. The very systems meant to protect society are turned against it. People lose faith in courts, police, and government itself. When fairness dies, despair quickly takes its place.

In a society ruled by immoral leaders, loyalty becomes more important than honesty or skill. Promotions are given to those who flatter the ruler, not those who deserve them. Positions of power are handed out like prizes to the most obedient followers. Talented people who refuse to lie are pushed aside. Over time, the government fills with cowards, liars, and thieves. The few honest people who remain are either forced to join the corruption or leave in shame. A kingdom built on such rot cannot stand forever.

Fear and distrust poison relationships between citizens. Under a corrupt throne, people learn to hide their thoughts. Speaking too freely can cost you your job, your freedom, or even your life. Friendships and families are torn apart by suspicion. Teachers must watch what they say. Workers must watch who they trust. Parents must be careful what they teach their children. Truth becomes dangerous. Lies become survival. Living in such a world breaks the human spirit little by little.

Religious institutions are often dragged into the corruption as well. Some leaders of faith are threatened into silence. Others are bribed with money, power, or promises of influence. True teachings of kindness and justice are twisted into messages of obedience and fear.

Sacred symbols are used to justify immoral acts. Those who stand firm in their beliefs are labeled as enemies. In time, faith itself becomes another tool of control. People lose not only their trust in government but also in their spiritual foundations.

Despite the leader's iron grip, no throne of corruption lasts forever. Injustice carries within it the seeds of rebellion. People can be fooled for a time, but not forever. Their suffering builds silently. One day, someone speaks out. Then another. Then a hundred more. A spark of courage catches fire across the land. The people remember what true freedom feels like. They realize that fear is not stronger than hope. Movements begin quietly but grow unstoppable with time.

History shows countless examples of corrupt leaders falling from power. Some are overthrown by revolution. Others are brought down by their own greedy and foolish mistakes. Few die peacefully in their beds. Most are remembered with shame, their grand palaces crumbling into dust. Statues are torn down. Their names are cursed instead of praised. No matter how high they climbed, their fall is certain. The people's memory is long, and justice, though delayed, will come.

A throne built on lies must be constantly defended with more lies. A ruler who gains power through fear must constantly inspire greater fear. They cannot rest. They cannot trust anyone, not even their closest friends.

Betrayal becomes a daily threat. Sleepless nights and growing paranoia become the ruler's companions. Their palaces become prisons. Their golden crowns become heavy chains. In seeking to rule over others, they end up ruled by their own terror and guilt.

Citizens who once celebrated their leader's rise may one day regret their silence. They realize too late that liberty is fragile and must be protected every day. It is easy to cheer when someone promises quick solutions. It is much harder to ask hard questions and demand honest answers. A healthy society needs brave people willing to stand up against injustice, even when it is unpopular or dangerous. Freedom is never given freely by the powerful. It must be claimed and defended by the people.

Education is one of the strongest weapons against the corruption of the throne. When people are taught to think critically, to question authority, and to value truth, they are harder to deceive. Knowledge shines light into the darkest places. It reveals lies and exposes injustice. Leaders who fear an educated public are often the most corrupt. They try to control what people learn and believe. But once knowledge is awakened, it is very hard to silence again.

Art, music, and literature also play powerful roles in resisting corruption. In times of darkness, artists find ways to speak truth in hidden ways. A painting can inspire rebellion. A song can awaken courage. A book can spark a revolution. Stories remind people of what is good, beautiful, and just. They keep the spirit of freedom alive even when it is under attack. Immoral leaders may burn books and silence songs, but ideas cannot be so easily destroyed.

The battle against corruption is never truly over. Every generation faces the choice: to accept lies or to fight for truth. To bow in fear or to stand in courage. Liberty is not just a gift from the past but a duty to the future. Leaders who seek power for selfish reasons will always exist. But so will the people who refuse to be ruled by fear. In the end, it is the spirit of the people, not the throne, that determines the fate of a nation.

Liberty Twisted: Freedom or Control?

True liberty is a force that empowers people. It gives individuals the chance to speak their minds, follow their dreams, and live without fear of oppression. True liberty lifts people higher, allowing them to build better lives for themselves and their communities. However, when immoral leaders come into power, they twist the meaning of liberty. They turn it into something dark, something it was never meant to be. Instead of using freedom to serve the people, they use the word "freedom" as a tool to control them. They change its meaning until it no longer brings hope, but confusion and fear.

When leaders are selfish, they know they cannot rule by force alone. Instead, they pretend to defend freedom while quietly taking it away. They speak loudly about "rights" and "choices," but behind the scenes, they create systems that limit real choice. They encourage people to think they are free while making decisions that lock them into narrow paths. This false sense of freedom keeps people quiet. They believe they still have power, even as their true options disappear one by one. In this way, liberty is not destroyed openly. It is corrupted from within.

One of the most common tricks of immoral leaders is to redefine what liberty means. They claim that liberty is about doing whatever you want without limits. They encourage selfishness, greed, and division. They say that caring about others is weakness. They teach that freedom means taking as much as you can, even if it hurts others. But this is not true liberty. Real freedom requires responsibility. Real freedom understands that we must respect the rights of others if we want our own rights to be safe. Twisting liberty into selfishness only brings chaos and suffering.

Immoral leaders also use the idea of "freedom" to attack critics and silence opposition. Whenever someone points out their corruption or cruelty, they respond by shouting about liberty. They claim that any attempt to hold them accountable is an attack on "freedom." They tell their followers that true patriots must ignore injustice to protect liberty. In reality, they are using the love people have for freedom as a shield for their wrongdoing. By doing this, they poison the very idea of liberty itself, making it harder for people to recognize real threats to their rights.

Control disguised as freedom is one of the most dangerous forms of tyranny. When people believe they are free, they are less likely to resist. Immoral leaders create rules and systems that seem harmless but are designed to trap citizens. They offer choices that are no choices at all. They create fake elections, where all the candidates serve the same corrupt power. They offer "free speech," but punish those who say anything real. They pretend to support free markets but rig the economy so that only a few can ever succeed. This is not freedom. It is control hidden behind a mask.

Another tactic is to focus on personal freedoms while ignoring social freedoms. Leaders might say, "You are free to buy whatever you can afford," but they make sure that only a few have the money to afford anything important. They might say, "You are free to start a business," but only if you can pay impossible fees and bribes. They might say, "You are free to speak," but only if you agree with the powerful. By focusing on shallow freedoms and ignoring real barriers, they create an illusion of liberty that hides deep inequality and injustice.

Twisted liberty often divides society instead of uniting it. When freedom is defined as pure selfishness, people stop caring about each other. Communities break apart. Trust disappears. Everyone is encouraged to fight for their own advantage, no matter the cost to others. This makes it easier for immoral leaders to stay in power. A divided people are weaker. They are too busy fighting each other to notice the growing chains around them. By twisting liberty into selfishness, leaders destroy the very bonds that make true freedom possible.

True liberty depends on truth, but twisted liberty depends on lies. Immoral leaders flood society with false information. They create confusion so people no longer know what is real. They call lies "truth" and truth "lies." They say that questioning authority is dangerous. They say that independent thinking is unpatriotic. When people can no longer trust what they hear, they become easier to control. Lies become the walls of the prison built in the name of freedom. Only the truth can break those walls down and restore real liberty.

In societies where liberty has been twisted, people often feel powerless without understanding why. They sense that something is wrong but cannot put it into words. They still go to work, vote, and speak their minds in small ways. But deep down, they know that the big decisions are out of their hands. They know that their leaders do not truly listen. They know that their choices are meaningless. This quiet despair is the true mark of corrupted liberty. It is the feeling of living in a prison you cannot see.

Over time, twisted liberty changes the values of a nation. People begin to believe that selfishness is strength and kindness is weakness. They celebrate wealth, no matter how it was gained. They look down on those who are struggling, blaming them for their own pain. Compassion, justice, and honesty become rare. Immoral leaders encourage this change because it keeps people weak and divided. A nation that forgets the true meaning of liberty is easy to rule with fear and lies. It becomes a place where cruelty is rewarded and fairness is forgotten.

The education system often becomes a target for those who twist liberty. They rewrite history to make past injustices seem justified. They teach students that questioning authority is wrong. They promote a version of freedom that ignores responsibility and compassion. In doing so, they raise a new generation that does not know what real liberty looks like. Without education based on truth and critical thinking, freedom cannot survive. Knowledge is essential for protecting liberty from corruption.

Twisted liberty also poisons relationships between citizens and their government. When leaders claim to offer freedom but deliver only control, trust breaks down. People stop believing in the system. They stop participating in democracy. They either give up completely or turn to dangerous alternatives. Some may seek safety by blindly following any new leader who promises change, even without thinking carefully. Others may fall into despair and isolation. Either way, the strength of the nation crumbles when real freedom is lost.

The media plays a huge role in either protecting or twisting liberty. Immoral leaders seek to control newspapers, television, and the internet. They spread propaganda dressed up as news. They attack journalists who ask hard questions. They encourage people to distrust any source of information they do not control. A free press is one of the greatest defenders of liberty. When it is silenced or corrupted, citizens are left in darkness. They cannot fight for freedom if they do not know what is happening around them.

Twisted liberty often uses symbols and slogans to trick people. Leaders wrap themselves in flags and sing songs about freedom, even as they take away rights. They build grand monuments and declare holidays, trying to distract from the truth. They make people feel proud of their country, even while they destroy its true values. Symbols of liberty are powerful, but when they are used without honesty, they become weapons of control. It is not enough to wave a flag or sing an anthem. True liberty lives in actions, not symbols.

In the face of twisted liberty, it is easy to feel hopeless. It is easy to believe that real freedom is gone forever. But history shows that liberty can be reclaimed. It requires courage, truth, and a willingness to stand up even when it is dangerous. It requires people who refuse to accept lies, even when it would be easier to stay silent. True liberty is always worth fighting for because it lifts everyone up, not just a few. It creates a world where everyone has the chance to live fully and freely.

Restoring real liberty begins with education and truth-telling. It begins with teaching people what freedom really means: not just the right to do whatever you want, but the right to live in dignity, safety, and fairness. It means remembering that rights come with responsibilities. It means rebuilding trust, community, and compassion. Leaders who truly love liberty must serve the people, not rule over them. They must protect the weak, not exploit them. They must tell the truth, even when it is hard.

Liberty is too precious to be left in the hands of the selfish. It belongs to every person, rich or poor, strong or weak. It must be defended every day, not just celebrated on special occasions. Freedom is not a gift given by leaders. It is a responsibility carried by the people. When liberty is twisted into control, it is up to the people to untwist it. They must remember the true meaning of freedom: the right to live fully, truthfully, and together. Only then can liberty truly lift us up.

The Water Deception: Nature's Hidden Truth

Water is often seen as the purest and most essential element in our lives. We drink it, we bathe in it, and we depend on it for everything from growing our food to cleaning our homes. Water seems simple, something we rarely question. But behind its clear appearance, there may be a hidden story. Over time, human greed and carelessness have changed how we access and understand water. Immorality does not stop at politics or business; it can even poison the elements we rely on most. Water, the symbol of life itself, has become a target for manipulation and deception.

In ancient times, people viewed water as sacred. Rivers, lakes, and oceans were respected, even worshipped. Communities gathered near water sources because they understood how precious they were. But as civilizations grew, so did human arrogance. People stopped seeing water as a gift and began treating it as a resource to be owned, sold, and controlled. Those with power began to claim rivers, lakes, and wells for themselves, shutting others out. What once belonged to everyone became the property of a few. This shift from respect to control marked the beginning of water's corruption.

Today, many people still believe that water is a basic right. We turn on our taps and expect clean water to flow. We buy bottled water believing it is pure and safe. But the reality is more complicated. In many parts of the world, water is not clean. It is full of chemicals, waste, and pollution caused by industries that care more about profit than public health. Companies dump toxins into rivers and lakes, knowing that cleaning them up would cost money. They hide the truth from the public, allowing greed to poison the water supply.

Governments, too, have been guilty of water deception. Some allow companies to pollute freely in exchange for campaign donations or economic promises. Others fail to maintain the systems that keep water clean and safe. Old pipes leak lead and other dangerous substances into drinking water. Treatment plants break down or are poorly managed. Officials sometimes hide these problems from citizens to avoid blame or expensive repairs. When the truth finally comes out, it is often after many people have already gotten sick. Water, the very thing meant to sustain life, becomes a silent killer.

Bottled water companies have built entire empires on the myth of purity. They advertise their products as cleaner and safer than tap water. They show beautiful mountains, forests, and sparkling springs on their labels. But studies have shown that much bottled water is no cleaner than regular tap water—and sometimes it is even worse. In some cases, companies simply bottle tap water and sell it back to the public at outrageous prices. They create fear around public water systems to boost their sales, while doing little to truly protect people's health.

In poor communities, the deception around water becomes even more dangerous. In many parts of the world, clean water is a luxury, not a basic right. People must walk miles just to reach a water source, which may not even be safe. Meanwhile, wealthy industries and neighborhoods have access to unlimited clean water. Governments and corporations often ignore the needs of the poor, seeing no profit in helping them. This deep inequality shows how immorality has twisted even the most basic elements of survival into tools for control and oppression.

Water privatization is another way that greed distorts the natural world. In some countries, companies have bought the rights to public water systems. They control who gets water and how much they must pay. When profits come first, human needs are ignored. Prices go up, quality goes down, and those who cannot pay are left to suffer. Water, which should be free and abundant, becomes a luxury item. The rich can afford it, while the poor must struggle or go without. This exploitation of water shows the darkest side of human ambition.

Pollution is not the only danger hidden in our water. In some cases, governments and industries add chemicals to water supplies without fully understanding the effects. Fluoride, for example, is added to prevent tooth decay, but debates continue over whether it might also cause health problems. Pesticides from farms seep into groundwater, carrying harmful chemicals far from their original source. Factories leak heavy metals into rivers and lakes. Even medicines flushed down toilets can find their way into drinking water. We are only beginning to understand the long-term effects of these hidden dangers.

Another layer of deception is the false belief that technology alone can fix water problems. Leaders promise high-tech filters, new purification systems, and advanced chemical treatments. While technology can help, it often becomes an excuse to avoid solving the root causes of pollution and greed. True protection of water would mean stricter rules, better enforcement, and less waste. It would mean valuing nature itself, not just treating water like another commodity to be managed. Without this shift in attitude, no amount of technology can undo the damage we continue to cause.

Climate change is making the water deception even worse. As droughts become more common and rivers dry up, competition for water is increasing. Rich countries and companies are buying up water rights in poorer nations, securing their own futures while leaving others to suffer. Deserts spread. Crops fail. Families are forced to leave their homes in search of water. Yet many leaders refuse to act, focused only on short-term profits. The global water crisis is not just a natural disaster; it is the result of decades of greed, denial, and corruption.

Education about water is also lacking. Schools may teach basic facts about the water cycle, but few students learn about the politics and economics of water. They do not hear about the corporations buying up water rights. They do not learn how industries pollute or how governments fail to act. Without knowledge, people cannot defend themselves. They cannot demand better laws or safer practices. Silence and ignorance allow the deception to continue. An informed public is the greatest weapon against the corruption of water.

The media plays a role in hiding water's hidden truths. News outlets often focus on dramatic disasters—like floods or droughts—while ignoring the slow poisoning of water supplies. They rarely investigate who profits from water shortages or who covers up pollution. When stories about water do appear, they are often simplified or forgotten quickly. Real journalism about water would mean following the money, asking hard questions, and exposing the systems of greed. Without a strong media, water deception remains in the shadows.

The way we think about water must change. It is not just a product to be bought and sold. It is a sacred trust, something every living creature depends on. If we continue to treat water as a commodity, we will face a future of growing inequality, suffering, and conflict. But if we recognize water as a shared right, we can build systems based on fairness and sustainability. We can choose leaders who protect nature instead of exploiting it. We can demand businesses act responsibly. It begins with seeing water clearly, not through the fog of lies and greed.

Individual actions also matter. Every time we waste water, we contribute to the problem. Every time we buy bottled water without questioning its source, we support companies that may not have our best interests at heart. Every time we stay silent about pollution or privatization, we allow the deception to continue. Change begins with small choices—using water wisely, supporting clean water initiatives, and speaking out against injustice. One voice may seem small, but many voices together can shake mountains.

Immorality touching the elements shows just how deeply corruption can spread. It reminds us that no part of life is safe when greed and selfishness go unchecked. Water should be above politics, above business, above corruption. Yet it has been dragged down like so many other parts of our world. Recognizing this reality is painful but necessary. Only by facing the truth can we begin to heal the damage. Only by understanding the deception can we protect the purity that water once promised.

The hidden truth about water is a warning. If we can allow even the simplest, most essential element to be corrupted, what else will we lose? The deception around water is not just about pollution or money. It is about losing respect for life itself. It is about forgetting that some things are too important to be bought, sold, or exploited. Water teaches us that the fight against immorality is not just about politics or power. It is about protecting the very foundation of life on Earth.

Water is life. Water is the truth. But when the truth is twisted, life itself is threatened. The water deception shows us that the battle for morality must reach every part of our world—even the parts we once thought were safe. It is a battle we must fight with knowledge, courage, and a deep respect for nature. If we lose the war over water, we risk losing everything. But if we can restore honesty and justice to our relationship with water, we have a chance to heal not just our rivers and lakes, but our very souls.

Everyday Immorality: Small Acts, Big Impacts

When people think about immorality, they often imagine huge scandals or serious crimes. They think of politicians lying to the public, companies stealing millions of dollars, or leaders starting wars for selfish reasons. These are the big, obvious examples. But the truth is, immorality also grows quietly, in small ways, every day. Simple acts of dishonesty, selfishness, and cruelty can build up over time. These small wrongs create an environment where bigger evils are more likely to happen. Everyday immorality, though easy to ignore, has a powerful impact on the world around us.

Think about lying. Many people tell "small" lies without even thinking twice. They lie to get out of trouble, to make themselves look better, or just to avoid an awkward conversation. They call these lies harmless. But each lie chips away at trust between people. When lying becomes normal, it becomes harder to know what to believe. Relationships weaken. Friendships fall apart. Communities grow suspicious of each other. A society built on lies cannot be strong. Even tiny untruths can slowly poison the connections that hold people together.

Selfishness is another form of everyday immorality. It can be as simple as cutting in line, hoarding supplies during a shortage, or refusing to help someone in need. At first, these actions seem small. One selfish act doesn't appear to hurt anyone. But when selfishness spreads, it changes the entire atmosphere of a community. People start to look out only for themselves. Cooperation fades. Kindness becomes rare. In a selfish world, trust disappears, and life becomes harder for everyone. Small selfish choices grow into a big culture of greed.

Cruelty in daily life also carries heavy consequences. Making fun of someone, excluding others, or speaking harshly can seem like minor acts. People might laugh it off or claim they were "just joking." But these moments leave scars. Words can hurt as much as physical wounds. Cruelty creates fear and sadness, pushing people into loneliness and anger. Over time, small cruelties build a cold, harsh world where people expect to be mistreated. When kindness is rare and cruelty is normal, communities crumble from the inside out.

Many people think that if their bad actions don't cause immediate harm, they don't matter. But morality isn't just about avoiding obvious damage. It's about creating an environment where goodness can grow. Every choice we make, no matter how small, either builds up or tears down the world around us. A casual act of kindness can inspire others to do good. A careless act of cruelty can encourage more harm. Every small decision matters more than we realize. We are either helping or hurting the society we live in, every day.

The problem with everyday immorality is how easily it spreads. When people see others lying, being selfish, or acting cruelly without consequences, they start to believe it's normal. They might think, "Everyone else is doing it, so why shouldn't I?" Immorality becomes contagious. Once it spreads through a community, it's very difficult to stop. New generations grow up thinking dishonesty and selfishness are just how life works. Breaking the cycle requires courage, awareness, and a commitment to choosing right over easy.

Excuses make everyday immorality even more dangerous. People find ways to justify their bad behavior. They say things like, "It's just a little lie," or "They deserved it," or "No one got hurt." These excuses allow immorality to hide in plain sight. They cover up the real damage being done. When people excuse their wrong actions, they avoid responsibility. Over time, their moral sense becomes weaker. They no longer see the difference between right and wrong clearly. Excuses slowly erase personal honor and accountability.

Technology has also made everyday immorality easier to commit and harder to notice. Online, people spread lies, insults, and cruelty behind screens. Cyberbullying, fake news, and online scams show how small acts of dishonesty can cause real-world harm. Because the internet feels distant and anonymous, people often behave worse online than they would in person. But the consequences are still real. Online actions can destroy reputations, spread hate, and even cause serious emotional harm. Everyday immorality has simply found new tools to grow.

Even small acts of dishonesty at work or school can create major problems. Cheating on a test, lying on a résumé, or stealing office supplies may seem minor. But these actions break trust between people and institutions. If cheating becomes common at school, the value of education falls. If dishonesty spreads in workplaces, teamwork suffers and businesses fail. Trust is the foundation of every strong institution. When everyday immorality eats away at trust, entire systems can collapse over time, just like a building with a weak foundation.

Peer pressure often encourages everyday immorality. Friends, coworkers, or classmates might pressure someone to lie, cheat, or bully others. They might make it seem cool or necessary to fit in. Resisting peer pressure is not easy, especially when people fear being judged or excluded. But giving in only makes the problem worse. Every time someone chooses to join in wrongdoing to avoid standing out, immorality grows stronger. Standing up for what's right, even when it's hard, is how individuals can start to reverse the damage.

Sometimes, everyday immorality begins with simply looking the other way. Seeing someone being bullied and doing nothing. Knowing about corruption at work but staying silent. Ignoring a friend's dishonesty because it's easier than confronting them. Inaction can be just as harmful as direct wrongdoing. Silence can be seen as approval. When good people stay quiet, evil grows louder and bolder. Choosing to act, even in small ways—speaking up, offering help, telling the truth—can make a huge difference in fighting immorality.

The road to major corruption often starts with tiny steps. History shows that tyrants and criminals didn't begin by committing huge evils right away. They started with smaller wrongs that seemed harmless at the time. As they got away with it, they moved on to bigger crimes. Everyday immorality works the same way. Small acts of dishonesty or cruelty, if left unchecked, can lead to much larger problems. Recognizing and stopping these small acts early is critical to preventing larger disasters later on.

Kindness and honesty in daily life can fight back against everyday immorality. Being truthful even when it's inconvenient. Helping others without expecting anything in return. Standing up against unfairness, even when it's unpopular. These small actions inspire others to act better too. Goodness can be just as contagious as immorality if people are brave enough to live it. Every small act of goodness adds up, like drops of water filling a river. A culture of morality grows when individuals choose to do what is right, even when no one is watching.

Teaching young people about everyday morality is crucial. Schools and parents must show that small choices matter. It's not enough to only punish big crimes; children must learn the importance of honesty, kindness, and courage in daily life. They must be taught that doing the right thing is not always easy, but it is always worth it. By building strong moral habits early, we can create a generation better prepared to resist the temptations of dishonesty and cruelty that surround them.

Understanding that we are all connected can motivate better daily behavior. Every time we are honest, kind, and unselfish, we strengthen the web of trust that connects society. Every time we are dishonest, cruel, or selfish, we weaken that web. Our actions affect not just ourselves but everyone around us. Seeing ourselves as part of a larger community helps us act with greater care. Morality is not just a personal choice; it is a gift we give to others by creating a world that is safer, kinder, and more just.

It's easy to feel powerless against the world's big problems. Corruption, injustice, and cruelty can seem too big to fight. But the truth is, we all have power in our daily choices. Every small decision matters. Every kind word, honest action, and brave stand against wrongdoing plants a seed of goodness. These seeds grow into forests over time. Everyday morality might not make headlines, but it builds the foundation for a better future. By refusing to participate in small wrongs, we make it harder for big wrongs to take root.

In the end, everyday immorality is not small at all. It shapes the kind of world we live in. It decides whether trust, kindness, and justice thrive—or whether dishonesty, selfishness, and cruelty take over. We must recognize the power we hold in every choice we make. By choosing honesty over lies, kindness over cruelty, and courage over fear, we can change the world in ways bigger than we ever imagined. The future begins with the everyday actions of ordinary people, including you and me.

Systems Built on Lies

When we hear the word "lie," we usually think about a single person telling an untruth to another person. But what happens when entire systems—like schools, governments, and companies—are built on lies? These lies don't just affect one conversation; they affect whole generations of people. When important institutions are based on falsehoods, immorality seeps into everyday life. People grow up surrounded by these wrong ideas, often without even realizing it. Lies become normal, expected, and even respected.

In schools, for example, students are supposed to learn facts, develop critical thinking, and prepare for life. But when a school teaches information that is outdated, biased, or even false, it builds a foundation of misunderstanding. If students are taught twisted versions of history, science, or ethics, they carry those false lessons into adulthood. They may never question what they were taught because they trust their teachers and the system. These early lies can shape their beliefs, actions, and worldviews for the rest of their lives.

History is often one of the first subjects where lies are hidden. Some schools present only one side of a historical story, leaving out important details or silencing other voices. They might glorify certain figures while ignoring the harm they caused. They might erase the contributions of certain groups. These lies shape how students see their country, their community, and themselves. When you control the way people understand their past, you control the way they imagine their future. Lies in education plant seeds of injustice and division.

Governments, too, often rely on lies to maintain power. Politicians may promise things they never plan to deliver. They may hide mistakes, cover up scandals, or twist facts to make themselves look good. When a government lies, it damages the trust citizens have in their leaders. Over time, people may become cynical, assuming that all politicians are dishonest. This cynicism weakens democracy itself because fewer people believe their voices matter. When lies rule politics, real solutions to problems become harder to find.

One of the most dangerous effects of lies in government is the creation of unjust laws and policies. Leaders who build their power on lies often pass rules that protect their interests instead of serving the people. They might spread fear or hatred to control public opinion. They might silence journalists or critics who try to reveal the truth. When laws are based on lies, they create real suffering. Entire groups of people can be oppressed because of false beliefs that were turned into official policies.

Companies are also guilty of building systems on lies. Advertisements often promise more than a product can deliver. Businesses might hide the harmful effects of their products or pretend to care about social issues only to boost profits. Workers may be lied to about their rights, wages, or opportunities for advancement. When businesses operate dishonestly, they create unfairness and inequality. Customers lose trust. Workers lose dignity. The economy becomes a game where only those willing to deceive can win.

Some of the biggest lies in companies involve environmental harm. A company might claim to be "green" or "sustainable" while secretly polluting the environment. This practice, called "greenwashing," fools customers into supporting harmful industries. It allows the destruction of nature to continue under the cover of good intentions. Lies like these don't just damage the planet; they damage people's ability to make informed choices. When corporations lie about their impact, they rob the public of the power to protect their own future.

The media can also be part of systems built on lies. News outlets sometimes focus more on attracting viewers than on reporting the truth. Sensational headlines, half-truths, and biased reporting can twist public understanding. When media companies choose profit over accuracy, they create confusion, fear, and anger among the population. People find it harder to know what is real. A society that can't agree on basic facts becomes divided and unstable. Lies in the media fuel hatred, distrust, and even violence.

One of the scariest things about systems built on lies is how invisible they can become. When people are raised in a system where dishonesty is normal, they often don't realize anything is wrong. The lies are taught as facts. The false beliefs feel like common sense. Questioning the system feels dangerous or wrong. In this way, immorality becomes baked into daily life. It hides behind rules, traditions, and authority figures, making it very hard to see and even harder to challenge.

Children are especially vulnerable to systems built on lies. They trust the adults around them to teach them what is right and true. If those adults pass down lies— whether by accident or by design—children accept them without question. These early lessons shape their sense of morality, justice, and truth. A child taught to believe in false ideas may grow into an adult who spreads those ideas to others, keeping the cycle alive. Breaking free from these lies takes enormous courage and critical thinking.

Critical thinking is one of the strongest tools against systems built on lies. It means asking questions, seeking evidence, and thinking carefully about what we are told. It means being willing to admit when something we believed was wrong. Systems built on lies depend on people not asking questions. They rely on blind trust and passive acceptance. Teaching critical thinking skills at home, at school, and in the community is essential to protecting truth and fairness in society.

Reform is possible, but it requires honesty, bravery, and persistence. It starts with individuals who are willing to seek the truth, even when it is uncomfortable. It continues with communities that demand transparency from their leaders, teachers, businesses, and media. Exposing lies can be dangerous because those in power often fight to protect their systems. Whistleblowers, activists, and journalists who reveal the truth often face threats or punishment. But their work is necessary to building a more just and honest world.

People must also recognize their own role in maintaining or challenging systems of lies. Sometimes, people benefit from falsehoods and are tempted to stay silent. A company executive might ignore corruption because it makes them rich. A politician might accept false ideas to gain votes. Even ordinary citizens might refuse to see injustice because admitting the truth would be uncomfortable. Changing systems built on lies requires not just blaming others but looking honestly at ourselves and our choices.

Education reform is a key part of breaking free from systems built on lies. Schools must be committed to teaching multiple perspectives, promoting critical inquiry, and correcting past falsehoods. Students should learn how to question information respectfully and responsibly. They should be encouraged to explore history, science, ethics, and media with open but discerning minds. When education is rooted in honesty and curiosity, it prepares future citizens to build systems based on truth, fairness, and justice.

Building new systems based on truth is not easy. It requires constant work, vigilance, and a willingness to correct mistakes. Even well-meaning institutions can slip into dishonesty if they are not held accountable. Regular checks, open conversations, and transparent decision-making processes are necessary. Truth must not be seen as a goal that is achieved once and forgotten; it must be a value that is protected and pursued every day, at every level of society.

Ordinary people have more power than they think to change systems built on lies. Every time someone demands the truth, refuses to spread misinformation, or supports honest leadership, they strengthen the foundations of a better society. Small actions add up. Choosing companies that act ethically, voting for honest politicians, supporting honest journalism—all these choices matter. Systems are made of people.

When people choose truth over lies, systems begin to change.

In the end, societies built on lies are fragile. They might look strong on the surface, but they are hollow inside. Truth is the foundation of real strength, real unity, and real progress. Building a world based on truth is not just about uncovering big lies; it's about nurturing honesty in every classroom, every office, every newsroom, and every government hall. The future belongs to those who are brave enough to demand truth and wise enough to live by it.

Recognizing and Resisting Immorality

Recognizing immorality is the first step toward resisting it. We cannot fight against something we don't see or understand. Many people grow up surrounded by certain behaviors, rules, or traditions that seem normal but are actually wrong or harmful. If no one teaches us to look carefully at the world around us, we might accept immorality as a regular part of life. That is why learning to recognize it is so important. Only by seeing clearly can we begin to make real changes for ourselves and for others.

Questioning what we are taught is one of the most powerful tools we have. This does not mean disrespecting every teacher, parent, or leader. It means thinking carefully about the lessons we are given. Are they fair? Are they true? Are they helping or hurting people? When we simply accept everything we are told without thinking, we make it easy for immorality to continue. When we ask questions, we open the door to discovering the truth and making better choices.

Critical thinking is another essential skill for recognizing immorality. Critical thinking means not just accepting information at face value. It means examining evidence, considering different points of view, and being willing to change your mind when presented with new facts. Critical thinkers are less likely to be fooled by lies or manipulation. They are better at spotting unfairness and injustice, even when it is hidden behind fancy words or powerful people. Critical thinking is a defense against the spread of immorality.

Sometimes immorality is easy to spot, like when someone commits a violent crime or cheats openly. But often, it hides in smaller, quieter places. It can hide in unfair rules, in jokes that make fun of certain people, or in businesses that quietly exploit workers. It can hide in traditions that hurt people or in laws that seem normal but treat some people unfairly. Recognizing immorality means looking beneath the surface. It means paying attention to who gets hurt and who benefits.

Standing up for truth and fairness is not always easy. It often means going against the crowd. It can mean disagreeing with friends, family members, teachers, or leaders. It can mean risking being misunderstood, mocked, or even punished. But standing up for what is right is one of the most important things a person can do. Every act of courage, no matter how small, weakens the power of immorality and strengthens the power of justice and truth.

One way to resist immorality is by speaking out. When we see something wrong, we should not stay silent. Silence often allows immorality to grow stronger. Speaking out does not always mean yelling or causing a scene. Sometimes it means asking a thoughtful question, making a calm statement, or offering a different point of view. Even a quiet voice can inspire others to think differently. Speaking out shines a light on hidden wrongs and encourages others to join the fight for fairness.

Another way to resist immorality is by setting a good example. Our actions can teach others as much as, or even more than, our words. When we act honestly, treat people fairly, and stand up for the vulnerable, we show others that it is possible to live with integrity. We show that goodness is not just an idea but a way of life. Being a good example may seem small, but it can have a powerful impact over time, inspiring others to choose goodness too.

It is also important to support others who are standing up against immorality. No one should have to fight alone. When we see someone speaking out for justice, we should encourage them, stand with them, and help amplify their voice. Immorality often tries to isolate those who resist it, making them feel small and powerless. But when people come together, they are stronger. Community is a powerful force against injustice and wrongdoing.

Learning about different perspectives can also help us recognize and resist immorality. Sometimes, we cannot see the harm in a system or behavior because we are not the ones being hurt. Listening to people from different backgrounds, experiences, and identities can open our eyes to injustice we might otherwise miss. It teaches us empathy and helps us understand the full picture. Compassion and understanding are strong weapons against the blindness that immorality depends on.

We must also be willing to recognize immorality in ourselves. It is easy to point out what others are doing wrong, but much harder to admit our own mistakes. Yet, true resistance to immorality begins with honesty about our own actions and beliefs. Are we treating others fairly? Are we standing up for what is right, even when it is inconvenient? Self-awareness and humility are crucial for anyone who wants to live a truly moral life.

Resisting immorality often requires long-term commitment. It is not something you do once and then forget. It is a daily choice to stay aware, to act with integrity, and to stand up for what is right. There will be days when it feels hard or even hopeless. There will be times when you wonder if your efforts make any difference. But every small act of goodness matters. Every act of resistance chips away at the structures of injustice and builds a better world.

Education plays a big role in recognizing and resisting immorality. A good education does not just teach facts; it teaches students how to think, question, and care about others. Schools that encourage debate, critical thinking, and empathy are helping build future generations that will resist immorality more effectively. Learning is not just about getting a good job; it is about becoming a responsible, thoughtful, and courageous human being.

Art, literature, and storytelling are powerful tools for helping people see and resist immorality. Stories allow us to step into other people's lives and see the world through their eyes. They help us understand injustice, cruelty, and heroism on a deep emotional level. A powerful book, movie, or painting can change hearts and minds in ways that arguments sometimes cannot. Artists and storytellers have a unique role to play in the fight against immorality.

Technology, too, can be used to resist immorality. Social media, for example, allows people to share stories of injustice and organize for change. Online platforms can spread truth quickly and widely. However, technology can also spread lies and hate just as easily. Using technology responsibly—fact-checking information, promoting honest voices, and standing against hate speech—is an important part of resisting immorality in the modern world.

Resisting immorality often means imagining a better world. It requires hope—the belief that change is possible, even when it is difficult. Hope gives people the strength to keep fighting when they are tired or afraid. Hope reminds us that even small acts of goodness can grow into big changes over time. Without hope, resistance becomes just survival. With hope, resistance becomes a path to a better, fairer world.

Finally, we must remember that resisting immorality is a shared responsibility. It is not just the job of heroes, leaders, or famous activists. It is the job of every person who cares about truth, fairness, and kindness. Every choice we make—how we treat others, how we speak, how we spend our money, how we vote—either strengthens or weakens the forces of immorality. Together, our everyday actions can build a society where truth and justice thrive.

Recognizing and resisting immorality is one of the hardest but most important things a person can do. It takes courage, patience, and determination. It requires us to be both thoughtful and brave, both kind and strong. But the rewards are great. By choosing to see the truth and act on it, we help create a world where everyone has a better chance to live with dignity, fairness, and hope.

A New Way Forward: Healing from Immorality

Healing from immorality is not just about looking back with regret; it is about moving forward with purpose. When we learn from past mistakes, we give ourselves the power to build something better. History is full of examples where societies ignored immorality until it caused great suffering. But it also shows us that change is possible. Healing starts when individuals choose to act differently, even when it's hard. Every good decision, every act of honesty, helps create a better future for everyone.

The first step in healing is personal responsibility. Each of us must look at our own actions and attitudes. Are we being fair and truthful in how we live our lives? Are we treating others with respect? Healing begins when individuals make moral choices, even in small, everyday situations. It's easy to blame leaders, systems, or history, but real change starts when regular people take ownership of their behavior. Small good deeds can add up to major transformations in a society.

Demanding honesty from those in power is another critical step. Leaders shape the rules and values of communities, schools, businesses, and governments. When leaders lie, cheat, or behave selfishly, their example spreads. That's why it's important for people to expect more from those in leadership positions. Citizens must hold their leaders accountable through questions, protests, elections, and public discussion.

Power without honesty leads to corruption, but power guided by truth can lead to real progress.

Healing also means understanding how deep the wounds of immorality run. Some damage caused by dishonesty, cruelty, or injustice lasts for generations. Healing these wounds takes time, patience, and real effort. It's not enough to simply say, "That was in the past." We must work actively to repair broken trust, address unfair systems, and ensure that the same mistakes are not repeated. True healing is not forgetting the past but learning from it to create a better future.

Education plays a major role in the healing process. When young people are taught critical thinking, compassion, and a sense of fairness, they are less likely to repeat the mistakes of the past. Good education encourages students to ask questions, understand different points of view, and seek truth even when it's uncomfortable. Schools that teach morality, history, and personal responsibility prepare the next generation to resist immorality and build stronger, more just societies.

Another important part of healing is forgiveness—but forgiveness does not mean ignoring wrongdoing. True forgiveness acknowledges the harm that was done while choosing not to be consumed by anger or hate. It allows individuals and societies to move forward without being trapped by the pain of the past. Forgiveness is powerful because it breaks cycles of revenge and bitterness. It opens the door for rebuilding trust and forming healthier, stronger communities.

Healing from immorality requires honesty about history, even when the truth is painful. Some people prefer to ignore or rewrite the past to make it seem less harsh. But healing demands facing reality. It demands admitting when harm was done and recognizing who suffered. Only by facing the full truth can we hope to correct wrongs and prevent them from happening again. Honesty, even when it hurts, is a key part of moving forward with integrity.

Communities that heal are communities that listen. Listening to the voices of those who have been hurt is essential. Their experiences teach important lessons about where immorality hides and how it affects real people. Listening shows respect and a willingness to change. It helps build trust, which is necessary for true healing. Without listening, wounds remain hidden, and problems stay unresolved. Listening turns pain into understanding and understanding into action.

Healing also involves making amends. When people or societies have caused harm, they must take steps to repair it. This might mean apologizing, offering restitution, changing unfair laws, or creating new opportunities for those who were hurt. Making amends is a sign of maturity and moral growth. It shows that words are not enough; actions must follow. True healing demands not just feeling sorry but doing what is needed to set things right.

Building a better future means creating systems based on truth, fairness, and compassion. Governments, schools, and businesses must be organized in ways that encourage honesty and punish corruption. Systems should reward those who act with integrity, not just those who gain the most power or money. Creating fair systems helps prevent immorality from growing back like a weed. It gives everyone a fair chance to succeed and live with dignity.

Healing requires courage. It takes bravery to admit mistakes, challenge unfairness, and choose a better way. It's much easier to stay silent or to do what's easy rather than what's right. But without courage, immorality thrives. Healing means stepping out of comfort zones and standing up even when it's scary. Brave people make the changes that others thought were impossible. Courage is the heartbeat of moral progress.

Hope is another essential part of healing. Without hope, it's easy to believe that things will never get better. But hope inspires action. It reminds us that no matter how bad things have been, improvement is possible. Hope gives energy to those working for fairness, honesty, and kindness. It lights the way forward when the road seems dark. Healing depends on hope because without it, people give up, and immorality wins.

Art, music, and storytelling can help in the healing process too. These forms of expression allow people to process pain, share their experiences, and inspire others to think differently. A powerful song or story can open hearts and minds in ways that facts and arguments cannot. Artists have an important role in healing from immorality by creating works that speak to truth, justice, and the human spirit.

Healing often starts small, at the level of individuals and families. A parent teaching their child to be honest, a student refusing to cheat, a worker standing up for fairness—these actions seem small but are incredibly important. Big changes usually grow from small beginnings. If enough individuals commit to moral living, the effects ripple outward, influencing communities, countries, and even the world. Personal change is the seed from which social change grows.

Part of moving forward is also understanding that healing is a journey, not a destination. There will always be challenges and setbacks. People will make mistakes. Systems will not change overnight. But every step toward greater honesty, kindness, and fairness matters. Healing is ongoing work, a process that requires persistence and patience. It's not about achieving perfection but about constantly striving to do better.

Healing from immorality leads to a more just, compassionate world. It creates societies where people trust each other, leaders act with integrity, and everyone has a chance to succeed fairly. It allows individuals to live with dignity and communities to thrive in peace. Healing makes it possible to replace cycles of hate and injustice with cycles of growth and hope. A healed society is not perfect, but it is strong, kind, and resilient.

In the end, a new way forward is built one choice at a time. Every honest word, every fair action, every brave stand adds to the foundation of a better future. Healing from immorality is not the work of a few heroes but the work of many people, each doing their part. Together, we can move beyond the mistakes of the past and build a world where truth, fairness, and kindness are not the exception—they are the rule.

Chapter Summary

Immorality is often seen as an abstract concept, a distant issue that doesn't affect our daily lives. However, as explored in The Throne and Liberty and Water Is Not What You Believe, immorality is present in the world in both grand and subtle ways. From corrupt leaders who promise liberty but deliver oppression, to the manipulation of something as fundamental as water for selfish gain, immorality is an ever-present force. It hides in plain sight, disguising itself as virtue, success, or normalcy. Yet, its effects are deeply destructive, causing harm to societies, the environment, and individuals.

Understanding immorality requires more than just recognizing its symptoms—it demands a willingness to engage in deep, uncomfortable reflection. It challenges us to question the things we are taught to trust, including the systems that govern our lives and the leaders who claim to represent us. Leaders who twist the concepts of liberty, justice, and fairness are a clear example of how immorality can infect even the most sacred ideals. By making us question what we've been told is right, we open our eyes to the realities of injustice, corruption, and the manipulation of power.

The systems that surround us, whether in government, education, or business, are often built on lies that go unchecked for years. These lies become so ingrained that they form the foundation of the world we live in, shaping our thoughts and actions in ways we might never even notice. As we recognize these lies, we begin to understand the need for real change. But change requires effort and courage—especially when it comes to confronting the systems and people that benefit from these lies. Fighting against immorality means standing up against those who try to deceive us for their own gain.

However, immorality is not just something external—it is also a reflection of our inner struggles. Each of us, in our own way, contributes to the culture of immorality through small acts of dishonesty, selfishness, or cruelty. These everyday actions might seem insignificant, but when they are repeated over time, they contribute to larger, more damaging systems. By examining ourselves and taking responsibility for our actions, we can begin to heal the damage we cause in our personal lives, relationships, and communities.

Healing the wounds of immorality begins with self-awareness and a commitment to acting with kindness, fairness, and truth. It is not enough to simply condemn immorality in others; we must also confront our own tendencies toward dishonesty, selfishness, and harm. When we choose to live by principles of integrity, we not only improve ourselves but also inspire others to do the same. Healing is a collective effort, and it starts with each individual choosing to do what is right, even when it is difficult.

The future of our world depends on our ability to see and resist immorality wherever it appears. As we become more aware of the ways in which corruption, deceit, and selfishness shape our world, we gain the power to change it. If we act with knowledge, compassion, and courage, we can begin to build a society where the throne truly serves the people, where liberty is genuine, and where even the most basic elements of life, like water, are free from manipulation. The journey toward a more just world is difficult, but it starts with the simple act of choosing to see the truth and live by it.

Ultimately, the fight against immorality is not just a battle against external forces but a call to action within ourselves. We cannot change the world if we are unwilling to confront the darkness within us. By recognizing and resisting immorality in all its forms—whether in our leaders, our systems, or ourselves—we can create a more honest, fair, and compassionate world. It starts with recognizing the truth, acting on it, and choosing to heal the harm we see around us. This is how we can truly build a better future for all.

Chapter Six

Compromise

In the modern world, compromise is often seen as a necessary part of life, especially in relationships, work, and social situations. However, when it comes to the most essential aspects of life—like our connection to the divine and the natural world—the concept of compromise takes on a much darker meaning. In this chapter, we will explore the idea that compromising the purity of God's teachings, and in particular, the purity of water, leads to a distortion of both physical and spiritual health. Water, in its purest form, is a sacred delivery system, carrying the divine teachings of God. The compromises made to the integrity of this sacred element are far more dangerous than most people realize.

Water has always been a symbol of life, purification, and renewal. But just as water can be tainted, so can our understanding of God's will. Compromising God's teachings, much like the compromise of water's purity, weakens the very essence of who we are. In this chapter, we'll explore how the distortion of water through human manipulation is an example of how broader compromises in society have affected not just our physical bodies, but our connection to the divine. Water is no longer just a life-sustaining element; it is now a medium that carries the impurities of the world, influencing everything it touches, including our minds and hearts.

The idea that God's will is transmitted through the purest form of water is not a metaphor but a profound truth. The chemicals, nanoparticles, and pollutants that have contaminated our water supply represent a deeper issue: the corruption of purity and the dilution of the divine. These contaminants not only affect our physical health but also impact our mental clarity and spiritual connection. Just as we would not compromise the purity of sacred teachings, we should never compromise the purity of our water. Both are necessary for our spiritual and physical well-being.

When we drink or bathe in water that has been tainted by human interference, we are essentially accepting the dilution of truth and purity. This compromises our ability to think clearly, act with wisdom, and stay connected to our higher purpose. Water, when altered, disrupts our cells, our thoughts, and even our very essence. This chapter explores the grave implications of these compromises, how they affect us individually, and how they impact society at large.

As we examine the dangers of compromising the purity of water, we must also examine the broader implications of compromise in our lives. Compromise can be subtle, often hidden under the guise of practicality or convenience, but it ultimately weakens our connection to God's will. This chapter is a call to return to purity—both in our physical world and in our spiritual lives. We must resist the temptation to accept the diluted forms of truth, water, and existence. Only by embracing the purest forms of life, as they were intended, can we reclaim our strength, clarity, and connection to the divine.

The Sacredness of Water

Water, one of the most essential elements on Earth, has been regarded as sacred by cultures across the globe for centuries. From ancient religious practices to modern-day environmental movements, water has always been a symbol of life, sustenance, and spiritual power. Every living thing on this planet depends on water for survival, and yet, its significance goes far beyond its role in sustaining life. Water has the ability to purify, to cleanse, and to renew—qualities that have made it sacred in the eyes of many people. In spiritual contexts, water represents not only physical life but also spiritual vitality, acting as a bridge between the physical and divine realms.

In almost every major spiritual tradition, water plays a critical role in rituals and beliefs. In Christianity, baptism is performed with water, symbolizing the cleansing of sin and the rebirth of the spirit. In Hinduism, the Ganges River is revered as a goddess, with its waters believed to have the power to purify one's soul and wash away past transgressions. In many Indigenous cultures, rivers, lakes, and oceans are seen as living entities, and their waters are treated with reverence, as they are believed to carry the wisdom of ancestors and the life force of the earth. Through these practices, water becomes more than a mere physical substance; it is imbued with spiritual significance, acting as a vehicle for divine connection and purification.

Water's purity reflects the nature of divine will. Just as water is naturally clear and untainted in its purest form, so too is God's will—pure, unchanging, and life-giving. The clarity of water mirrors the clarity of truth, which is vital for spiritual understanding and growth. In the same way that clean water nourishes the body, divine teachings nourish the soul. They provide the clarity needed to lead a virtuous life, free from the corruption of sin and misdirection. A pure heart, much like pure water, allows divine wisdom to flow freely, guiding the individual toward righteousness and peace.

The relationship between water and spiritual purity is not just symbolic. Water is often seen as a means of connecting with the divine, a conduit for transformation. In many spiritual practices, people use water to cleanse themselves before entering sacred spaces, as a way to prepare for spiritual growth. This cleansing is not only physical but mental and emotional. Just as water can wash away dirt from the body, it is believed that water can also wash away impurities from the soul, preparing individuals to receive divine wisdom. In this way, water serves as a mediator between the material world and the divine, allowing human beings to experience and embody divine teachings.

The sacredness of water also speaks to the interconnectedness of all things. Water is a universal element, found everywhere on Earth, in all living organisms, and in the atmosphere. This omnipresence of water reflects the idea that divine truth and purity are not confined to any one place or group of people. Just as water flows through rivers, streams, and oceans, divine wisdom flows through all of creation, available to everyone. The sacredness of water reminds us of the fundamental unity of all life and the spiritual interdependence between all beings, which are all nourished by the same source.

In addition to representing purity and renewal, water is also a symbol of transformation. In many cultures, water is seen as a force of change, capable of shaping landscapes and altering the course of life. Rivers carve out valleys, rain nourishes crops, and the ocean shapes coastlines. In spiritual terms, water represents the transformative power of God's will, which can cleanse the soul, heal wounds, and guide individuals toward a new path. Just as water is never static, constantly moving and changing, so too is the spiritual journey— always flowing, always evolving. The transformation that comes from embracing divine teachings is like the flowing of water, constantly renewing and reshaping our understanding of the world.

Water also has the power to connect us to the past, present, and future. Rivers, lakes, and oceans are often seen as timekeepers, carrying with them the stories of generations that have come before. In this sense, water symbolizes the continuity of life, carrying the lessons of the past into the present and ensuring that the wisdom of the ages is never lost. The purification that comes from water is not only for the individual but also for communities and entire cultures. As people bathe in or drink from sacred waters, they are reminded of their connection to the ancestors who revered the same waters, drawing on the power of generations of knowledge and spiritual insight.

The act of drinking water or bathing in it is a reminder of the basic, fundamental needs of the human body, but it also symbolizes a deeper spiritual nourishment. Just as the body requires water to thrive, the soul requires divine teachings to remain pure and aligned with God's will. Water serves as a symbol of this spiritual nourishment, as essential for the soul as it is for the body. In the same way that we would never knowingly consume contaminated water, we must ensure that the teachings we follow and the truths we accept are pure and untainted by the corruption of the world.

In modern times, the purity of water is often threatened by human actions. Pollution, contamination, and the manipulation of natural resources all contribute to the degradation of water quality. Just as we must be vigilant in ensuring that our physical water remains pure and untainted, we must also be cautious about the teachings we accept. It is easy for truth to become muddled and distorted, especially when it is influenced by external forces such as politics, greed, or personal agendas. Just as we must filter out the impurities from our water, we must also filter out the distortions and falsehoods that can obscure divine teachings.

In many ways, the contamination of water parallels the corruption of spiritual teachings. When water is polluted, it loses its ability to nourish and cleanse. Similarly, when God's teachings are distorted or diluted, they lose their transformative power. The purity of water serves as a reminder of the importance of maintaining spiritual clarity. Just as we seek to protect and preserve the purity of water for future generations, we must also work to preserve the integrity of divine teachings, ensuring that they remain pure and accessible to all who seek them.

The sacredness of water also teaches us about humility and reverence. Water does not demand recognition or glory; it simply exists to serve and nourish. In this sense, water reflects the nature of God's will, which does not seek personal gain or recognition but exists to serve the greater good of all creation. When we approach water with reverence and humility, we are reminded of the divine qualities of service, selflessness, and purity. By learning from the example of water, we can adopt these qualities in our own lives, striving to live in alignment with God's will and to serve others with humility and grace.

Water is also a symbol of renewal. Just as water can wash away dirt and impurities, it can also wash away spiritual burdens. In many spiritual traditions, water is used in rituals of renewal and rebirth, offering a fresh start to those who seek it. The purification of water reflects the cleansing of the soul, providing an opportunity for individuals to shed past mistakes, wrongdoings, and spiritual stagnation. Water offers the promise of new beginnings and the hope of transformation. In this sense, water is a constant reminder that no matter how polluted or corrupted our lives may seem, there is always the possibility for purification and renewal.

The sanctity of water calls us to respect and protect this vital resource, understanding its deeper significance as a life-giving and spiritual element. Just as we must preserve the purity of water for future generations, we must also safeguard the purity of divine truth. By doing so, we honor both the physical and spiritual nourishment that water provides, ensuring that it remains a sacred gift for all who seek to drink from its depths.

The sacredness of water also teaches us the importance of balance. Water is neither too much nor too little—it exists in perfect harmony with nature. In our own lives, we must strive for balance in our spiritual practices, ensuring that we are neither overwhelmed by the pursuit of perfection nor complacent in our faith. Water, in its purest form, teaches us that balance is essential for both physical health and spiritual well-being.

Finally, the sacredness of water reminds us of the interconnectedness of all life. Water flows through everything, touching every part of the Earth and every living being. In this way, it serves as a reminder of the divine presence that connects all things. Just as water nourishes and sustains life, so too does God's will sustain and nourish our souls. By recognizing the sacredness of water, we can deepen our connection to the divine and to all living beings, understanding that we are all part of a larger, interconnected whole.

The Impact of Water on the Body and Mind

Water is not just something we drink to quench our thirst—it's the very substance that allows our bodies to function. Comprising about 60% of the human body, water is involved in nearly every bodily process. It helps regulate temperature, flushes out toxins, supports digestion, and ensures that nutrients are transported to where they are needed. Every cell in our body depends on water to survive and thrive. Without it, our bodies would quickly shut down. But it's not only physical health that water influences—our mental and emotional health is equally reliant on this essential fluid.

Water is the medium through which our cells receive nourishment and oxygen, which are necessary for optimal function. The brain, being one of the most energy-demanding organs in the body, relies heavily on water to maintain its intricate processes. Even mild dehydration can lead to problems such as trouble concentrating, poor memory, and an increased risk of mental fatigue. A lack of sufficient water can cause our thinking to become foggy, and our emotional responses may become more erratic. This is because the brain, which is mostly made up of water, cannot work properly when its supply of water is compromised.

Just as the body's physical systems depend on water, so too does our mind. Water is essential for producing neurotransmitters, the chemicals that transmit signals in the brain. These neurotransmitters help us think clearly, make decisions, and regulate our mood. When the body is dehydrated, the production and function of these neurotransmitters become inefficient, resulting in reduced cognitive abilities, mood swings, and even depression. Water helps keep the mind clear, sharp, and focused. When it is compromised, mental and emotional clarity are often the first to suffer.

It's not just about the amount of water we drink—it's about the quality of the water we consume. Water that is contaminated with harmful substances, such as chemicals, heavy metals, and nanoparticles, can have detrimental effects on our bodies and minds. These impurities can disrupt cellular processes, interfere with hormonal balances, and even impact brain function. The chemicals found in polluted water can cross the blood-brain barrier and affect the brain's delicate chemistry, leading to cognitive decline, mood disturbances, and impaired memory. When water is polluted, it no longer serves as the life-giving substance it was intended to be.

The purity of water is akin to the purity of God's teachings in our lives. Just as pure, clean water nourishes the body and mind, God's truth purifies and nourishes our souls. When God's teachings are compromised, distorted, or diluted, they lose their ability to strengthen and guide us. Similarly, when we drink contaminated water, we allow harmful substances into our bodies that disrupt our natural balance and health. The analogy between water's purity and spiritual clarity is striking—just as polluted water harms our physical health, compromised spiritual teachings weaken our ability to make sound, ethical decisions and maintain emotional well-being.

Contaminated water can have long-term consequences on health that extend beyond the immediate effects. Chronic exposure to toxic substances in water can lead to issues like hormone imbalances, compromised immune function, and even cancer. The body slowly becomes poisoned, much like how the soul becomes poisoned when it is exposed to false teachings. Over time, both the physical and spiritual bodies can deteriorate without proper cleansing and nourishment. Just as we must take care to protect our bodies from polluted water, we must be vigilant in protecting our spiritual well-being from corruption and distortion of the truth.

One of the most insidious effects of contaminated water is its ability to subtly influence mental health. People often do not realize the link between their physical environment and their mental clarity. Many of the chemicals in polluted water, such as fluoride, chlorine, and lead, are known to have negative effects on brain function. These substances can contribute to anxiety, depression, and difficulty focusing. Over time, this mental fog becomes normalized, and people may begin to accept it as a part of life, unaware that the water they drink is contributing to their mental struggles. This highlights the importance of both physical and spiritual discernment—we must not allow harmful influences to quietly seep into our lives without questioning their effects.

The brain is highly sensitive to environmental changes, and it reacts to impurities in water by slowing down its processes. When the brain is overloaded with toxins from contaminated water, it becomes less efficient at processing information, leading to slower reactions, poor decision-making, and impaired judgment. This can have serious consequences in daily life, from missing important details to making impulsive decisions that harm relationships or careers. Similarly, when we allow false or misleading teachings to infiltrate our minds, we begin to make decisions that are out of alignment with our true purpose, weakening our ability to discern right from wrong.

In addition to physical and cognitive effects, contaminated water can also lead to emotional instability. Water that carries toxic substances can interfere with the production of serotonin and other mood-regulating chemicals in the brain. As a result, individuals who consume polluted water may experience mood swings, irritability, and even depression. The body becomes more susceptible to stress, and emotional responses become more extreme. In the same way, when we stray from God's teachings and allow negative influences to shape our beliefs, we become more emotionally volatile, unable to find peace or clarity in our decisions.

The importance of clean, pure water cannot be overstated. Water that is free from harmful contaminants supports the body in every aspect, from physical health to mental clarity. When we consume pure water, we give our bodies and minds the best chance to function at their highest potential. Just as pure water promotes clarity and vitality, God's teachings, when embraced in their purest form, offer the same benefits for our souls. When we follow the unadulterated truth, we experience greater peace, wisdom, and understanding. However, just as polluted water can poison the body, compromised teachings can pollute our spirits.

The widespread pollution of water sources, from industrial waste to agricultural runoff, has led to the introduction of harmful chemicals into the water supply. These contaminants do not just affect physical health—they also impact mental and emotional well-being. People may not realize that their health problems, whether they are physical, mental, or emotional, could be linked to the water they consume. In much the same way, spiritual contamination—through false teachings, manipulation, and the twisting of divine truth—can cause long-lasting harm to individuals and communities.

The body's need for clean water is a constant reminder of the importance of purity in all areas of life. Just as we would never intentionally drink water laced with toxins, we should be equally cautious about what we allow into our minds and spirits. The quality of water we drink directly impacts our ability to function and thrive. Similarly, the quality of teachings we follow influences our spiritual and emotional well-being. The closer we align ourselves with God's pure truth, the clearer and more peaceful our lives will be.

Contaminated water can have an insidious effect on families and communities. When water is compromised, it doesn't just affect one person—it affects everyone who drinks it. Similarly, when society allows falsehoods and distortions to dominate the cultural conversation, the entire community suffers. People become disconnected from their spiritual roots, unable to discern truth from deception. This loss of clarity leads to confusion, moral decay, and societal instability. Just as we must work to clean up polluted water sources, we must work to purify the teachings we encounter and share.

Ultimately, the purity of water and the purity of teachings are both essential for the well-being of the individual and the collective. Water is the lifeblood of the body, just as divine truth is the lifeblood of the soul. Both must be free from contaminants in order to support healthy living. We must be proactive in protecting the water we drink, ensuring that it is clean and pure. Similarly, we must protect our minds and spirits by seeking out the truth and rejecting any influences that would distort it. When both water and truth are pure, we experience greater clarity, health, and peace.

The Corruption of God's Will

God's teachings are meant to be pure, life-sustaining, and full of wisdom, just as water is intended to be pure and nourishing. Water, in its natural state, is clear and clean, designed by God to nourish and maintain all living beings. Similarly, God's teachings were given to us in their purest form to guide us, nurture our spirits, and promote a life of love, kindness, and understanding. However, just as water can be polluted and contaminated, God's will can be distorted over time, manipulated by human desires for power, control, and convenience.

Throughout history, we've seen how the original purity of God's teachings has been compromised for the benefit of those in power. Like water that has been tainted by chemicals and pollutants, God's word can become diluted or altered, misused to serve agendas that contradict the core principles of justice, peace, and love. The shift from pure teachings to distorted versions occurs when the truth is bent or selectively presented to maintain control over people. This not only harms individuals, but it also damages entire communities, leading them away from the path of righteousness and truth.

Just as polluted water can harm the body by introducing toxins that disrupt our systems, the corruption of divine teachings has a harmful effect on the mind, body, and soul. When God's word is twisted to fit personal or political agendas, it no longer serves its true purpose—nourishing the spirit and guiding us toward living a meaningful, fulfilling life. Instead, it becomes a tool for manipulation and control. People are led astray, their spiritual health compromised, just as polluted water makes the body sick and weak. The more we deviate from the purity of God's will, the more we suffer, individually and collectively.

This corruption doesn't happen all at once; it's a gradual process, much like the slow contamination of water sources over time. Small changes, misunderstandings, and misinterpretations build up, eventually resulting in a significant distortion of God's teachings. It's easy to overlook the small compromises, but these subtle changes accumulate, making it more difficult to see the damage until it becomes overwhelming. Just as a small amount of pollution in water can multiply and affect an entire water supply, small deviations from God's will can affect society in profound ways, eroding moral values and creating confusion.

The distortion of God's teachings is not always an intentional act of malice, but often a result of ignorance, misinterpretation, or negligence. Leaders, teachers, and institutions may unintentionally spread versions of God's will that are incomplete or misrepresented. This can happen when people fail to seek the truth in its entirety or when they allow personal biases to cloud their understanding. Just as water can become contaminated through neglect or carelessness, God's teachings can be misrepresented or misunderstood when we fail to diligently seek the truth and live in alignment with divine principles.

The impact of this corruption extends beyond individuals—it affects entire communities and societies. When God's teachings are distorted, the moral foundation of society becomes shaky. People may begin to adopt values that are far removed from the principles of love, justice, and peace. These deviations lead to societal unrest, division, and conflict. Just as polluted water can lead to widespread illness, a society that strays from the truth of God's teachings experiences moral decay, with people suffering from confusion, division, and a lack of direction. The consequences of this corruption are often not immediately visible, but they accumulate over time, creating a broken and disjointed world.

One of the key ways in which God's teachings are corrupted is through the use of religion as a tool for power. Throughout history, religious teachings have been manipulated by those in positions of power to maintain control over the masses. Instead of using God's will to inspire love and justice, some have twisted it to justify oppression, inequality, and violence. Just as water can be used for both nurturing and destruction, so too can divine teachings be used to either heal or harm. The power to distort these teachings has caused immense suffering, both spiritually and physically, to countless people throughout the ages.

In many cases, the corruption of God's will is also fueled by greed and self-interest. Just as water can be polluted by industrial waste or agricultural runoff for the sake of profit, so can God's teachings be distorted to serve the selfish desires of individuals or institutions. These corrupt teachings may promise power, wealth, or status, but they ultimately lead to spiritual bankruptcy. People are misled, chasing after hollow promises instead of seeking the true peace and fulfillment that come from living in alignment with God's will. This is why the fight for spiritual purity is so important—we must recognize when God's teachings have been compromised and work to reclaim their original truth.

Another aspect of this corruption is the way in which society has embraced convenience over purity. In a world driven by instant gratification and short-term gains, many people seek a watered-down version of spirituality that is easy to consume and doesn't require much effort. Just as we might settle for tap water filled with contaminants because it's easy to access, many people settle for a version of God's will that fits their desires and avoids the discomfort of true spiritual growth. This convenience, however, comes at a great cost—just as contaminated water leads to physical illness, a shallow understanding of divine teachings leads to spiritual emptiness.

The distortion of God's teachings also affects the way individuals view themselves and others. When people are taught a twisted version of divine will, they begin to internalize values that may not align with the truth. They may see themselves as unworthy or flawed, or they may adopt prejudiced views toward others. This is particularly harmful when it comes to issues like love, justice, and equality. Just as polluted water affects the body's ability to function properly, distorted teachings prevent individuals from understanding their true worth and their ability to create positive change in the world.

In today's world, where misinformation and manipulation run rampant, it is more important than ever to stay vigilant in seeking the truth of God's will. We must actively challenge the distortions that exist in society and strive to reclaim the purity of divine teachings. Just as we filter water to ensure its purity before drinking it, we must carefully filter the information we receive and seek to align our beliefs with the truth of God's word. Only through this conscious effort can we ensure that we are living in alignment with divine will, both in our personal lives and in society as a whole.

The pursuit of purity—whether in water or in spirituality—requires dedication and discernment. We cannot afford to be passive when it comes to protecting ourselves from corruption. Just as we must protect our bodies from polluted water, we must protect our souls from distorted teachings. This means questioning what we are taught, searching for deeper understanding, and being willing to reject anything that leads us away from the truth. By doing so, we can rebuild our spiritual foundation and restore the purity of God's teachings in our lives.

God's will, when understood and followed in its purest form, has the power to heal and transform the world. It brings clarity, peace, and harmony to the mind and soul, just as clean water revitalizes the body. But when corrupted, it loses its ability to guide and nourish us. The distortion of divine teachings has far-reaching consequences, affecting not just individuals but entire societies. As we work to purify both the water we drink and the teachings we follow, we will find a greater sense of purpose, fulfillment, and connection to God's true will.

Ultimately, the task of reclaiming purity—whether in water or in spirituality—requires a commitment to truth, clarity, and integrity. We must resist the urge to compromise or accept diluted versions of what is right. By doing so, we can help restore the original beauty and power of both God's will and the water that sustains us. This is the path to true health, peace, and spiritual fulfillment.

How Chemicals and Pollutants Alter Our Connection to the Divine

Water, in its purest form, is a vital element that sustains not only our physical bodies but also our spiritual well-being. It has long been viewed as a conduit for life and a symbol of purity and renewal in many spiritual traditions. However, just as pollutants and chemicals disrupt the natural balance of our bodies, they can also interfere with our ability to connect with the divine. These toxic substances prevent the free flow of energy and clarity, blocking our access to higher understanding and spiritual insight. In much the same way that polluted water harms our physical health, spiritual pollution distorts our connection to God and His teachings.

Chemicals in our water supply, such as pesticides, industrial byproducts, and pharmaceuticals, can alter the way our bodies function. These pollutants don't simply stay in our bodies—they can interfere with our minds and our emotional health. When our physical systems are disrupted, it becomes harder to maintain a clear, peaceful state of mind, which is necessary for spiritual growth and connection to the divine. In a similar way, corrupted ideologies and distorted interpretations of divine will can pollute our spiritual clarity. They cloud our judgment, make us lose sight of truth, and block the flow of spiritual energy, leading us away from God's purpose for us.

The flow of divine energy is meant to be as pure and unobstructed as water flowing through a natural stream. However, just as industrial runoff can poison a river, the introduction of false beliefs, twisted teachings, and misguided ideologies can pollute our spiritual connection to the divine. When we allow these pollutants into our minds, they block the channels through which spiritual guidance flows. Our ability to receive clear understanding from God becomes clouded, and we may struggle to discern right from wrong, truth from deception. Over time, this spiritual pollution can erode our faith and make it harder to align ourselves with God's will.

In our physical bodies, pollutants can cause a range of problems, from fatigue and headaches to chronic illness and organ damage. Similarly, spiritual pollutants disrupt our internal harmony, causing confusion, doubt, and inner conflict. When we lose our connection to the divine, we feel disconnected and lost. This sense of spiritual fragmentation often leads people to search for answers in places that cannot offer true healing, like materialism, fame, or power. Just as water that is tainted can no longer quench thirst, a soul that is polluted by false beliefs cannot find true peace or fulfillment. We need pure spiritual nourishment, just as our bodies need clean water to thrive.

The impact of spiritual pollutants is not always immediate. Just as it takes time for water to become visibly polluted, the effects of false teachings and toxic ideologies often build up gradually. Initially, we may not notice the change in our connection to the divine, but over time, we begin to feel a sense of emptiness or disconnection. This sense of spiritual thirst is similar to the dehydration we experience when our bodies are deprived of pure water. When we are disconnected from God's teachings, we may find ourselves wandering, searching for meaning in superficial or fleeting experiences. Our sense of purpose fades, and we struggle to find clarity in our lives.

In addition to blocking our connection to God, polluted water can also prevent us from fully embracing the life that God intends for us. When our minds and spirits are clouded by external pollutants, we fail to recognize the abundance of blessings and guidance that are constantly available to us. Just as water carries nutrients and oxygen to our cells, divine wisdom is meant to nourish our souls and guide us toward righteousness. However, when we allow ourselves to become spiritually polluted, we stop absorbing the nourishment that is meant to empower us. Our spiritual vitality diminishes, and we become vulnerable to the influences of negativity and falsehood.

One of the most damaging effects of spiritual pollution is the loss of clarity. Just as polluted water becomes murky and difficult to drink, a polluted spirit loses its ability to see the truth. When our spiritual vision is clouded, we are more likely to accept false teachings, believe in illusions, and make decisions that lead us away from God's will. This spiritual blindness makes it difficult to navigate life's challenges and discern the right path forward. Without clear sight, we may find ourselves stuck in unhealthy patterns, repeating mistakes and feeling disconnected from our true purpose. The clarity that comes from a pure connection to the divine is essential for making wise decisions and living a life of integrity.

To reclaim our spiritual purity, we must first acknowledge the pollutants in our lives and take steps to remove them. Just as we must filter and purify water to make it safe to drink, we must filter out false beliefs and distorted teachings that have crept into our minds. This requires self-awareness, introspection, and a willingness to challenge the narratives we've been taught. We must actively seek the truth of God's will, examine our beliefs, and cleanse ourselves from anything that leads us away from His guidance. Only then can we restore the flow of divine energy and begin to live in alignment with God's purpose for us.

Another important aspect of restoring our spiritual connection is recognizing the role that external influences play in our lives. Just as water can be contaminated by pollutants in the environment, our spiritual clarity can be compromised by the negative influences around us. Whether it's harmful media, toxic relationships, or societal pressures, these external forces can cloud our judgment and prevent us from hearing the still, small voice of God. To protect our connection to the divine, we must be mindful of the influences we allow into our lives. We need to guard our minds, hearts, and spirits from the pollution of negativity, and seek environments that foster spiritual growth and clarity.

The connection between clean water and spiritual purity extends beyond just the immediate effects of pollutants. Over time, exposure to contaminated water leads to chronic health problems, and similarly, exposure to false teachings leads to long-term spiritual harm. As we allow ourselves to be polluted by toxic ideologies, we create a disconnection that becomes harder to heal. Spiritual wounds from exposure to these pollutants can take years to recover from, just as it can take a long time for polluted ecosystems to heal.

However, with effort, dedication, and a return to purity, both our bodies and spirits can be restored.

In many ways, we are responsible for the quality of both the water we drink and the teachings we allow into our minds. Just as we have the power to choose clean water over polluted sources, we also have the responsibility to choose truth over falsehood. It's not enough to simply avoid the most obvious forms of pollution—we must actively seek out purity and protect ourselves from the subtle, insidious forces that seek to distort our connection to God. This requires vigilance and commitment, as well as a willingness to continually question and examine the information we receive. Only through this conscious effort can we restore our connection to the divine and live in alignment with God's will.

The effects of spiritual pollution are far-reaching, not just for individuals but for entire communities. Just as contaminated water affects entire ecosystems, polluted teachings can have a ripple effect, spreading confusion and misunderstanding throughout society. When a community's collective connection to the divine is compromised, it creates a culture of division, conflict, and moral decay. This is why it is so important to not only focus on personal purification but also work to purify the environments in which we live. By sharing the truth and living in accordance with God's will, we can help restore clarity and spiritual purity to the world around us.

Restoring the purity of water and the purity of our spiritual connection is a lifelong process. Just as clean water must be continually protected from pollutants, our spiritual clarity must be nurtured and preserved over time. We must remain vigilant in guarding our minds and hearts against the influences that seek to pollute us. This requires intentional action, such as seeking knowledge, practicing mindfulness, and living with integrity. The effort to protect our spiritual connection to the divine is ongoing, but the rewards of living in alignment with God's will are immeasurable.

In the end, just as pure water revitalizes and sustains our bodies, a pure connection to the divine revitalizes and sustains our souls. The more we cleanse ourselves of spiritual pollutants, the more we open ourselves to receiving God's guidance and wisdom. By embracing purity, we restore the flow of divine energy and live in harmony with God's will. This connection is the source of true fulfillment and peace, just as clean water is the source of life.

The Weaponization of Water

In the modern world, water, once regarded as a pure and life-sustaining resource, has been transformed into a tool of control. What was once a symbol of purity, renewal, and divine gift has now become a means of manipulation and power. The contamination of water with harmful chemicals, pollutants, and toxins has not only disrupted ecosystems and endangered public health, but it also reveals the darker side of human governance and corporate greed. Water, which should flow freely and healthily, now reflects the greed and corruption that dominate many of the systems that govern our world. Governments and corporations use it as a weapon, poisoning it to maintain control, manipulate populations, and further their own agendas. This weaponization of water is a grave example of how immorality pervades even the most sacred elements of our environment.

Water is essential to every living being. It nourishes the body, cleanses the soul, and symbolizes life itself in various spiritual traditions. Yet, today, we see this life-sustaining resource being tainted by pollutants designed not just to harm, but to exert control over those who depend on it. The introduction of chemicals into public water supplies, for example, affects not only the physical health of the population but also their mental and emotional well-being. The introduction of fluoride, chlorine, and various industrial byproducts into drinking water has long been a controversial practice. These chemicals are presented as necessary for public health and sanitation, but they also raise questions about their long-term effects on human biology and behavior. Water that was once meant to nourish is now increasingly viewed as a tool to manipulate, to create dependence, and to control the masses.

The true weaponization of water goes beyond the chemical pollution we see in our public utilities. In some regions of the world, access to clean water is deliberately restricted to exert power over populations. Water scarcity is increasingly being used as a means of control, with governments and corporations hoarding water resources, pricing it out of reach for the poor, and intentionally withholding it from communities in need. This denial of basic human needs—clean water—becomes a tool to further the interests of the powerful while keeping the marginalized in a state of dependence and poverty. The unequal distribution of water resources highlights the deep immorality that runs through the systems that govern our world. By turning water into a scarce commodity, those in power can maintain control over the people, exacerbating inequality and perpetuating suffering.

The effects of weaponized water are not just physical but psychological. The constant awareness of contamination and scarcity creates a climate of fear and anxiety. Populations that once had access to clean water may now live in fear of the health consequences of drinking contaminated water, or the stress of knowing that clean water may become even scarcer. This fear is a psychological weapon, sowing distrust in public institutions and creating a feeling of helplessness among the people. Governments and corporations that control water supplies can use this fear to manipulate public opinion, justify increasing prices, or even pass laws that protect their interests at the expense of the well-being of the people. When water, the most fundamental resource, becomes tainted with toxic chemicals and scarcity, it creates a population vulnerable to manipulation.

The contamination of water is a direct reflection of the corruption and immorality within our systems. Just as pollution of the water system is often hidden or disguised as harmless, the manipulation of water resources is often masked as good governance or corporate responsibility. The truth, however, is that these actions are a direct assault on the sanctity of life itself. Water, which should be an equalizer, a resource that flows freely to nourish all, is being treated as a commodity to be bought and sold. In many ways, this parallels the corruption of divine teachings—what was meant to be a gift for all is being twisted, manipulated, and controlled for the benefit of a select few.

The parallels between the weaponization of water and the distortion of moral and spiritual truths are alarming. Just as the pollution of water harms the body, the pollution of truth harms the soul. Both are the result of greed, selfishness, and the desire for control. Water, when pure, represents clarity and renewal. It cleanses, heals, and revitalizes. Similarly, divine truth, when preserved, is a source of clarity, wisdom, and direction. But just as water can be contaminated with chemicals, divine teachings can be corrupted by false ideologies, distorted interpretations, and the manipulation of truth. The weaponization of water, then, becomes a metaphor for the ways in which we allow sacred resources—both physical and spiritual—to be exploited for the benefit of the few.

The reality of weaponized water is seen in the way some corporations exploit water for profit. Bottled water companies, for example, often extract water from natural sources at no cost, only to sell it back to consumers for a profit. This privatization of water is another example of how something so essential to life has been turned into a commodity, controlled by corporate interests rather than being treated as a public resource. The widespread availability of bottled water is marketed as a convenience, but behind the scenes, it represents a fundamental shift in how we value and access this life-giving resource. Water, once a shared gift, is now a luxury for those who can afford it, while the rest are left to deal with the consequences of pollution and scarcity.

One of the most disturbing aspects of the weaponization of water is how it targets vulnerable communities. In many parts of the world, particularly in impoverished regions, access to clean water is a daily struggle. Water sources are often contaminated with industrial waste, sewage, or chemicals, leading to health crises, including waterborne diseases. In some cases, governments or corporations knowingly allow this contamination to persist because they view these populations as expendable or unworthy of the same access to clean water as others. This inequity is not just a failure of governance; it is a deliberate act of injustice, where the basic human right to clean water is denied to the most vulnerable.

The weaponization of water also extends to the environmental impacts of pollution. As industries discharge harmful chemicals into rivers, lakes, and oceans, the entire ecosystem is affected. Fish and wildlife that depend on clean water are harmed, and entire aquatic ecosystems can be destroyed. These environmental impacts have far-reaching consequences, affecting food sources, local economies, and biodiversity. The poisoning of water is not just a physical threat to human health, but a long-term ecological crisis that will have lasting effects for generations to come. This environmental devastation, often caused by the greed of corporations and governments, highlights the widespread disregard for the sacredness of nature and the sanctity of life.

This disregard for water's purity and sanctity is not limited to industrial pollution. In some cases, water is intentionally contaminated with chemicals as a form of control. The introduction of fluoride into public water supplies, for example, is controversial because of its potential effects on human health. While fluoride has been promoted as a preventive measure for dental health, critics argue that its presence in drinking water is an infringement on personal freedom and bodily autonomy. Whether or not one agrees with the benefits of fluoride, the issue highlights how water is manipulated to serve the interests of those in power, without regard for the well-being of the people.

In light of these issues, it is clear that the weaponization of water is a profound moral crisis. Water, which should be a source of life, has become a source of harm. This reflects a larger trend in society, where things that are meant to nurture and sustain us are being twisted and used for control. The contamination of water is not just an environmental issue—it is a moral issue. It is a direct attack on the sanctity of life and the rights of people to access the resources they need to live. And just as polluted water harms the body, so too does the pollution of truth harm the soul.

To reclaim the sanctity of water, we must first acknowledge the damage that has been done and take steps to reverse it. This requires not only cleaning up the physical pollution in our water systems but also purging the spiritual and moral pollution in our societies. We must demand that governments and corporations stop exploiting water for profit and instead work to ensure that it remains a resource accessible to all. This may involve policies to protect water sources, regulate pollution, and ensure that everyone has access to clean water, regardless of their economic status. But it also involves a deeper recognition of the sacredness of water and the need to protect it, not just for our survival, but for the well-being of future generations.

The weaponization of water is a reflection of a larger moral crisis in our world. When we allow greed, power, and corruption to dictate how we treat the resources that sustain life, we lose touch with the true purpose of these gifts. Water is not just a commodity—it is a divine resource that should be treated with reverence and respect. If we are to restore the sanctity of water and all that it represents, we must stand against the forces that seek to exploit it. We must protect it, purify it, and restore it to its rightful place as a source of life and renewal. Only then can we begin to heal the harm that has been done and restore balance to the world around us.

The Moral Implications of Compromised Water

Water, in its purest form, is essential for both physical and spiritual well-being. It represents clarity, renewal, and connection to life itself. When we accept the dilution of water's purity, we are not just allowing a physical substance to lose its integrity—we are also accepting a deeper moral compromise. Just as watered-down spiritual teachings can lead us astray from God's will, polluted water erodes our connection to the divine and to our true selves. This dilution creates a gradual breakdown of what is pure and sacred, leading us further away from the truth. Accepting this compromise is not a small matter; it is an invitation to begin losing touch with what really matters—our health, our integrity, and our faith.

Compromised water may seem like a minor issue at first, but it is a reflection of a larger pattern. Just as small amounts of chemicals can disrupt the purity of water, small compromises in our beliefs, behaviors, and decisions can gradually weaken our connection to God. Each sip of polluted water is a reminder of how we allow impurities into our lives, whether through the media we consume, the teachings we accept, or the choices we make. When water is contaminated, its ability to nourish and cleanse is compromised. Similarly, when our hearts and minds are filled with false teachings or distractions, our ability to receive the pure wisdom of God's will is diminished. We begin to lose clarity, and over time, our connection to the divine becomes clouded.

The contamination of water is not just an environmental issue; it is a moral issue. The presence of harmful chemicals in our drinking water represents a violation of the sanctity of life. Just as pure water should nourish the body and soul, our spiritual life should be nourished by the purity of truth. When we accept that which has been diluted or tainted—whether in our water or in our beliefs—we are choosing to settle for less than what was originally intended. God's teachings, like pure water, are meant to cleanse and renew us, but when they are diluted or distorted, they lose their power. This compromise in both our physical and spiritual life leaves us vulnerable to illness, confusion, and a disconnection from what is truly important.

One of the greatest moral implications of compromised water is how it affects our health. Water, the fundamental life source, is meant to heal and sustain us. When polluted water enters our bodies, it has far-reaching consequences. Chemicals such as lead, chlorine, and pesticides can disrupt our body's natural processes and impair our ability to function. Just as polluted water weakens the body, accepting compromised teachings weakens our faith. The consequences are not always immediate, but over time, the erosion of integrity, both physical and spiritual, becomes more evident. When we choose to ignore the purity of water, we are, in effect, choosing to accept an inferior version of life—one that is devoid of the nourishment and renewal that purity provides.

The moral compromise we make when accepting contaminated water extends beyond personal health. It impacts the world around us, especially the most vulnerable populations. Communities that are already disadvantaged often bear the brunt of polluted water, experiencing higher rates of illness and suffering. The moral question is not just about individual health, but about justice, fairness, and compassion for those who have no control over the quality of their water. Similarly, when we accept spiritual teachings that are diluted or manipulated for convenience or control, we allow the most vulnerable among us—those searching for truth—to be misled. The consequences of this moral compromise extend far beyond the individual, affecting communities, families, and society as a whole.

Compromised water, both in the physical and spiritual sense, also damages the very fabric of our relationships. Water connects all life, and its purity can bring us together in shared experiences of renewal and healing. But when water is polluted, it creates division. The water we drink is no longer something we can all share with confidence; instead, it becomes a source of anxiety and division, as some have access to cleaner water than others. This division mirrors how spiritual and moral compromises can divide us as well. When truth is diluted or compromised, people begin to distrust one another, as their understanding of the divine and of right and wrong becomes fragmented. We are no longer united in our shared beliefs or our shared humanity, and this division weakens the bonds that hold us together.

One of the most insidious aspects of accepting diluted water is how it affects our ability to make clear, moral decisions. Just as polluted water clouds our judgment and impairs our body's ability to function, compromised teachings cloud our minds and hearts. We begin to question what is right and wrong, and the clarity that once guided our choices fades away. The process of accepting compromised water is gradual. At first, we may not notice the impact, but over time, it becomes clear that we are not as healthy, clear-minded, or spiritually connected as we once were. As with any moral compromise, the longer we accept the impurities in our water or beliefs, the harder it becomes to recognize the truth and reclaim what was lost.

The erosion of personal integrity is one of the most significant moral consequences of accepting polluted water. Personal integrity is built on the foundation of purity—whether that purity is in the form of water, truth, or our beliefs. When we compromise on one thing, it becomes easier to compromise on others. Just as drinking contaminated water may seem harmless in the moment but leads to long-term harm, accepting diluted spiritual teachings may seem harmless at first, but it slowly eats away at our sense of right and wrong. Over time, we lose the strength to stand firm in our beliefs, and our sense of personal integrity weakens. The more we accept impurities, the more we lose touch with the purity that should guide our actions.

The moral implications of compromised water extend to the way we view the world and our role within it. Water is a fundamental symbol of life and connection. When we accept its corruption, we are also accepting a worldview that is disconnected from the divine. We are saying that purity and truth are not worth protecting. By accepting compromised water, we are also accepting a worldview that prioritizes convenience, profit, and power over the sanctity of life. This perspective leads to a world where purity is undervalued, and the moral cost of compromise is ignored. In this world, we lose the ability to see the divine in the simple, everyday elements of life.

The moral compromise of accepting polluted water can also be seen in how it affects our faith. Water, in many religious traditions, is used for cleansing, purification, and renewal. It is a symbol of the Holy Spirit and the divine presence. When we allow water to be polluted, we also allow our connection to the divine to be polluted. Just as clean water is needed for physical cleansing, spiritual purity requires the clean teachings of God's word. When we accept diluted teachings or make moral compromises, we lose the clarity and strength of our faith. The erosion of this purity weakens our spiritual connection, leaving us feeling disconnected from God and from our true purpose.

Our faith is rooted in the belief that God's teachings are pure, true, and life-giving. Just as we depend on pure water for our physical survival, we depend on the purity of divine wisdom for our spiritual survival. When we accept that which has been diluted or corrupted, we are choosing to forsake the very teachings that were meant to sustain us. Compromised water represents the spiritual compromises we make when we choose to accept half-truths or watered-down versions of God's word. These compromises weaken our faith, making it harder to discern the truth and to live according to God's will.

As we come to understand the moral implications of compromised water, it becomes clear that the choice to accept diluted or contaminated water is a reflection of the choices we make in our lives. It is a choice to accept less than what God intended for us—less than the purity, clarity, and nourishment that we need. When we accept compromised water, we are accepting a gradual erosion of everything that is good, true, and pure. Just as polluted water can harm the body, compromised teachings can harm the soul. To restore purity in our lives, we must reject the compromises and impurities that have crept in, both in our physical and spiritual environments.

The final step in reclaiming our connection to the divine is to reject the compromise of polluted water and diluted teachings. Just as we must work to purify the water we drink, we must work to purify our minds and hearts from the contamination of falsehoods and distractions. This requires a return to the purity of truth—the truth of God's word and the truth of our own divine connection. Only by rejecting the compromises of this world can we restore our integrity, health, and faith. By doing so, we reclaim the clarity, purity, and nourishment that we were meant to receive from both water and God's teachings.

The Dangers of Accepting a Diluted Reality

The act of compromising is something that often starts small but builds up over time. When we compromise on the purity of water, we allow contaminants to enter our bodies. Similarly, when we compromise on our beliefs or moral standards, we allow diluted truths to enter our minds and hearts. These compromises lead to a distorted reality—a reality that is less than what was intended for us. Over time, we begin to accept this less-than-ideal version of life, and it becomes difficult to recognize what purity truly looks like. The danger of accepting a diluted reality is that it gradually distorts our perception of what is true, healthy, and divine. What may seem like a small compromise at first can slowly lead us away from God's original design for our lives.

In the case of water, we know that contamination has immediate and long-term effects on our health. Polluted water can lead to illness, disease, and a weakened immune system. Similarly, when we accept diluted truths in our spiritual lives, it weakens our ability to discern what is right from what is wrong. The gradual acceptance of these diluted realities leads to spiritual illness, causing us to lose our clarity, focus, and connection to God. Just as our bodies depend on pure water to function optimally, our souls depend on pure, unaltered truth to guide us. When we start accepting lies, half-truths, and compromises, our spiritual health is put at risk, and we become disconnected from the divine.

When water becomes polluted, its ability to cleanse, nourish, and heal is diminished. In the same way, when we accept a compromised version of reality, the truths that once nourished and protected our minds and hearts are weakened. We begin to view the world through a distorted lens, one that no longer reflects the clarity of God's will. Over time, this distorted reality becomes our new normal. We no longer question the impurities that have seeped in, and we begin to live in a world where compromise is the norm. This process of accepting less than what is pure and true leads to confusion, misdirection, and spiritual decay. It is only by rejecting these compromises and returning to the unaltered truth that we can restore our connection to God and to the life we were meant to lead.

When we accept a diluted version of reality, it affects not just our spiritual lives but our physical lives as well. Polluted water, for instance, doesn't only harm the body—it also affects the mind. The contaminants in water can lead to brain fog, fatigue, and impaired cognitive function. Similarly, when we accept diluted truths in our lives, we begin to experience a kind of spiritual brain fog. We lose the ability to think clearly about our purpose, our values, and our relationship with God. We may find ourselves questioning what is truly important, struggling to distinguish between truth and falsehood. This mental confusion keeps us from making the decisions that align with God's will, and it impairs our ability to live in harmony with our higher purpose.

The dangers of accepting a diluted reality extend beyond individual health and well-being. As we begin to accept compromises, we normalize them in our communities. Just as polluted water becomes widespread, so too do diluted truths spread across society. What was once considered pure and sacred becomes tainted, and the collective consciousness becomes clouded. We begin to live in a world where compromise is the standard, and the pursuit of purity and truth seems like an impossible ideal. When entire communities begin to accept diluted realities, the moral fabric of society begins to unravel. What was once a society founded on shared values and clear moral principles becomes fractured and confused, and people lose their way.

The process of accepting a diluted reality happens gradually, almost imperceptibly. At first, the compromises seem small and harmless—perhaps just a minor change in behavior or a small shift in belief. But over time, these small changes add up, and the original purity is lost. This is how compromise works in our lives: it often doesn't start with a dramatic event, but with a slow, steady erosion of what is true and good. Just as a small amount of pollution can gradually contaminate a body of water, small compromises can slowly pollute our minds and hearts. Over time, the effect becomes more noticeable, and it becomes harder to reverse the damage.

A diluted reality can also create a false sense of security. When we accept a compromised version of reality, we begin to believe that it's acceptable or even normal. We may convince ourselves that the impurities in our water or in our beliefs don't matter, that they are just part of life. But this false sense of security is dangerous because it keeps us from seeking the truth and striving for purity. We begin to settle for less, convinced that the diluted version of life is all we can have. This mindset prevents us from striving for the fullness of life that God has intended for us. It keeps us trapped in a cycle of accepting what is mediocre, rather than reaching for the excellence that comes with living in alignment with God's will.

The danger of a diluted reality is not just that it distorts our perception of the world; it also distorts our sense of self. When we accept compromises, we begin to lose touch with who we truly are. We are made in the image of God, meant to live with clarity, purpose, and integrity. But when we start accepting diluted truths, we begin to lose sight of our divine nature. We start to believe the lies that tell us we are not worthy or that we are incapable of living a pure, righteous life. These false beliefs erode our sense of self-worth and keep us from becoming the people God intended us to be. Accepting a diluted reality prevents us from living up to our full potential and from stepping into the abundant life that God has promised us.

One of the most insidious aspects of a diluted reality is how it affects our relationships. Just as polluted water can contaminate everything it touches, a diluted truth can corrupt our connections with others. When we accept lies and half-truths, we begin to relate to others through a distorted lens. We start to believe that dishonesty, manipulation, and compromise are normal parts of relationships. This mindset leads to broken trust, misunderstandings, and division. Our relationships suffer because we are no longer operating from a place of purity and truth. The more we accept a diluted version of reality, the more our relationships become strained and disconnected from the love, respect, and honesty that they should be built on.

The dangers of a diluted reality are not only spiritual and emotional; they are also intellectual. When we accept compromised truths, we limit our ability to think critically and to understand the world as it truly is. The purity of knowledge is like pure water—it nourishes and enlightens the mind. But when knowledge is tainted by falsehoods or misunderstandings, it leads to confusion and ignorance. This lack of clarity prevents us from making sound decisions, solving problems effectively, and understanding the deeper truths of life. In a world filled with diluted realities, we must be vigilant and discerning, seeking out the truth even when it is hard to find.

Rejecting a diluted reality requires courage and intentionality. It requires us to look beyond the surface and to seek out what is pure and true. Just as we must purify our water to restore its health and vitality, we must purify our minds and hearts to restore our spiritual health. This process requires us to reject the compromises that have slowly seeped into our lives and to make a conscious effort to live according to the unaltered truth. It means returning to God's word, seeking His guidance, and allowing His purity to cleanse our minds and hearts. By rejecting a diluted reality, we reclaim the clarity, purpose, and fulfillment that God intends for us.

The first step in rejecting a diluted reality is to recognize it for what it is. We must become aware of the compromises we have made, whether in our personal lives, our relationships, or our spiritual practices. This awareness allows us to take the necessary steps to change course and to return to a life of purity and truth. It requires us to ask difficult questions, to challenge the status quo, and to seek out what is real and authentic. Once we recognize the diluted reality we've been living in, we can begin the process of purification and restoration.

By rejecting a diluted reality, we free ourselves from the chains of compromise and confusion. We begin to see the world through a clearer, purer lens—one that reflects the truth of God's will. This clarity allows us to make decisions that align with our higher purpose, to build relationships based on honesty and respect, and to live in a way that is true to our divine nature. When we reject the lies and half-truths that have polluted our minds, we open ourselves up to a life of abundance, peace, and fulfillment. Only by living in alignment with pure truth can we experience the fullness of life that God intends for us.

Reclaiming Purity: Restoring Water and Spirit

Purity is something we often take for granted until it is compromised. Just as we rarely think about the water we drink until it becomes contaminated, we often neglect the importance of living a pure life until we notice the negative effects. Reclaiming purity starts with awareness—becoming conscious of what has contaminated our bodies, minds, and souls. The first step in restoring purity is recognizing where compromises have been made. Whether it's the water we drink or the way we live our lives, we must identify the sources of pollution and be willing to take action. The process of purification involves both a conscious effort and a willingness to make difficult choices, but it is the only way to restore our connection to our true selves and to God's divine will.

Just as water flows freely and cleanly in nature, we are designed to live in alignment with purity and truth. However, over time, we accumulate layers of impurities—whether they be physical toxins in our bodies or spiritual falsehoods that cloud our understanding. To reclaim purity, we must take steps to remove these impurities, just as we would purify polluted water. The purification process begins with a decision—a decision to stop accepting diluted or false versions of reality. In the case of water, this might mean choosing filtered water over what comes from the tap. In our spiritual lives, it means seeking the truth and rejecting the lies, half-truths, and compromises that have crept in over time. By making this decision, we take the first step toward reclaiming purity in all areas of our lives.

The process of purifying our lives is not quick or easy. Just as cleaning polluted water requires time, effort, and the right tools, purifying our hearts and minds requires dedication. It involves identifying harmful influences and actively removing them from our lives. This could mean reevaluating the media we consume, the people we surround ourselves with, and the beliefs we hold. We must be willing to confront the aspects of our lives that have been tainted by compromise, whether in our personal choices, our relationships, or our understanding of spiritual truth. This is where the true work begins. Purification is not a one-time event, but a lifelong process. It requires patience, self-reflection, and the strength to make hard decisions for the sake of our well-being.

One of the most important steps in reclaiming purity is returning to the source of all truth—God's teachings. Just as water comes from its source in nature, our spiritual nourishment comes from God's divine wisdom. By reconnecting with the untainted word of God, we allow ourselves to be washed clean and restored. This process of reconnecting with the truth might involve prayer, meditation, or studying scripture. It's about opening ourselves up to the wisdom that has been passed down through the ages and aligning ourselves with God's divine will. In doing so, we begin to rid ourselves of the impurities that have clouded our vision and our hearts. Purifying our lives means going back to the foundation of our faith and allowing it to guide our actions and thoughts.

Another way to reclaim purity in our lives is by practicing mindfulness and intentionality. Just as we make careful choices about the water we drink, we must be intentional about the thoughts, actions, and decisions we make every day. Living mindfully means being aware of the impact of our choices and striving to make those choices align with our higher purpose. This can be as simple as choosing to spend time in nature, taking time to pray or reflect, or being intentional about the way we treat others. Every action we take is an opportunity to align ourselves with purity, and the more mindful we are, the easier it becomes to stay on the path of spiritual restoration. Mindfulness allows us to notice when we are veering off course and gently guide ourselves back to the truth.

Reclaiming purity also requires a commitment to personal growth and transformation. It's not enough to simply acknowledge the impurities that have crept into our lives—we must actively seek to grow and change. This involves a willingness to confront our own shortcomings and a commitment to becoming better people. Just as a polluted body of water cannot remain stagnant if it is to be restored, we cannot remain stagnant in our spiritual lives. We must be open to change, growth, and renewal. This might involve seeking support from others, whether through mentorship, counseling, or community. It might involve making changes in our habits or our environments that support our growth. Purity is not about perfection, but about striving to become the best versions of ourselves, in alignment with God's will.

Another essential aspect of reclaiming purity is forgiveness. Both forgiving others and seeking forgiveness for ourselves can be incredibly purifying.

Holding on to resentment, anger, and unforgiveness creates emotional pollution that blocks our connection to God and to others. Just as polluted water cannot cleanse anything, a heart filled with unforgiveness cannot truly heal or grow. By choosing to forgive others and ourselves, we allow the flow of divine love and healing to enter our lives. Forgiveness frees us from the toxic grip of bitterness and allows us to move forward with a heart that is open, pure, and ready to receive God's grace. It's an essential step in the purification process, one that helps us restore our spiritual health and reconnect with God's will.

Part of reclaiming purity is also acknowledging the importance of self-care. Just as we would not drink polluted water, we should not neglect our own well-being—physically, mentally, or spiritually. Self-care is a crucial part of the purification process because it helps us maintain our connection to our higher purpose. Taking care of our bodies, minds, and spirits allows us to live in a state of balance and harmony. It enables us to be more effective in serving others and in fulfilling God's will. This might mean getting enough rest, eating nourishing foods, engaging in physical exercise, and taking time for spiritual practices. Self-care is not a selfish act, but an essential part of living a pure and healthy life.

Restoring purity in our lives also involves creating boundaries. Just as we protect ourselves from drinking contaminated water, we must protect ourselves from negative influences. Boundaries allow us to maintain our spiritual, emotional, and mental health by keeping out what does not align with our higher purpose. These boundaries may include limiting exposure to toxic people, unhealthy environments, or harmful habits. Creating boundaries is an act of self-respect and self-love, allowing us to protect our purity and maintain the clarity we need to stay connected to God's truth. By setting these limits, we give ourselves the space to grow, heal, and flourish.

Purification also requires us to cultivate gratitude. When we focus on the blessings in our lives, we begin to appreciate the purity that still exists, even amidst the challenges and compromises of the world. Gratitude helps us shift our focus from what is polluted to what is pure and good. It reminds us of the gifts that God has given us and encourages us to live with a sense of reverence and appreciation. Practicing gratitude helps us to stay grounded and centered in truth, even as we work through the process of purification. It also deepens our connection to the divine, as we recognize the abundance of blessings that flow from God's love.

As we continue the process of purifying our lives, it's important to remember that perfection is not the goal. Just as water purification is an ongoing process, our spiritual purification is a lifelong journey. We may slip up, we may face setbacks, but the key is to stay committed to the process. Every step we take toward purity is a step closer to reclaiming our divine connection. The goal is not to become flawless, but to keep moving forward, guided by the principles of truth, love, and grace. By staying committed to this journey, we begin to experience the peace and clarity that come from living in alignment with God's will.

To reclaim purity, we must also practice patience. The purification process takes time, and it's important not to rush or force it. Just as it takes time for water to clear and become pure, it takes time for our lives to reflect the truth and purity that we desire. We must trust that the process is happening, even when it feels slow. Patience is essential because it allows us to trust in the journey and remain faithful to the process. It teaches us that purity is not something we achieve overnight, but something we work toward with intentionality and faith.

Finally, reclaiming purity requires a deep commitment to faith. It is through faith that we find the strength to reject compromise, to pursue the truth, and to restore our connection to the divine. Faith is the foundation of the purification process, giving us the courage to face the challenges ahead and the hope to keep moving forward. It is through faith that we are reminded that purity is possible, no matter how polluted the world around us may seem. With faith, we trust that God will guide us through the process and that, in time, we will be restored to the purity and clarity that is our birthright.

Chapter Summary

In this chapter, we explored the dangers of compromising the purity of water and how this mirrors the compromise of God's teachings. Water, in its purest form, is a delivery system for life and divine wisdom. It sustains our bodies and symbolizes the life-giving truth that comes from God. When water becomes contaminated, it no longer serves its intended purpose, just as when God's word is distorted, it no longer fulfills its divine function in our lives. The purity of water reflects the purity of truth. When we allow it to become polluted—either physically or spiritually—we lose access to its benefits, leading to a disruption of both our physical well-being and our spiritual connection. In the same way that pure water is essential for life, pure teachings are essential for a thriving faith.

Contaminated water is not just a physical concern; it is a reflection of a deeper issue. The pollutants in our water—whether they come from chemicals, nanoparticles, or other toxic substances—are a direct result of human greed and disregard for the sacredness of life. These pollutants infiltrate our water supply, and in a similar way, the purity of divine wisdom can be compromised by human intervention. When we distort or dilute God's teachings for convenience, personal gain, or societal pressure, we are contaminating the very essence of what makes us whole. The chapter draws a parallel between the pollution of water and the pollution of our spiritual lives. Both are harmful, and both diminish our ability to function at our highest capacity. When we accept these compromises, we allow the forces of corruption to infiltrate every part of our existence, undermining our health, our relationships, and our relationship with the divine.

One of the most concerning aspects of accepting contaminated water or diluted teachings is the slow, often imperceptible erosion that occurs. Just as we may not immediately feel the effects of drinking polluted water, we may not notice the subtle damage done to our spiritual lives when we accept compromised truths. Over time, however, the consequences become clear. The impurities in water can cause long-term damage to our bodies, leading to illness and a weakened immune system. Similarly, distorted teachings can lead us away from God's will, causing confusion, lack of purpose, and spiritual sickness. The compromises we make—whether knowingly or unknowingly—accumulate over time, ultimately clouding our judgment and disconnecting us from the life-giving power of pure water and pure truth.

This chapter also highlights the role that personal responsibility plays in maintaining both physical and spiritual purity. Just as we must actively choose clean, uncontaminated water, we must actively seek out and protect ourselves from diluted or false teachings. The world around us is full of distractions, falsehoods, and pollutants that can easily lead us astray. It is up to each individual to discern what is pure and true. This requires vigilance, critical thinking, and a willingness to reject anything that compromises the purity of our physical health or our faith. Our responsibility is not just to protect ourselves, but also to help others recognize the dangers of contamination—whether it be in the water they drink or the beliefs they hold. By standing firm in our commitment to purity, we can create a ripple effect that spreads to others, fostering a world that values truth, clarity, and connection to the divine.

The call to action in this chapter is to refuse compromise in all its forms. We are called to reject diluted or distorted teachings and to actively pursue purity in all aspects of our lives. This does not mean living in a bubble or avoiding difficult truths, but rather embracing the unaltered, life-giving wisdom that God offers. We are challenged to seek out truth, to cleanse ourselves from spiritual toxins, and to nurture our connection to God with intentionality and care. Just as we would never knowingly drink contaminated water, we must never accept teachings or beliefs that lead us away from divine guidance. The path forward requires us to be discerning, proactive, and steadfast in our commitment to purity, recognizing that the purity of our minds, bodies, and spirits is essential for living in alignment with God's will.

In conclusion, this chapter emphasizes that the journey to spiritual and physical purity is not an easy one, but it is necessary for our well-being. By choosing purity over compromise, we can restore our connection to God's will and protect the sanctity of life. The process requires self-awareness, discipline, and a deep commitment to truth. As we reject the dilution of water and teachings, we reclaim the purity that God intended for us. In doing so, we create a world where divine wisdom flows freely—like pure water—nourishing our souls and guiding us toward a higher purpose. The call to action is clear: we must remain vigilant in our pursuit of purity, knowing that it is only through this pursuit that we can fully align ourselves with the divine and live in harmony with the world around us.

Chapter Seven

Faithfulness

Faithfulness is a powerful concept that encompasses loyalty, steadfastness, and trustworthiness. It is a quality we seek in our relationships with others, but more importantly, it is something we must cultivate in our relationship with God. This chapter explores faithfulness in the context of water, one of the most essential elements of life. Just as water is pure, life-giving, and everlasting, so too should our faithfulness to God's teachings be. When we remain loyal to the purest form of water, we are ultimately aligning ourselves with God's divine will, receiving His unwavering support and guidance in our lives.

Water is the foundation of all life. From the creation of the earth to the formation of living beings, water has played an essential role in sustaining life. It is not only the physical sustenance that we rely on, but also a spiritual symbol of purity and truth. Water represents the original material from which all things were created. The purity of water mirrors the purity of God's truth, and just as we depend on water for our survival, we must depend on God's truth to nourish and guide us.

The concept of faithfulness in relation to water is significant because water is both the Alpha and the Omega, the beginning and the end. Water is present in all things and is essential to the existence of life itself. It is a constant, eternal force, just as God's presence is eternal and unwavering. The purity of water symbolizes the divine wisdom and strength that flows through the universe. By being loyal to the purest form of water, we are, in effect, being loyal to God's will and aligning our lives with His divine plan.

Our relationship with water is deeply personal. Our bodies consist of approximately 99% water on a nanoscale, which reflects the close connection between water and life. This deep integration of water within us serves as a reminder that we are all interconnected with the Creator and the sustaining force of life. To remain loyal to the purest form of water is to honor the divine presence within ourselves and to commit to the purity and truth that God provides.

Water's eternal nature is a powerful reminder that without the basic elements that make up water, there would be no life. Water is formed when two hydrogen elements come together, symbolizing the divine interaction of creation. King Hydrogen and His Son—

represented in the fundamental particles of hydrogen and oxygen—are the creators of water. Without them, there would be no water, and without water, there would be no life. Thus, faithfulness to water is a reflection of our faithfulness to the divine force that sustains all life.

Water as the Source of Life

Water is the essential element that supports all life on Earth. It is found in every living thing, from the smallest bacteria to the tallest trees. Without water, nothing could survive. It hydrates the land, feeds the rivers, fills the oceans, and nourishes the air we breathe. Water shapes landscapes, creates weather, and sustains the balance of nature. It carries nutrients that allow plants to grow and animals to thrive. It provides the environment where many creatures live and reproduce. Water's movement through rain, rivers, and clouds is part of a great cycle that repeats endlessly. This beautiful, continuous cycle makes life possible everywhere on the planet. Without it, Earth would be a dry, dead world floating in space. Water is not just a convenience; it is a necessity for every form of life that has ever existed.

Water forms the foundation of every living organism. In humans, water makes up about seventy percent of our body weight. It helps cells keep their shape and carry out their important jobs. Blood, sweat, saliva, and tears are all mostly water. It helps regulate our body temperature, digest food, and remove waste. Inside plants, water carries minerals and nutrients from the roots to the leaves. In animals, it carries oxygen through the blood. Water is involved in every chemical reaction that keeps living things alive. Without it, cells would shrivel up and die. When we understand how deeply water is involved in every part of life, we start to realize that water is not something separate from us. It is part of who we are. Life without water is impossible because life is, in many ways, water itself.

Water is the basic building block of existence. Every living system depends on water to survive and thrive. Water acts as a solvent, meaning it dissolves many substances and allows chemical reactions to occur. Life's processes, like digestion and energy production, rely on these reactions. When plants make food through photosynthesis, they need water. When animals eat plants or other animals, they need water to process that food. Even the air contains water vapor, which helps regulate temperature and weather patterns. Water's ability to bond with other elements makes it the perfect medium for life. Without water, none of the complex systems that make life possible could work. Water's unique properties are why life exists in the first place. It holds together the web of existence with invisible threads.

Without water, life as we know it would cease to exist. Imagine a world with no rivers, no lakes, and no rain. The land would dry up and crack. Plants would wither and die. Animals would follow soon after. Humans could not survive without clean, fresh water to drink. Even if there were food, we would not be able to digest it without water. Our bodies would overheat without sweat to cool us down. We would lose our ability to think clearly, move, and survive. Water loss leads to dehydration, organ failure, and death. Every ecosystem on Earth—from the Amazon rainforest to the Arctic tundra—depends on water. No water means no life. It is that simple and that serious. This truth should inspire deep respect and careful protection of water.

Staying loyal to the purity of water is more important now than ever. Water pollution from factories, farms, and cities threatens the quality of the water we depend on. Chemicals, trash, and waste enter rivers and oceans, poisoning the creatures that live there. Contaminated water can cause serious diseases in humans and animals. Polluted water harms soil quality, plant life, and the delicate balance of ecosystems. Protecting water's purity means protecting life itself. We must act with care and respect, understanding that everything we pour onto the ground eventually finds its way back to the water cycle. Loyalty to water's purity means choosing sustainable actions and avoiding careless waste. It means treating water as the precious, sacred resource that it truly is.

Loyalty to the purity of water is a sacred duty that connects us to something greater than ourselves. Water is not just a material resource; it is a spiritual one. In many cultures and religions, water is a symbol of life, renewal, and blessing. Baptisms, purification ceremonies, and sacred baths all show water's importance to the human spirit. When we pollute or waste water, we break the sacred bond between ourselves and the Earth. Protecting water honors the Creator who gave us life through this vital substance. It is an act of gratitude, faith, and stewardship. Loyalty means guarding water's purity for the sake of all life, present and future.

Through loyalty to pure water, we remain connected to the Creator. The very first chapters of many sacred texts mention water as the beginning of creation. Water was there before mountains, forests, or animals. It covered the earth and received the first blessings of life. By honoring water, we honor the original gift of life. Every time we drink, bathe, or witness a river's flow, we have the chance to remember this connection. Purity is not just physical cleanliness; it is spiritual faithfulness. Remaining loyal to water keeps us grounded in gratitude and connected to the Source of all life.

Water is not only essential; it is also sacred. It reminds us of our small place within the vast design of creation. We depend on something we did not create and cannot replace. Water humbles us, teaches us respect, and invites us to live with gratitude. Its flowing nature reminds us of life's continuous movement and renewal. Water's softness teaches us strength without force. Its clarity reminds us to seek purity in our thoughts and actions. Its necessity reminds us of the importance of caring for things we cannot live without. Through water, we learn deep lessons about living well and wisely.

The story of creation always begins with water. Long before cities, kings, or technology, there was water. In ancient times, rivers and seas were seen as sacred. People built temples near springs and lakes, understanding water's power and mystery. Civilizations like Egypt, Mesopotamia, and the Indus Valley grew around rivers. Their success depended on honoring and managing water wisely. When water was plentiful and pure, people thrived. When water was scarce or polluted, people struggled or perished. These ancient lessons still hold true today. Water remains at the heart of our survival and success.

Adam and Eve, the first humans, lived in a paradise rich with water. Rivers flowed through the Garden of Eden, making it fertile and beautiful. This image shows that water is a symbol of divine blessing. It nourishes not just the body, but also the soul. Fresh, flowing water was part of humanity's first home. It sustained the plants and animals, providing food, beauty, and life. The importance of water in this story shows that it is a foundational part of the divine design. Losing water's purity means losing the paradise that once was.

Everyone consists of about ninety-nine percent water at the molecular level. This means that every movement, thought, and heartbeat is powered by water. Even though we often think of ourselves as solid beings, at the smallest level, we are mostly liquid.

Water molecules form the spaces between proteins, the walls of cells, and the flow of energy inside us. Without water, life's chemistry cannot happen. We are, in many ways, walking oceans. Understanding this fact deepens our respect for water. Protecting water means protecting the very fabric of our existence.

Water is the only eternal material on Earth. Everything else wears down, rusts, or decays. Water, however, continues its cycle without end. It evaporates from the sea, forms clouds, falls as rain, and fills rivers again. This endless journey across sky, land, and sea symbolizes renewal and hope. No matter how harsh the season, water always returns. Its cycle mirrors the cycles of life, death, and rebirth. Water's eternity teaches us that life, too, is part of a greater, unbreakable cycle. By staying loyal to water, we stay loyal to life's enduring flow.

Two hydrogen atoms and one oxygen atom form water, the miracle molecule. This simple combination creates a substance with unique properties: surface tension, solvent power, temperature regulation, and more. Water can absorb heat without changing temperature quickly, making it perfect for stabilizing climates. It can dissolve salts, sugars, and gases, allowing life's processes to happen smoothly. It climbs against gravity in plants and breaks down mountains over time. This tiny molecular bond holds the secret to Earth's flourishing beauty. Without hydrogen and oxygen's perfect match, life could never have begun.

Without "King Hydrogen" and "His Son," there would be no water. Hydrogen is the universe's most abundant element, formed in the first few minutes after the Big Bang. Oxygen came later, forged in the hearts of ancient stars. Their meeting created water—a substance perfectly suited for life. This cosmic story shows that even the smallest elements, when combined rightly, can achieve greatness. Water is a legacy of the stars, a gift from the universe to Earth. Protecting water is respecting the ancient dance that gave rise to us all.

Water is everywhere, even when we cannot see it. It hides in the air as invisible vapor. It rests inside rocks as tiny droplets. It moves beneath our feet in underground rivers. It waits frozen inside glaciers and snow. Water's invisible presence teaches us to value what we cannot always see. Life often depends on quiet, hidden forces. Water's silent work nourishes crops, cools the land, and shapes the world. It reminds us that the most important things are often those we take for granted.

Remaining faithful to the purity of water means taking action. It means refusing to dump waste into rivers, refusing to use chemicals that poison groundwater, and refusing to waste water thoughtlessly. It means planting trees that protect water sources, supporting clean water initiatives, and educating others about water's value. Every choice we make can either protect or endanger water. By choosing wisely, we show our loyalty. Protecting water today ensures that future generations will also experience its blessings tomorrow.

Loyalty to water teaches loyalty to all creation. Water connects all living things: animals, plants, people, and ecosystems. A raindrop that nourishes a forest may later feed a river, a town, or a thirsty traveler. Water ties the world together in invisible bonds of life. By protecting water, we protect the intricate web that sustains us all. Our loyalty to water becomes loyalty to the Earth, loyalty to life, and loyalty to the Creator who entrusted us with this sacred gift.

The Eternal Nature of Water

Water is often referred to as the Alpha and the Omega—the beginning and the end—because it has been part of existence from the very start and will remain until the very end. When we think about water, we realize that it never truly disappears. It simply changes forms, moving from liquid to vapor to ice and back again. This endless cycle shows us that water, like God's wisdom, is eternal. Water was present at the dawn of creation, and it will be here for the generations to come. Every river, ocean, and raindrop whispers the story of something that cannot be destroyed, something that keeps renewing itself endlessly. Through its nature, water teaches us that true power lies in patience, persistence, and quiet strength, always moving, always present, always alive.

If we look closely at the world around us, we can see the eternal nature of water in action. Rivers carve through mountains over millions of years, shaping valleys and forming landscapes. Oceans cover most of the planet and hold mysteries that scientists still do not fully understand. Rain falls on the ground and nourishes plants, animals, and humans, starting life anew every day. In all of these natural wonders, water is working behind the scenes, reminding us that some of the most powerful forces in life are the ones we often take for granted. Just as we sometimes forget to appreciate God's constant care, we may also forget the miracle that is water.

The water cycle is an incredible process that demonstrates water's eternal journey. Water from oceans and lakes evaporates into the air, forming clouds. These clouds travel across the skies, releasing rain, snow, or hail back to the Earth. The water then flows through rivers, seeps into the ground, or returns to the oceans, where the cycle begins again. This cycle has been repeating for millions of years without ever stopping. Even when we cannot see it, the water is always moving, always working. In the same way, God is constantly moving through our lives, shaping events and guiding us, even when we are unaware.

The eternal nature of water also shows us the importance of resilience. No matter what obstacles stand in its way, water finds a path. It can carve through rock, seep into the tiniest cracks, and wear down even the hardest surfaces over time. Water does not resist change—it adapts, flows, and transforms. This resilience teaches us to be flexible and patient. Life is full of challenges, but like water, we can find ways to move forward. Trusting in God's eternal wisdom, we learn that setbacks are not the end but simply a new beginning, another part of the greater cycle of life.

Water's eternal journey also reflects the idea of purification. As it moves through the water cycle, water is naturally filtered and cleansed. Evaporation leaves impurities behind, and rain brings fresh water to the Earth. In our spiritual lives, we also undergo a process of purification. Through experiences, challenges, and lessons, we are refined and strengthened. Water reminds us that no matter how muddy or impure we may feel at times, there is always a chance for renewal. God's grace, like the rain, washes over us, giving us new life and new purpose.

Even on a microscopic level, water's eternal nature is astonishing. Scientists have found water molecules that have been on Earth for billions of years. Some of the water we drink today may have passed through the bodies of dinosaurs or ancient forests. Every molecule of water has a story stretching back to the beginning of time. This incredible thought reminds us that we are connected to history, to creation, and to God through the simple act of drinking or touching water. In every drop, there is a trace of eternity, a whisper of the endless cycle of life and spirit.

Water also symbolizes baptism, a powerful act of spiritual renewal. In many faith traditions, water is used to cleanse the soul, washing away sin and marking the start of a new life. Baptism through water is a visible sign of an invisible truth: that God's eternal love offers us a fresh beginning. Just as water constantly renews itself, we too are offered the chance to begin again, to leave behind old mistakes, and to embrace a future filled with hope. Water's eternal nature gives us the confidence that God's promises never run dry.

Throughout the Bible, water is used as a symbol of God's eternal presence. From the parting of the Red Sea to the living water that Jesus offers, water is seen as a gift that sustains, protects, and renews. These stories remind us that God's care flows endlessly, never pausing or weakening. Just as water nourishes the body, God nourishes the soul. By staying connected to the source, we are refreshed, strengthened, and able to grow. Water is not just a symbol of life—it is life, moving and eternal, just like the Creator.

The oceans, covering over 70% of the Earth's surface, are another powerful reminder of water's eternal nature. The waves rise and fall in a rhythm that has lasted for millions of years. Tides move with the pull of the moon, showing a harmony that is beyond human control. When we stand before the ocean, we can feel its power and vastness. It humbles us and reminds us that we are part of something much greater. The same awe we feel before the sea is the awe we should feel before the eternal wisdom and love of God.

Snow and ice, though frozen, are also part of water's eternal journey. Glaciers, some millions of years old, hold ancient water trapped in solid form. These icy giants slowly move and reshape the land beneath them, even though they appear still. In our own lives, there are times when God's work seems hidden or slow, but that does not mean it is absent. Like glaciers, the eternal nature of water teaches us that even silent, unseen movements can change the world over time. Trusting the process brings peace.

Water's ability to exist in three forms—liquid, vapor, and solid—also teaches us about the mystery of eternity. In the same way that water takes different shapes yet remains the same substance, God can reveal Himself in many ways while remaining unchanged. Sometimes He is the refreshing rain, sometimes the mighty river, and sometimes the quiet mist. Each form meets us where we are, giving us what we need. Water's transformations show us that eternity is not boring or static—it is rich, full of wonder, and endlessly creative.

When we drink water, we are participating in the eternal cycle. That simple act connects us to the past, the present, and the future. The water inside us has been part of countless lives and will continue its journey long after we are gone. In this way, we are all caretakers of eternity. We are responsible for respecting and honoring the gifts we have been given. Water's eternal presence reminds us to live wisely, to cherish what is sacred, and to protect what has been entrusted to us.

Water also reflects the idea of mercy. No matter how polluted or dirty water becomes, it can always be purified. Similarly, no matter how far we stray from our faith, there is always a way back. God's mercy, like clean water, is always available if we seek it. This lesson teaches us not to give up on ourselves or others. Just as polluted rivers can be restored to health, broken lives can be healed. The eternal flow of water promises that renewal is always possible, no matter how great the damage.

In times of drought, when water becomes scarce, people realize just how precious and necessary it is. Spiritually, there are times when we feel dry or distant from God. These "spiritual droughts" remind us not to take His presence for granted. They teach us to seek, to pray, and to thirst for truth and connection. When the rain finally comes, it brings relief and joy, just as spiritual renewal fills us with hope and life again. Water's eternal return after drought mirrors God's faithfulness in answering our deepest needs.

Storms, floods, and heavy rains show the mighty side of water's nature. They can be frightening and overwhelming, but they also bring important changes. They clear old growth, replenish dry land, and create opportunities for new life. In the same way, challenges and trials in life can feel like floods, but they often lead to growth and renewal. God uses even the storms of our lives for good purposes. Water's eternal strength teaches us that even chaos can be part of a greater plan for renewal.

Rainbows after storms remind us of God's promises. When water droplets catch the light just right, they create a beautiful arc of colors in the sky. This phenomenon is both a scientific wonder and a spiritual symbol. After the flood, God gave the rainbow as a sign of His eternal covenant with humanity. Each time we see a rainbow, we are reminded that God's promises are everlasting. Just as water cycles endlessly, His faithfulness never fails, bringing color and hope after every storm.

At night, the sound of a river, a fountain, or rain on the roof can bring comfort and peace. These sounds remind us of water's gentle, steady presence. Even when the world feels uncertain, the rhythm of water continues. This quiet faithfulness is a reflection of God's eternal care. He does not always shout to get our attention; often, He speaks through the quiet, the steady, and the constant. Water teaches us that sometimes the most powerful forces are the ones that work patiently and lovingly in the background.

In the end, water's eternal nature points us back to the source of all life—God Himself. Every river, ocean, raindrop, and glacier tells a story of renewal, resilience, mercy, and love. Water is not just necessary for physical survival; it nourishes the soul by reminding us of eternal truths. When we honor the gift of water, we honor the Creator who gave it to us. Living in gratitude, awareness, and respect for water leads us to live in closer harmony with God, whose wisdom and love are truly without end.

Water and the Creation of Humanity

From the very beginning of the world, water has been a powerful and life-giving force. Before anything else was formed, water covered the surface of the earth. It moved, flowed, and prepared the land for the life that would one day fill it. The Bible tells us that in the earliest moments of creation, the Spirit of God hovered over the waters. This image shows us that water was not just a background detail—it was an essential part of the world God was shaping.

When God created Adam, the first human being, He formed him from the dust of the earth. Yet dust alone could not make a living soul. It was the breath of life that filled Adam, and water that nourished and sustained him. Without water, Adam would have been no different from the dry earth he was made from. Water completed the creation, making the human body able to live, grow, and move. It was through water that life truly began.

Eve, the mother of all living, was created from Adam's side. Her creation too depended on water. Just as Adam's body needed the moisture and nutrients that water provides, so did Eve's. From the start, water flowed through their bodies, giving energy, strength, and the ability to multiply. Their blood, their breath, their very cells were filled with the life-giving presence of water. Without it, there could be no humanity at all.

Water not only allowed Adam and Eve to live, but it was also central to the world they were placed in. The Garden of Eden, described as a lush and fertile place, was fed by a mighty river. This river split into four great branches, watering the land and bringing life to everything it touched. Trees grew tall, fruits ripened on the branches, and flowers bloomed, all because water moved beneath and around them.

The river in Eden was more than just a source of physical nourishment. It symbolized the connection between humanity and God. As the river gave life to the garden, God's presence gave life to Adam and Eve. Water stood as a reminder that they were dependent on something greater than themselves. They could not survive on their own. They needed the steady flow of water just as they needed the constant care of their Creator.

Throughout their time in Eden, Adam and Eve walked beside the flowing waters. They drank from the river, bathed in its coolness, and saw their crops grow because of its abundance. Every splash, every ripple, every drop was a testimony to God's goodness. The water reminded them that life was a gift, something to be cherished and respected. It taught them gratitude for the unseen forces that sustained them.

When Adam and Eve disobeyed God and were cast out of Eden, their connection to water did not end. Even though they entered a harsher, less forgiving world, water remained essential. They still needed it to live, to farm, to raise their children. The rivers, lakes, and rain that God provided were signs that His mercy had not left them. Even after the Fall, God continued to sustain life through water.

As humanity grew and spread across the earth, people continued to settle near water sources. Early civilizations sprang up along great rivers like the Nile, the Tigris, and the Euphrates. These rivers gave them food, transportation, and fertile soil. Without water, these early peoples could not have survived. Their closeness to water reflected the same truth Adam and Eve knew: water is life.

In many cultures, water also took on a sacred meaning. It was not just a tool for survival, but a symbol of cleansing, renewal, and blessing. Religious ceremonies often included washing with water to represent purification. Baptism, for example, uses water to symbolize the washing away of sin and the beginning of a new life. These traditions remind us that our spiritual lives are as deeply tied to water as our physical bodies are.

The human body itself is a testament to our dependence on water. Our blood, sweat, and tears all contain water. Every organ relies on it to function properly. Scientists say that the human body is made up of about 60% water. This fact shows that we are, in many ways, walking vessels of water. From our first breath to our last, we carry within us the same element that covered the earth at the dawn of creation.

Even today, water continues to shape our world and our lives. It falls from the sky as rain, feeding crops and filling rivers. It moves through underground streams, nourishing roots and plants we never see. It evaporates into the air, forming clouds that shade and water the earth. Every part of the water cycle is a silent miracle that keeps life moving forward.

Our spiritual connection to water is just as strong today as it was for Adam and Eve. Many religious traditions still use water in sacred rituals. Whether it is baptism, ritual washing, or simply offering a prayer by a river, water reminds us of the divine gift of life. It calls us back to humility, showing us that no matter how advanced we become, we still rely on the simple gifts of the natural world.

Water also teaches us lessons about persistence and strength. A river may seem gentle, but over time, it can carve through stone. A steady rain can change the landscape of a mountain. Water's power is often hidden, but it is unstoppable. In the same way, our faith and connection to God may seem quiet, but with time, they shape our hearts and lives in ways we cannot always see.

The importance of water in creation is a call to respect and protect it. Polluting rivers, wasting water, or ignoring the needs of others dishonors the gift we have been given. Just as Adam and Eve were stewards of Eden, we are stewards of the earth today. Caring for water sources is not just about survival; it is an act of gratitude and obedience to the Creator who first gave us life.

Looking back to the story of creation, we see that water was not just an accident or a minor detail. It was part of a grand design. Water was prepared before humanity arrived, ready to sustain, nourish, and bless. Every drop was part of God's plan to provide for His creation. Water, like life itself, is a sacred trust, a reminder that we are part of something much larger than ourselves.

In the end, the story of water and humanity is the story of life itself. It reminds us that we are connected to the earth, to each other, and to the Creator. It shows us that even the most basic needs—like the need for water— carry deep spiritual meaning. Water teaches us about dependence, about humility, and about hope. It flows through the pages of history just as it flows through our veins.

Water continues to whisper the same truth it did in the beginning: we are not our own source of life. We are sustained by forces beyond our control, gifts we did not create. In every sip of water, every river we cross, every storm we see, there is a reminder of the Creator's love and provision. Water is a teacher, a giver, and a living connection to the divine story that began before time itself.

The Purity of Water as a Symbol of Divine Truth

Water, in its purest form, represents the highest form of clarity. Pure water, free from contamination, holds a symbolism that transcends its physical properties. Just as pure water sustains our bodies by quenching thirst, the pure truth of God sustains our souls by offering guidance, wisdom, and nourishment. The clarity of water reflects the clarity that we need in our spiritual lives—truth that cleanses and restores us.

When water is clean, it is transparent and untainted. We can see through it without obstruction. Similarly, divine truth is transparent. It is not clouded by confusion or deception. In a world full of distractions and falsehoods, we often find ourselves searching for clarity. Just as we seek pure water to stay healthy, we must seek the purity of God's truth to maintain spiritual health. Only by embracing this truth can we live fully, grounded in understanding and wisdom.

The Bible describes water as a life-giving element from the very beginning of creation. In Genesis, it is through the waters that the Earth is formed and sustained. The Earth itself is 71% water, showing how deeply intertwined life is with this essential substance. Water, like divine truth, nourishes and gives life to all things. Without it, the Earth would be barren, and life as we know it would not exist. In the same way, without God's truth, we cannot thrive spiritually.

Pure water flows freely from springs and rivers, just as the pure truth of God flows freely for all who seek it. This abundance of water serves as a reminder that divine truth is available to everyone. It is not hidden or reserved for only a select few. When we approach God's teachings with humility and openness, we find that His truth is as abundant as the water in the world—ready to nourish those who are thirsty for understanding.

The purity of water also represents the purity of the heart and mind that is required to understand God's truth. Just as clean water is essential for our physical well-being, a pure heart is necessary to receive and comprehend the divine wisdom that God offers. If we allow impurities like pride, selfishness, and doubt to cloud our hearts, we cannot fully appreciate the beauty of His truth. It is only when we purify our hearts through prayer, reflection, and humility that we can truly understand the depth of God's wisdom.

In the same way that water cleanses our bodies, the pure truth of God cleanses our souls. It washes away confusion, sin, and the burdens of guilt. Water is used in many religious rituals, such as baptism, to symbolize the purification of the soul. When we seek God's truth, it acts as a cleansing force, washing away the impurities that prevent us from living in alignment with His will. This purification allows us to become more like Christ and to live according to the divine plan.

Just as we rely on water to sustain our physical health, we must rely on God's truth to sustain our spiritual health. Without water, our bodies would wither and die, just as without truth, our spirits become weak and disconnected from God. The importance of truth cannot be overstated—it is the foundation upon which our faith is built. When we neglect the search for truth or allow falsehoods to infiltrate our minds, we risk losing our connection to the divine source of life.

The water cycle—evaporation, condensation, and precipitation—is a natural process that ensures the continuous renewal of water on Earth. In the same way, God's truth renews us continually. Just as water is always available in different forms, from rain to rivers, God's truth is always present in different ways, through scripture, prayer, and the guidance of the Holy Spirit. This ongoing process of renewal helps us stay grounded in the purity of God's wisdom.

Water, when it becomes contaminated, loses its purity and is no longer safe to drink. Similarly, when we allow falsehoods or distortions of truth into our lives, our spiritual well-being suffers. Just as we avoid drinking polluted water to protect our health, we must avoid false teachings that lead us astray. Our spiritual health depends on our ability to discern truth from error and to remain faithful to the pure, untainted wisdom that God offers.

God's truth is constant, just as water is constantly cycling through the Earth. No matter what happens, God's truth remains unchanged. Water may take different forms, from vapor to liquid to ice, but its essence remains the same. Likewise, the truth of God is unchanging, eternal, and always relevant, no matter what challenges we face in life. It is this consistency that makes God's truth a reliable foundation for our lives.

The clarity of pure water also symbolizes the clarity that comes from understanding divine truth. When the water is clear, we can see the bottom, and nothing obstructs our view. Similarly, when we live in the light of truth, we can see clearly the path God has set before us. Without truth, we live in darkness, stumbling through life with no clear direction. But with God's truth as our guide, we can walk confidently, knowing that we are following the right path.

In many ancient cultures, water was viewed as a sacred element, representing the divine and the life force. Water was used in rituals and ceremonies to purify and bless. This reverence for water highlights the deep connection between water and the sacred. Just as water was seen as sacred, so too is the truth of God sacred. It is not to be taken lightly or manipulated for personal gain. It must be respected, cherished, and upheld as a holy gift from God.

The symbolism of water extends beyond its physical properties to its spiritual significance. Water has the power to refresh, renew, and restore. Similarly, God's truth has the power to refresh our spirits, renew our faith, and restore our connection to Him. Just as we thirst for water, we also thirst for the living water of God's word, which satisfies our deepest spiritual hunger and fills us with His presence.

Water, in its purest form, represents the untainted, unaltered truth of God. Just as water flows freely, the truth of God is available to anyone who seeks it. It does not discriminate based on race, wealth, or status. The purity of water reminds us that God's truth is available to all, and it is through our faith and obedience that we can drink deeply from this well of wisdom.

When we seek out pure water, we demonstrate our understanding of its value. Similarly, when we seek out God's truth, we acknowledge its worth and recognize that it is the key to spiritual life. Water may be abundant, but it is still precious. In the same way, God's truth is abundant, but we must value it, seek it, and protect it, so it can continue to nourish us throughout our lives.

Finally, just as water flows from one place to another, God's truth is meant to flow through us to others. When we are filled with the pure truth of God, it overflows from our hearts and touches the lives of those around us. Like a river that nourishes the land, the truth we share nourishes the hearts of others, helping them to grow in faith and understanding. The more we embrace God's truth, the more we are able to share it with the world.

Our Bodies and the 99% Water Connection

Our bodies are astonishingly made up of about 60% water on the surface level, but when we dive deeper into a nanoscale, that percentage jumps to an extraordinary 99%. This remarkable fact reveals just how deeply interconnected we are with the element that sustains all life—water. It's a constant reminder that we are not separate from nature, but a part of it, intricately woven into the natural world. Just as water shapes the land, it also shapes our very existence. We are made of water, and through this, we are reminded of the Creator who designed us with such intentionality and purpose.

This deep connection to water serves as a visual representation of the spiritual connection between ourselves and God. Just as water is vital for our physical survival, so too is God's wisdom essential for our spiritual well-being. Without water, our bodies would cease to function, and without divine truth, our spirits would wither. By understanding the role water plays in maintaining our physical lives, we can draw parallels to the role of faith and wisdom in sustaining our spiritual lives. It is through this connection to water that we are reminded of our dependence on God for all that sustains us.

The human body is composed of various organs and systems, each relying on water to perform their functions. Water carries nutrients to our cells, helps regulate body temperature, and eliminates waste. These essential roles that water plays within our bodies illustrate the ways in which God's wisdom sustains and directs us. Water's ability to nourish, cleanse, and restore is a reflection of the transformative power of divine truth. Just as we need water to keep our bodies in balance, we need spiritual wisdom to keep our lives in harmony with God's plan.

Water is also essential for the brain, which is composed of about 75% water. This demonstrates just how much water affects our thoughts, emotions, and cognitive processes. Our minds depend on water to think clearly, make decisions, and regulate our emotions. In the same way, God's wisdom is the foundation for clear thinking, sound judgment, and emotional balance. Without this wisdom, our minds can become clouded, just as dehydration can lead to mental confusion and difficulty concentrating. This connection between water and the mind serves as a powerful reminder of the importance of staying spiritually nourished.

The circulation of water within the body also mirrors the flow of God's wisdom in our lives. Water circulates through our bodies, reaching every cell, ensuring that everything functions optimally. Similarly, God's wisdom flows throughout our lives, touching every aspect of our being. Just as water's movement sustains our physical life, God's wisdom sustains our spiritual life, ensuring that we remain healthy and grounded in His truth. Without the flow of water through our bodies, we would experience dysfunction. Similarly, without the flow of God's wisdom in our lives, we would struggle to find meaning and purpose.

Water has the ability to cleanse and purify, a feature that is mirrored in the cleansing power of God's truth. When we are spiritually depleted or weighed down by sin, it is God's wisdom that purifies us and restores our inner peace. Just as water flushes toxins from our bodies, God's wisdom helps us remove the impurities from our hearts and minds. This purification process is essential for maintaining a healthy spiritual life, just as regular hydration is essential for maintaining a healthy body. Both processes keep us functioning at our highest potential.

The way water adjusts to its surroundings also reflects how divine wisdom works in our lives. Water takes the shape of whatever vessel it occupies, filling every nook and cranny. In the same way, God's wisdom is adaptable and can fill every part of our lives. No matter where we are in our spiritual journey, God's wisdom is there, waiting to fill us and guide us. Whether we are facing challenges or experiencing joy, His wisdom flows into our hearts, providing us with the guidance and clarity we need to navigate every situation.

Water is also symbolic of the baptismal cleansing of the soul. In Christian faith, baptism represents a washing away of sin, and water is the medium through which this purification takes place. This act signifies the importance of water not only as a physical necessity but also as a spiritual symbol. Just as our bodies are cleansed through physical water, our spirits are cleansed through the living water of God's truth. This transformation is essential for our growth and renewal in faith, reflecting the profound connection between our physical and spiritual lives.

The 99% water composition of our bodies also highlights the interconnectedness of life. Just as our bodies rely on water for survival, every living thing on Earth depends on water in some way. The Earth itself is covered by over 70% water, and this balance is crucial for the health of the planet. Water's abundance and importance in all forms of life underscore the fundamental truth that we are all interconnected. Our bodies are not isolated entities but part of a larger, interconnected system that reflects God's design for the world. This interconnectedness reminds us of our responsibility to live in harmony with nature and to recognize the divine order in all things.

The role of water in our bodies is not limited to physical health; it also has a profound impact on our emotions and well-being. Water is often associated with calmness and tranquility, and being near water has been shown to reduce stress and promote relaxation. This connection between water and emotional health reflects the peace that God's wisdom brings into our lives. When we are filled with His truth, we experience a sense of peace that surpasses understanding. Just as water can calm the body, God's wisdom can calm the soul, bringing balance and serenity to our hearts.

Water's importance extends beyond its biological functions; it is also symbolic of the spiritual nourishment we need to thrive. Just as water sustains life by providing hydration, God's wisdom sustains our spirits by providing direction and purpose. Without the right nourishment, our bodies become weak and vulnerable. Similarly, without spiritual nourishment, our souls become weak and disconnected from the divine. The 99% water connection within our bodies serves as a constant reminder of our need for spiritual sustenance, which can only be found in God's truth.

The dependency we have on water to sustain our physical lives should prompt us to reflect on how much we depend on God's wisdom to sustain our spiritual lives. Our bodies are fragile and require constant hydration to function properly. Similarly, our spirits are fragile and require constant nourishment from God's word to stay strong and healthy. This connection between water and wisdom highlights our need for a continuous relationship with God, one that is nurtured through prayer, reflection, and seeking His guidance.

The fact that water is essential to life yet often taken for granted serves as a reminder of how we should value the wisdom of God. Water is everywhere, and we often don't think twice about its availability. In the same way, God's wisdom is always available to us, yet we sometimes overlook its importance. We may become so focused on the immediate needs of life that we forget to seek His guidance. Just as we need water to live, we need God's wisdom to thrive spiritually. It is essential to remember that just as we must drink water regularly to stay healthy, we must seek God's wisdom regularly to stay spiritually nourished.

The way that water maintains balance within our bodies is also symbolic of the balance that God's wisdom brings to our lives. Water helps to regulate our body temperature, maintain hydration levels, and remove waste, ensuring that everything functions properly. Similarly, God's wisdom helps to regulate our emotions, actions, and thoughts, maintaining balance in our spiritual lives. Without the guidance of God, we would struggle to maintain this balance, just as our bodies would struggle to maintain their health without the proper hydration and nourishment.

Our bodies' dependence on water, and the intimate relationship we share with this vital element, should inspire us to cultivate a deeper relationship with God. Water nourishes us, heals us, and supports us in every aspect of our lives. Similarly, God's wisdom nourishes, heals, and supports us in our spiritual journeys. As we recognize the profound connection between our bodies and water, let us also recognize the profound connection between our spirits and God's divine wisdom. Both are essential for living a life of purpose, fulfillment, and peace.

In conclusion, the 99% water composition of our bodies is a powerful reminder of the intricate relationship between ourselves, nature, and God. Just as water sustains our physical lives, God's wisdom sustains our spiritual lives. Our dependence on water is a reflection of our dependence on divine truth. Water is a constant presence in our lives, just as God's wisdom should be a constant presence in our hearts. May we always remember this connection and seek the purity of water and wisdom to guide us through life.

The Role of King Hydrogen in Creation

Water, the essence of life, is formed when two hydrogen atoms combine with an oxygen atom. This simple yet profound chemical reaction is more than just a scientific process; it is a reflection of the divine order that governs creation. The pairing of hydrogen and oxygen to form water symbolizes harmony, unity, and balance, which are key principles in both the natural world and spiritual life. In this process, King Hydrogen and his companion oxygen work together to create something that sustains all life. This simple chemical reaction, when observed through the lens of faith, reminds us of the Creator's intricate design, a design that weaves together every part of creation, from the tiniest atom to the grandest galaxy.

King Hydrogen, being the most abundant element in the universe, plays a foundational role in the creation of water. As the smallest and lightest atom, hydrogen is both humble and powerful. It represents the beginning, the starting point of many processes, including the creation of life itself. Hydrogen's role in the formation of water can be seen as a metaphor for the Creator's role in bringing life into existence. Just as hydrogen is essential to the formation of water, so too is God essential to the creation and sustaining of all life. This divine interaction is a constant reminder that God is present in every detail of creation, down to the smallest particles that make up the world around us.

Water is a substance that is vital for all forms of life, and it is formed through the joining of two hydrogen atoms and one oxygen atom. This precise combination is not random but reflects an intelligent design. It is no accident that water is the substance that sustains life. The combination of hydrogen and oxygen, through a bond that is both strong and delicate, mirrors the relationship between the Creator and His creation. Just as the bond between hydrogen and oxygen creates a substance that is essential for life, so too does God's wisdom and love create a foundation for the life that He has given us.

The creation of water through the interaction of hydrogen and oxygen can also be seen as a symbol of divine cooperation. The two hydrogen atoms and the oxygen atom work together, each playing its role in the creation of something greater than the sum of its parts. This divine cooperation is reminiscent of the unity between God the Father and His Son. Just as the elements of water work together in perfect harmony, so too do the Father and Son work in unity to bring life and purpose to all that exists. This divine cooperation is a reminder that unity and collaboration are essential principles that should be reflected in our own lives.

The formation of water through the bonding of hydrogen and oxygen is also a powerful symbol of transformation. In its gaseous form, hydrogen and oxygen are individual elements that are separate from one another. However, when they come together, they transform into water, a substance that is capable of sustaining life. This transformation mirrors the way that God can take the individual parts of our lives, which may seem insignificant or disconnected, and bring them together to create something beautiful and purposeful. Just as water is essential for life, God's transformative power is essential for the spiritual growth and flourishing of His creation.

Hydrogen, as the simplest element, is symbolic of the humility that is required for great creation. It is a reminder that greatness often comes from simplicity, and the most profound truths are often found in the most basic elements of life. In the same way, God often uses the humble and the ordinary to accomplish His greatest works. The role of hydrogen in the creation of water is a reflection of how God uses the small and seemingly insignificant things in our lives to create something much greater. This serves as a reminder that no part of creation is too small or unimportant in the eyes of the Creator.

The presence of water on Earth is essential to the existence of life, and its creation through the combination of hydrogen and oxygen highlights the divine wisdom that governs all of creation. Water's role in sustaining life cannot be overstated; it nourishes plants, animals, and humans, providing the foundation for all living things. The fact that water is formed through the interaction of just two hydrogen atoms and one oxygen atom demonstrates the simplicity yet profound significance of God's creation. This simple process is a powerful reminder of the Creator's hand in every part of the world, as He provides what is needed for life to flourish.

The relationship between King Hydrogen and oxygen in the creation of water also mirrors the relationship between the Creator and His creation. Water is a substance that flows and moves, shaping the land and sustaining life wherever it goes. In the same way, God's wisdom flows through all of creation, shaping and sustaining the world and all living things. Just as water flows through rivers and oceans, bringing life wherever it goes, so too does God's wisdom move through our lives, shaping us and guiding us toward growth and understanding. The creation of water is a reminder that God's influence is everywhere, sustaining life and shaping the world in ways we may not always understand.

The role of hydrogen in the creation of water also highlights the importance of the smallest elements in the grand design of creation. Just as hydrogen, the smallest of the elements, plays a key role in creating water, so too do the small and often unnoticed aspects of our lives play important roles in our spiritual journey. The creation of water serves as a reminder that even the smallest acts of kindness, the smallest moments of faith, and the smallest choices can have a profound impact on our lives and the lives of others. In the same way, hydrogen's seemingly simple role in the formation of water is crucial to the existence of life.

Water, formed through the combination of hydrogen and oxygen, is essential not only for sustaining life but for its creation. The fact that life as we know it would not exist without water emphasizes the divine significance of this element. Water's ability to nourish, purify, and transform reflects the way in which God's love nourishes, purifies, and transforms us. Just as water has the power to bring life, so does God's love and wisdom have the power to create new life within us, shaping us into the people He intends for us to be.

The bond between hydrogen and oxygen in the creation of water is also a symbol of the power of unity. The two hydrogen atoms and one oxygen atom must come together to create water, and in doing so, they create something that is greater than the sum of its parts. This divine principle of unity is seen throughout creation, where different elements and forces come together to form something beautiful and purposeful. In our own lives, we are reminded that unity with God and with each other is essential for living a life of purpose. Just as hydrogen and oxygen must unite to form water, we must unite with God and with one another to create lives that are meaningful and fulfilling.

The role of hydrogen in the creation of water also teaches us about the importance of balance. Water is a substance that is both life-giving and destructive. It nourishes crops and quenches thirst, but it can also flood lands and cause destruction. This balance reflects the way in which God's wisdom, while always good, must be approached with humility and reverence. Just as water must be handled with care and respect, so must we approach God's wisdom with reverence and gratitude. The creation of water reminds us that God's gifts must be used wisely and with respect for the delicate balance that exists in the world.

Water, created through the interaction of hydrogen and oxygen, is a powerful symbol of God's presence in the world. Just as water is essential for life, so too is God's wisdom essential for our spiritual survival. The creation of water through the combination of these elements reflects the way in which God uses the simplest and most fundamental parts of creation to bring about His will. It is through this divine interaction that life is sustained, and it is through God's wisdom that our spiritual lives are sustained.

The creation of water, with its divine interaction between King Hydrogen and oxygen, is a reminder of the Creator's involvement in every aspect of our lives. Water is not just a substance that exists; it is a symbol of God's care, provision, and wisdom. Just as water is formed through the joining of two hydrogen atoms and one oxygen atom, our lives are shaped by God's wisdom, love, and purpose. The divine interaction that creates water is a reminder that God is present in every part of creation, from the smallest atom to the vast oceans, and that His presence sustains us at every moment of our lives.

In conclusion, the role of King Hydrogen in the creation of water is a powerful symbol of the Creator's hand in the world. Water is not just a physical substance; it is a reminder of the divine wisdom and love that sustain all of creation. Just as hydrogen and oxygen come together to form water, God's wisdom and love come together to form the foundation of our lives. This divine interaction reminds us that we are never alone, and that God is present in every detail of our lives, working to sustain us and bring us into harmony with His will.

The Need for Faithfulness in All Aspects of Life

Faithfulness is a principle that stretches far beyond our loyalty to God or the natural world. It is something that should guide every part of our lives, whether in the way we interact with others, the way we manage our responsibilities, or the way we uphold our values. Faithfulness is not just about staying committed to one thing but is a fundamental aspect of who we are as individuals and as part of a greater community. It is an unshakable foundation that keeps us grounded, no matter what challenges or temptations we face. Just like the importance of water in sustaining life, faithfulness sustains our relationships, integrity, and trust.

In our relationships with others, faithfulness plays a pivotal role. Loyalty and trust are the building blocks of any healthy relationship, whether it's with family, friends, or colleagues. When we are faithful to those we care about, we demonstrate a commitment to their well-being and a desire to support them, no matter what. This commitment creates stability, allowing relationships to grow and strengthen over time. Just as water flows through all living things, faithfulness should flow through every interaction we have. It nurtures and fosters meaningful connections, making us reliable partners in life.

Faithfulness also extends to our commitments and promises. When we make a commitment, whether in personal relationships or in professional settings, we are called to honor our word. A promise is like a seed planted in the soil of trust, and faithfulness is the water that nourishes it to grow. If we fail to keep our promises, the trust that was once flourishing can wither. Just like a garden needs consistent care to thrive, our promises need faithfulness to be realized. Remaining faithful to our word not only honors others but also cultivates our own sense of integrity and reliability.

Faithfulness is crucial in our spiritual lives as well. In our relationship with God, faithfulness is a reflection of our trust in His wisdom and guidance. The Bible teaches that God is always faithful to us, no matter the circumstances, and that we are called to respond in kind. This means that we must remain steadfast in our devotion to Him, even when life becomes difficult or when we face challenges. Just as water is essential for sustaining life, faithfulness is essential for sustaining our relationship with God. It keeps us connected to His presence and ensures that we remain grounded in His truth.

When we are faithful to God, we open ourselves to His guidance and support. Faithfulness invites God's presence into our lives, and through that presence, we receive the wisdom and strength to navigate life's challenges. The more faithful we are to Him, the more He can work in and through us. Faithfulness, in this sense, is not a one-time act but a continuous commitment to trust and obey God's teachings. The more we cultivate faithfulness in our hearts, the more we will see God's faithfulness reflected in the way He works in our lives.

Faithfulness also involves being true to our values and beliefs, especially when the world around us may challenge or contradict them. In a world that often shifts with changing opinions and pressures, faithfulness provides a solid foundation. When we stay true to what we know is right and good, we strengthen our moral compass and guide others by our example. This is especially important in times of uncertainty or moral dilemmas. Just like a river carves its path through rock, our steadfastness in our principles creates a legacy of integrity that can influence those around us.

The need for faithfulness is not limited to our relationships and spiritual lives. It is just as essential in our personal growth and self-discipline. To become the best version of ourselves, we must be faithful to our goals, dreams, and the habits that lead us toward them. Whether it's dedicating ourselves to studying, exercising, or improving our skills, faithfulness is the driving force behind sustained effort. Success is not built on fleeting motivation but on a commitment to remain faithful to our purpose, even when progress seems slow. Just like water continually shapes the land over time, our faithfulness shapes our character and our future.

In times of hardship, faithfulness becomes even more critical. When faced with challenges or setbacks, it's easy to become discouraged or lose focus. However, it is in these moments that faithfulness plays a vital role in helping us persevere. Just as water can erode and reshape the hardest stones over time, faithfulness helps us endure life's trials and emerge stronger. Faithfulness provides the strength to keep going, even when the path is unclear, and reminds us that every difficulty is an opportunity for growth.

Faithfulness also helps us maintain stability in a world that is constantly changing. The environment, relationships, and even societal norms can shift, but our faithfulness to our values, commitments, and relationships provides a constant. This stability is essential for personal peace and fulfillment. When everything else around us is uncertain, our faithfulness to what matters most can provide the clarity and assurance we need to navigate through the storm. Just like water remains a source of life through all seasons, faithfulness remains a source of strength in every circumstance.

Building trust is one of the most important outcomes of faithfulness. In any relationship, trust is the glue that holds everything together. When we are faithful, we prove ourselves worthy of that trust, and over time, trust deepens, creating stronger bonds between individuals. This is true not only in our relationships with people but also in our relationship with God. Trust in God is built through faithfulness—trust that He will provide, guide, and protect us, no matter what. Just like water is trusted to nourish us, faithfulness allows trust to grow and thrive.

Remaining faithful is also about being patient. Faithfulness does not demand immediate results; instead, it allows for growth and development over time. Like a plant that requires water, sunlight, and patience to grow, faithfulness nurtures our lives and relationships slowly but surely. When we remain faithful, even in the absence of immediate rewards, we allow the seeds of our efforts to take root and bear fruit. Patience, combined with faithfulness, leads to lasting success and fulfillment.

Faithfulness is not about perfection but consistency. It is not about always getting things right but about continuing to try, no matter how many times we may fail. Each time we return to our commitments with sincerity and determination, we reinforce our faithfulness. Like the steady flow of water, which does not rush but flows consistently, our faithfulness is built through persistent effort. Each small act of faithfulness adds up over time, and, together, they create a life that reflects our commitment to what we believe in.

In every area of life, faithfulness helps us build character. It teaches us responsibility, discipline, and integrity, which are essential qualities for living a meaningful and fulfilling life. Faithfulness in the little things leads to trust in the bigger things, and each act of faithfulness strengthens our character. This character becomes the foundation for everything we do, enabling us to live with purpose and make decisions that reflect our highest values. Faithfulness shapes who we are, transforming us into people who can be trusted by others and trusted by ourselves.

Just as water cleanses and refreshes, faithfulness refreshes our spirits and strengthens our resolve. When we remain faithful to our values, commitments, and relationships, we are not only doing what is right— we are also nurturing our inner selves. Faithfulness helps us stay aligned with our purpose and renews our focus, allowing us to continue on our journey with renewed strength and clarity. In this way, faithfulness becomes a source of renewal, helping us persevere through life's challenges and emerge stronger on the other side.

The need for faithfulness is, ultimately, a call to live with integrity and consistency in all areas of life. When we remain faithful to our commitments, relationships, and values, we create a life that is grounded in trust, purpose, and stability. Whether we are navigating the complexities of human relationships, facing challenges in our spiritual lives, or working toward personal goals, faithfulness is the key that unlocks success and fulfillment. Just as water flows consistently, sustaining all life, faithfulness sustains our lives, keeping us grounded and connected to the divine purpose that guides us.

Loyalty to Water, Loyalty to God

Loyalty is a quality that is deeply rooted in the way we connect with both the natural world and the divine. Water, in its purest form, is essential for life. It sustains us physically, keeps our bodies functioning, and enables growth in all living things. Just as water is indispensable for our physical survival, God's truth is essential for our spiritual survival. This parallel between water and truth reminds us that loyalty to the purest form of water should mirror the loyalty we show to God's will in our lives. Just as we depend on water daily, we must depend on God's guidance and truth.

When we are loyal to water, we recognize its power to refresh, cleanse, and nourish. Water sustains all life, and without it, there would be no growth, no renewal, and no vitality. In the same way, God's teachings provide us with the strength to grow spiritually, to renew our hearts, and to be cleansed from the impurities of the world. Water does not hesitate to flow to those who need it, and similarly, God's truth is always available to those who seek it. Loyalty to water, therefore, is a reminder of our need to remain faithful to the spiritual truth that nourishes our souls.

Loyalty to water means understanding its value, recognizing that it is not something to be taken for granted. We know that water can be scarce and that its preservation is vital for the survival of all living creatures. This understanding leads us to respect water, to care for it, and to use it wisely. Similarly, loyalty to God's truth requires a deep respect for what is sacred. Just as we conserve and protect water, we must protect the purity of the teachings that sustain our spiritual well-being. Both water and God's truth require us to act with responsibility and reverence.

Faithfulness to water also involves a daily commitment. We cannot survive without water, and just as we make sure to drink water daily, we must also make time each day to connect with God through prayer, reflection, and study of His word. This daily practice of loyalty to both water and God creates a rhythm in our lives that aligns us with the source of life itself. By establishing this routine, we not only nourish our bodies with water but also nourish our spirits with God's guidance, ensuring that we remain grounded and faithful.

Just as water cleanses the body and refreshes the soul, God's truth has the power to cleanse our hearts and renew our minds. Loyalty to water symbolizes a commitment to spiritual purity. When we drink water, we take it into our bodies, allowing it to cleanse and restore us. In the same way, when we accept God's truth, we take it into our hearts, allowing it to purify our thoughts and actions. Loyalty to water, therefore, becomes a symbol of our willingness to let God's truth shape our lives and guide our decisions.

Water is essential for life on Earth. From the tiniest plant to the largest animal, every living being relies on water for survival. This universal need for water underscores its importance, reminding us that life is interconnected, and we must care for the resources that sustain us. Likewise, God's truth is universal. It is the same for everyone, and it is accessible to all who seek it. Just as we are all united by our need for water, we are united by our need for God's truth. Loyalty to water reflects our recognition of the interconnectedness of all life and our responsibility to stay faithful to the source of all truth.

In our modern world, it is easy to take water for granted. We have access to clean water at the turn of a faucet or the press of a button. However, this convenience should not diminish our appreciation for water's life-giving properties. Similarly, we often take God's truth for granted, assuming that it will always be there when we need it. However, just as we must actively conserve and protect water, we must actively seek and preserve God's truth in our lives. Loyalty to both requires us to stay vigilant and to prioritize what truly matters.

Our loyalty to water is a reflection of our understanding that life is fragile. Water is the foundation of life, and without it, we would not exist. This fragility reminds us that we must be mindful of how we use and share water, understanding its role in sustaining not just our own lives but the lives of all creatures on Earth. In the same way, God's truth is a gift that sustains our spiritual lives. It is fragile in its purity and can be easily distorted or neglected. Our loyalty to God's truth is rooted in the understanding that it is precious and must be preserved with care.

Water has the ability to transform landscapes, shaping the Earth over time. Through its steady flow, water carves valleys, builds rivers, and nourishes plants and animals. In the same way, God's truth has the power to transform our lives. Just as water shapes the Earth, God's truth shapes our hearts, minds, and actions. Loyalty to water is a reminder that, over time, the small, consistent acts of faithfulness to God's truth can lead to profound changes in our lives. Even the smallest drop of water can make a difference, and similarly, even the smallest act of faithfulness can have a lasting impact.

Loyalty to water also means understanding that water is a gift. It is something that we are entrusted with, not something we own. Water flows freely, sustaining all who come into contact with it. In the same way, God's truth is a gift that we are entrusted with. It is not ours to control but ours to share with others. Just as water is meant to be shared, God's truth is meant to be spread, to bring life and healing to those who are thirsty for it. Loyalty to both water and God's truth calls us to be good stewards, sharing these gifts with generosity and love.

Faithfulness to water and faithfulness to God are intertwined. When we honor water, we are reminded of the sacredness of life itself. Water symbolizes the constant renewal and provision that we receive from

God, and by showing loyalty to water, we affirm our commitment to God's will. Similarly, when we live faithfully according to God's teachings, we acknowledge the life-giving power of His truth. Both water and God's truth are gifts that sustain us, and loyalty to them is a recognition of the divine order that exists in the world.

The act of drinking water is an intimate act, one that sustains us from the inside out. It is a personal experience, much like our relationship with God. Each sip of water nourishes us, and each prayer or moment of spiritual reflection nourishes our souls. Just as we trust water to fulfill our bodily needs, we trust God to fulfill our spiritual needs. Loyalty to water, therefore, is a reflection of our trust in God's provision and care. Both water and God's truth work within us, transforming us from the inside out.

Water flows freely and abundantly, never hesitating to reach those in need. This characteristic of water reminds us that God's truth is always available, flowing freely to all who seek it. We do not need to earn God's truth or hoard it—it is a gift that is offered freely to all. Our loyalty to water reminds us that we should also be generous with the truth that God has given us. Just as water quenches the thirst of the body, God's truth quenches the thirst of the soul.

Loyalty to water and God is also an act of gratitude. We do not own water, yet we benefit from it every day. It is something that we often take for granted, but without it, life would be impossible. Similarly, God's truth is a gift that we often overlook. Our loyalty to both is a way of expressing gratitude for these precious gifts. Just as we show thanks for water by using it wisely, we show thanks for God's truth by living according to it, sharing it with others, and living lives that reflect His teachings.

Ultimately, loyalty to water is a reflection of our loyalty to God. Water sustains our physical life, and God's truth sustains our spiritual life. Both are essential, both are gifts, and both require us to act with reverence and care. By staying loyal to water, we are reminded to stay loyal to God's truth, understanding that both offer life, growth, and transformation. Loyalty to water and loyalty to God are intertwined, and through both, we find the nourishment that we need to thrive spiritually and physically.

Chapter Summary

In this chapter, we delved into the profound concept of faithfulness, specifically exploring how it relates to water, a vital element that sustains all life. Water, in its purest form, serves as a powerful symbol of divine truth. Just as water is essential for physical survival, God's wisdom and teachings are indispensable for our spiritual well-being. This comparison reminds us that our faithfulness to water reflects our faithfulness to God and His eternal will. Water sustains us physically, while God's guidance sustains us spiritually, and both are essential for thriving in life.

We also learned that water, in its eternal cycle, is symbolic of God's timeless nature. Just as God is the Alpha and the Omega, the beginning and the end, water too cycles through the Earth in an unbroken rhythm. It is constantly renewing, replenishing, and sustaining life. Water is a reminder of the constant, unchanging presence of God in our lives. As water cycles through the Earth and nourishes everything it touches, God's presence sustains and nurtures our souls, regardless of the circumstances around us.

Our bodies are made up of 99% water at a cellular level, which emphasizes our deep connection to both the physical and spiritual realms. The water within us connects us to the natural world and to the divine Creator. This intimate relationship with water underscores our dependence on both the physical world and spiritual truth. Water is not just an external resource; it is within us, constantly flowing and sustaining our bodies. Just as we care for the purity of water, we must also honor the purity of the divine truth that flows within us, helping us grow and thrive spiritually.

The chapter highlighted the importance of being faithful to the purest form of water, which serves as a symbol of our commitment to divine truth. Just as we ensure that the water we consume is clean and pure, we must also ensure that the spiritual truth we hold on to remains untainted and aligned with God's teachings. Faithfulness to the purest form of water becomes a reflection of our commitment to living according to God's wisdom. By staying loyal to both water and God's truth, we strengthen our relationship with the Creator and open ourselves up to His guidance and protection.

Faithfulness in all aspects of life is essential for building a solid foundation of trust and spiritual growth. Whether we are talking about our relationship with water or our relationship with God, loyalty and consistency are key to our development. Just as water is essential to our physical well-being, God's truth is essential to our spiritual health. When we remain loyal to the purest forms of both, we are better equipped to navigate life's challenges, knowing that we have the unwavering support of God's guidance.

Ultimately, our loyalty to water is a reflection of our loyalty to God. As the Creator and Sustainer of all life, God provides us with everything we need, including the wisdom that guides us through life. Just as we are faithful to water, which nourishes and sustains us, we must also remain faithful to God, who provides us with the wisdom and strength to fulfill our purpose. By aligning ourselves with the divine will, we open ourselves to the guidance necessary to live a life that is pure, true, and in accordance with God's purpose for us.

In summary, this chapter underscored the deep connection between water, faithfulness, and our relationship with God. Through our loyalty to water, we learn how to remain loyal to God and His teachings. Water, in its purest form, symbolizes the divine truth that sustains us spiritually. As we honor the purity of water, we honor the Creator, and through faithfulness in all aspects of life, we invite God's guidance and support into our hearts.

Chapter Eight

Victory

Victory is often viewed as the ultimate achievement, the moment when one triumphs over all obstacles. But true victory is not simply about winning battles or overcoming challenges in the physical world—it is about a deeper, more spiritual victory. The kind of victory that transcends earthly matters and aligns us with the forces of the universe. To attain this kind of victory, one must join the Army of the Light, a powerful and divine force that guides us toward true freedom, protection, and enlightenment. The Army of the Light is not bound by physical limitations or time—it is an eternal force that commands the universe, shaping the very elements around us.

This chapter explores the concept of true victory, one that is achieved not through sheer force or manipulation, but through alignment with divine purpose. By joining the Army of the Light, we tap into the limitless power of creation itself. This army has the ability to control everything in the universe—stars, planets, oceans, and even the weather. Through this power, we gain insight into the mysteries of existence and unlock the potential to overcome every obstacle that stands in our way.

The Army of the Light is not just about power; it is about protection. It safeguards the very essence of life—water. As the fundamental source of all life, water must be protected from threats that arise from the misuse of human knowledge. Chemicals, nanotechnology, and other forms of destructive technology pose a danger to the purity of water, and by extension, the purity of all life. Understanding this protection allows us to see the greater purpose of the Army of the Light, which acts as a shield to preserve the integrity of life itself.

Through this chapter, we will also explore the true nature of water and its connection to our lives. Water is not just a substance we drink to stay alive; it is the source of all energy, all life, and all wisdom. It is the matrix and the prison, the Alpha and the Omega, and it holds the key to unlocking our true potential. By understanding water's role in our lives, we can begin to understand how to harness its power for victory.

Finally, we will examine how the concept of water as both a matrix and a prison reveals the duality of existence. Water is eternal, and everything in existence is intrinsically tied to it. By recognizing this, we can begin to comprehend the deeper meanings of victory, power, and love. Victory is not just about personal achievement—it is about understanding the greater purpose of life and aligning ourselves with the forces that govern the universe.

The Army of the Light – Guardians of the Universe

The Army of the Light stands as an eternal and all-powerful force, unlike any military power known to humanity. While earthly armies are limited by the laws of nature and the physical constraints of technology, the Army of the Light operates beyond these boundaries, drawing its strength from the very fabric of the universe. This army is a force of creation, not destruction, with a singular focus on the protection of life and the preservation of the cosmic balance. Through their deep understanding of the universe's workings, they have the power to control elements such as stars, planets, oceans, and even the weather. Their reach is limitless, and their capabilities extend beyond human imagination. They are the guardians of all that exists, ensuring that everything operates in harmony with the divine design.

The Army of the Light is not driven by the same desires that often motivate earthly forces—greed, conquest, or power. Instead, their purpose is higher and purer. Their mission is to protect life in its most sacred form, to defend the purity of all living beings and the natural order of the universe. Unlike the armies of the world, which may seek power for their own benefit, the Army of the Light seeks only to serve a divine and cosmic purpose. They understand that everything in the universe is interconnected, and by maintaining the balance of life, they ensure that the cycle of creation and destruction continues in a way that sustains all things. Their work is selfless, devoted to preserving the fundamental essence of life.

One of the most vital responsibilities of the Army of the Light is the protection of water. Water is not just a physical substance; it is the essence of life itself. All living beings, from the smallest microbe to the largest animal, are made up of water. Life cannot exist without water, and without clean, pure water, existence as we know it would cease to be. The Army of the Light understands this in the deepest way. They know that the very foundation of life is built upon water, and that every living being's survival depends on its purity. This is why they dedicate themselves to the protection of water, ensuring that it remains free from contamination, corruption, or misuse. By doing so, they safeguard the delicate web of life that spans across the universe.

The ability of the Army of the Light to command such vast and powerful forces—stars, planets, oceans, and even the weather—is not a simple manifestation of power; it is a reflection of their divine purpose. They are not merely warriors; they are protectors and custodians of the cosmic order. Their influence is woven into the very fabric of creation. They are the ones who ensure that the natural order is maintained and that no force, whether from within the universe or beyond it, can disrupt the harmony of existence. Their power extends beyond the physical realm, tapping into the spiritual and metaphysical forces that shape reality. They are the guardians of life's balance, and their influence is felt in every corner of the universe.

What makes the Army of the Light so unique is that they are not driven by personal ambitions or desires. Unlike earthly armies, which are often motivated by the pursuit of power or control, the Army of the Light exists to fulfill a divine mandate. Their mission is one of service, not self-interest. They do not seek fame or glory, but instead strive to maintain the purity of life and the balance of the cosmos. Their strength is not measured in the number of battles they win, but in the preservation of the natural order and the safeguarding of the forces that sustain life. Their work is ongoing, a quiet force that operates in the background to protect what is most sacred.

The role of the Army of the Light is not just to intervene when disaster strikes or when balance is threatened; their mission is proactive. They work to prevent chaos and destruction before it happens. By maintaining a constant watch over the universe and its delicate systems, they ensure that no force—whether natural or unnatural—can tip the balance into destruction. This constant vigilance is what makes them the ultimate protectors. They do not wait for something to go wrong; they are always on guard, always working to preserve the cosmic order and the purity of all that exists. Their actions may be unseen, but their impact is profound.

In their guardianship of life, the Army of the Light also plays a critical role in the defense of water. Water is vulnerable to contamination, and the threat of pollution is ever-present. As humanity's technological advancements continue to grow, the potential for harm to water sources increases. The Army of the Light works tirelessly to counteract these threats, ensuring that water remains pure and capable of sustaining life. They act as a shield, protecting the most essential resource from the dangers that come from misuse and exploitation. Their efforts are vital, as the health of the planet's water systems is directly tied to the survival of all living creatures.

The Army of the Light's commitment to safeguarding water is not merely about preventing pollution. They also work to ensure that the natural cycles of water—evaporation, condensation, and precipitation—continue uninterrupted. These cycles are the lifeblood of the planet, sustaining ecosystems and ensuring that water is available to nourish all life. By maintaining these cycles, the Army of the Light ensures that life on Earth remains balanced and that the planet's ecosystems continue to thrive. Their protection of water goes beyond simply keeping it clean; it is about ensuring that the planet's water systems remain functional and that all living beings can continue to benefit from the life-sustaining properties of water.

Water, as the fundamental building block of life, holds immense power. It is the source of all creation, and through it, all living beings are connected. The Army of the Light recognizes this profound truth and acts accordingly. Their power to manipulate water, to protect it, and to maintain its purity is a direct reflection of their commitment to preserving life. Water is sacred to them, and they understand that in order to protect life, they must first protect water. Without it, nothing would exist. Therefore, the Army of the Light takes great care in ensuring that water remains unspoiled, ensuring that the life force of the universe continues to flow freely.

The Army of the Light's efforts are not limited to water alone. They also work to protect other vital elements of life, including the atmosphere, the earth, and the celestial bodies. Each element is part of a delicate web that sustains life. The Army of the Light ensures that these elements remain in harmony, preventing any one force from overwhelming the others. They intervene when necessary, but they also work in subtle ways to ensure that the balance of creation is maintained. Their work is often invisible to the naked eye, but its effects are felt in every breath of air, every drop of water, and every heartbeat.

Their role as protectors of life extends beyond the physical realm. The Army of the Light is also concerned with the spiritual and energetic aspects of existence. They understand that the purity of life goes beyond the physical body—it includes the soul, the mind, and the spirit. By ensuring that the natural forces remain intact and undisturbed, they allow for the flourishing of spiritual growth and the development of consciousness. The Army of the Light is not just concerned with the survival of life; they are also focused on the flourishing of all beings, helping them to reach their highest potential and live in harmony with the divine.

As guardians of the universe, the Army of the Light operates in complete alignment with divine principles. Their actions are guided by love, compassion, and wisdom. They do not seek power for its own sake, but rather they use their abilities to serve the greater good. Their influence is felt throughout the universe, and their presence ensures that life continues to evolve in a way that is harmonious with the divine plan. They are not simply warriors; they are healers, nurturers, and protectors, dedicated to ensuring that all life—physical, emotional, and spiritual—remains in balance.

While the Army of the Light is immensely powerful, they do not wield their power recklessly. They understand the responsibility that comes with their position and act with great care. They intervene only when necessary, ensuring that their actions do not disrupt the natural flow of life. They are careful stewards of the universe, always mindful of the delicate balance between creation and destruction. Their actions are always purposeful, always aimed at maintaining harmony and ensuring that the forces of darkness are kept at bay.

The power of the Army of the Light lies not just in their ability to control the physical world, but in their deep understanding of the spiritual realm. They know that true victory is not about domination; it is about alignment with the divine forces that govern the universe. By staying true to this purpose, they are able to maintain the balance of life and prevent the forces of chaos from taking hold. They are not mere warriors— they are guardians of the eternal truth, protectors of the essence of life itself.

The Army of the Light's role as protectors extends far beyond Earth. They are the guardians of the entire cosmos, ensuring that the divine order is maintained across all realms and dimensions. They understand that the universe is vast and interconnected, and they act as the stewards of this grand design. Their work transcends time and space, and their influence reaches across galaxies and beyond. They are the protectors of the infinite, ensuring that the cycle of creation continues uninterrupted.

Ultimately, the Army of the Light's purpose is to ensure that life, in all its forms, continues to thrive. Their role is not one of conquest or destruction, but of protection and preservation. By maintaining the purity of water, the balance of the elements, and the harmony of the universe, they ensure that life continues to evolve and grow in alignment with divine principles. Their actions are guided by love, wisdom, and compassion, and they work tirelessly to protect the essence of life itself. In doing so, they offer us all the opportunity to live in peace, harmony, and victory.

The Power of Water

Water is not just a physical substance we drink or use to bathe; it is the very foundation of life. All living organisms on Earth—whether plant, animal, or human—are made up of water. This simple yet profound truth highlights the significance of water in the maintenance of life. Without water, life as we know it would cease to exist. It is the medium through which nutrients are transported, energy flows, and systems work in harmony. Water, in its essence, is the source of all that is living, connecting every being to the fundamental forces of nature. This makes water not only crucial to survival but also an essential element for growth, development, and transformation.

The importance of water goes beyond its physical presence. Water holds the unique ability to transform life in ways we are only beginning to understand. It can shape landscapes, nourish crops, and even heal. Water is the driving force behind the natural cycles that sustain the environment. Through the process of evaporation, condensation, and precipitation, water ensures that the Earth remains fertile and capable of supporting life. It sustains ecosystems, supports the growth of plants and trees, and provides nourishment to every living creature. Without water, the entire web of life would collapse, as it is the fundamental building block upon which all existence is based.

What makes water so special is its ability to adapt and change. Water takes on different forms—liquid, solid, or gas—depending on its environment, but it always remains vital. Whether it is a raging river, a quiet pond, or the moisture in the air, water has the power to shape its surroundings. It can carve mountains, erode rock, and even influence the weather. In this way, water is not merely a passive element but an active force capable of creating and transforming the world. It connects the different realms of existence, binding together the physical, emotional, and spiritual dimensions of life in a way that no other element can.

One of the most profound aspects of water is its role as the ultimate connector. It is through water that life is created, as it provides the essential nutrients and environment for growth. From the first cell that formed in the primordial oceans to the complex organisms that now roam the Earth, water has always been the catalyst for life. It is the womb of creation, where the essence of life is nurtured and protected. Through this connection, water serves as the bridge between the physical and spiritual realms, allowing energy to flow freely and sustain the life force that resides in every living being.

Water's connection to energy is what makes it so sacred. All living beings are forms of energy, and it is water that facilitates the flow of that energy throughout the body. The human body, for example, is about 60% water, and this water is constantly in motion, circulating nutrients and oxygen, carrying away waste, and maintaining internal balance. This movement of water within the body mirrors the flow of energy in the universe. It is through water that energy is transferred and transformed, allowing life to continue. The energy that sustains the body and the soul is intrinsically tied to water, which acts as the conduit for this life-giving force.

The soul, too, is a form of energy, and it is intimately tied to the element of water. Water is the vehicle through which the soul connects to the physical world, and it is through water that the soul's energy is nourished and maintained. This connection is not just metaphorical but deeply spiritual. Water is the symbol of purity, clarity, and renewal. It is a reminder that our essence, our soul, is constantly being renewed, just as water flows and renews the land. The purity of water reflects the purity of the soul, and it is through this purity that we maintain our connection to the divine and the universe.

The Army of the Light understands the sacredness of water and its vital role in sustaining life. They recognize that water is not just a resource but a fundamental force that ties all living beings together. The purity of water is essential for the survival of life, and it is the Army of the Light's responsibility to protect this resource. They know that without clean, pure water, the fabric of life would unravel, and all living beings would suffer. This understanding is why they are so dedicated to preserving the purity of water, ensuring that it remains untainted by pollution or corruption. Their mission is to guard the sanctity of water, knowing that it is the lifeblood of the universe.

The Army of the Light does not take the protection of water lightly. They understand that water is vulnerable, easily tainted by human activity, natural disasters, or malevolent forces. Pollution, contamination, and misuse threaten the purity of water, and the Army works tirelessly to prevent these threats. They recognize that water cannot be separated from life, and therefore, any harm to water is harm to all living beings. By protecting water, they protect not just the planet but the entire cosmos. Their duty to safeguard this precious resource is a reflection of their commitment to preserving the balance of life.

Water also holds a deep spiritual significance that goes beyond its physical properties. In many cultures and traditions, water is seen as a symbol of spiritual purification and renewal. It is often associated with healing, cleansing, and transformation. In rituals and ceremonies across the world, water is used to wash away negative energies, clear the mind, and restore balance. This symbolic role of water is an extension of its deeper purpose in the universe. Water is not just a physical element; it is a spiritual force that connects us to the divine and the energies of the cosmos.

The connection between water and energy is also evident in the way water influences emotions and consciousness. Water has the power to calm the mind, soothe the spirit, and promote clarity. The sound of water flowing, the sight of a serene lake, or the feeling of water on the skin can bring a sense of peace and balance. This effect on the mind and emotions is not coincidental. Just as water supports the physical body, it also supports the emotional and spiritual well-being of individuals. The flow of water mirrors the flow of emotions, helping to restore equilibrium when life becomes turbulent.

As the ultimate connector, water does not just unite individuals or ecosystems; it also connects the past, present, and future. Water is timeless. It flows through the ages, carrying with it the memories of ancient civilizations and the promise of future generations. The water you drink today may have flowed through the lands of distant ancestors, and the water that nourishes future generations will have once passed through your own body. This continuity creates a deep sense of connection to the past and the future, reminding us that we are part of something much larger than ourselves. Through water, we are all connected across time, space, and existence.

Water also acts as a powerful teacher. It shows us how to adapt, how to flow with the challenges of life, and how to persist even in difficult circumstances. Water does not resist change; instead, it flows around obstacles, carving its path through rock and earth. This ability to adapt and overcome is a lesson for all living beings. Like water, we too must learn to flow with life's challenges, to remain fluid and adaptable in the face of adversity. Water teaches us that we do not have to fight against the current; instead, we must learn to navigate it with grace and wisdom.

The Army of the Light sees water as a divine gift, a force that must be respected and protected. Their commitment to safeguarding water is a reflection of their deep reverence for life itself. They understand that the purity of water is directly tied to the health and well-being of all living beings. By protecting water, they protect the essence of life, ensuring that it remains pure and untainted for generations to come. This dedication to water is one of the many ways the Army of the Light works to preserve the delicate balance of the universe and maintain the harmony of existence.

Water, as a life-sustaining force, holds the key to understanding the interconnectedness of all things. It teaches us about the flow of energy, the importance of purity, and the need for balance. Through water, we learn that life is not static but ever-changing, constantly evolving and transforming. Water is a reminder that life, in all its forms, is connected, and that we are all part of a greater whole. The Army of the Light understands this profound truth and works to ensure that water remains pure, a source of life, energy, and renewal for all beings across the universe.

In the end, the power of water is not just in its physical form but in its spiritual significance. Water is the lifeblood of the Earth, the medium through which energy flows, and the connector between the physical and spiritual realms. It sustains all life, nurtures growth, and renews the spirit. The Army of the Light, through their vigilance and dedication, ensures that this precious resource remains pure and protected, honoring its role as the foundation of all existence. In protecting water, they protect life itself. Through their efforts, they offer us a glimpse into the profound interconnectedness of the universe and the sacredness of the forces that sustain us.

The Protection of Water from Earthly Threats

Water, despite its vital importance, is under constant threat, largely due to human actions. One of the most significant risks to the purity of water is the misuse of technology. From the chemicals we release into our rivers and oceans to the pollutants in the air that eventually settle into our water sources, human activity has dramatically increased the likelihood of contamination. The very technology that was created to enhance our lives has, in many cases, become the catalyst for the destruction of the environment. Pollution is not just a local problem—it is a global one. Industrialization, overpopulation, and improper waste disposal have all contributed to the degradation of our water systems. If left unchecked, these threats will continue to worsen, making it harder for clean, safe water to reach the living organisms that rely on it.

Chemicals are among the most dangerous contaminants that pollute water. These substances often end up in rivers, lakes, and oceans through agricultural runoff, industrial processes, and improper waste disposal. Pesticides, fertilizers, and industrial chemicals seep into the water, making it unsafe for consumption by animals and humans alike. The long-term effects of chemical pollution are devastating. When these chemicals enter the food chain, they cause harm to every organism, from the smallest fish to the largest mammals. In some cases, these toxic substances accumulate in the bodies of organisms, leading to severe health problems, reproductive issues, and even death. The Army of the Light recognizes that every drop of polluted water is a threat not just to life on Earth but to the delicate balance that sustains all creation. This is why they make it their mission to combat chemical pollution and protect water sources.

Another major threat to water comes from industrial waste. Factories and plants produce vast amounts of waste that, when improperly managed, find their way into water bodies. Heavy metals, plastics, and other industrial byproducts can have a catastrophic effect on water quality. These pollutants can take years, if not centuries, to break down, leaving lasting damage on aquatic ecosystems. Marine life is particularly vulnerable, as toxic substances in water can lead to the death of fish and other sea creatures. Even after these pollutants settle in the ocean floor, they continue to affect the environment, impacting the food chain and the biodiversity of marine life. The Army of the Light sees these industrial pollutants as one of the greatest threats to the survival of life itself, and they work relentlessly to ensure these threats are neutralized before they cause irreversible harm.

Plastic pollution is another serious issue that affects water sources around the world. Single-use plastics, such as bottles, bags, and straws, are disposed of improperly, and much of it ends up in the ocean. As plastics break down into smaller particles, they release harmful chemicals into the water, poisoning aquatic life. Marine animals often mistake plastic for food, leading to ingestion, injury, and death. Plastics also block the gills of fish, causing suffocation, and disrupt the ability of aquatic plants to photosynthesize, which is crucial for the production of oxygen. The Army of the Light, understanding the gravity of the situation, works to safeguard the purity of water by confronting the proliferation of plastic waste and removing it from water sources before it has a chance to spread.

In addition to chemicals and plastics, emerging technologies such as nanotechnology also pose a threat to the purity of water. While nanotechnology has the potential to revolutionize industries and improve human life, it also introduces new risks. Nanoparticles, when released into water sources, can be extremely difficult to remove. These tiny particles have the ability to penetrate cell membranes and disrupt biological processes. Their small size makes them nearly invisible to current filtration systems, meaning that even the most advanced water purification methods might not be effective in removing them. As nanotechnology continues to advance, the Army of the Light remains vigilant, ensuring that any harmful applications of this technology are neutralized before they can contaminate the water supply.

The Army of the Light understands that water contamination is not just a matter of pollution but also of corruption. Corruption can take many forms—whether it's through the deliberate poisoning of water sources for strategic purposes or the exploitation of water as a commodity for financial gain. In regions where access to clean water is scarce, some may choose to monopolize water resources, selling it to those in desperate need at inflated prices. This exploitation of water is not just an ethical issue; it is a violation of the natural order. The Army of the Light works to prevent such exploitation, ensuring that water remains a shared resource, available to all who need it, free from corruption and greed.

In their role as protectors of water, the Army of the Light takes proactive measures to prevent contamination before it occurs. They use advanced technologies and divine powers to purify water, remove pollutants, and restore balance to ecosystems that have been harmed. Their abilities go beyond human understanding, as they have access to powers that transcend the limitations of earthly technologies. The

Army can harness the forces of nature itself to cleanse water, using wind, earth, and fire to neutralize toxins and restore the purity of water sources. By guarding the waters, they ensure that these essential resources remain clean, safe, and abundant for all living creatures.

The Army also intervenes when natural disasters threaten the water supply. Hurricanes, floods, and droughts can all have devastating effects on water sources, leading to contamination or depletion. In the aftermath of such events, the Army of the Light works swiftly to restore order, clearing away debris, purifying water, and ensuring that life can continue to thrive. Their intervention is swift and precise, often preventing the worst-case scenarios from becoming a reality. Whether it's protecting a water source from contamination during a flood or ensuring that a drought-stricken region has access to clean water, the Army of the Light plays an essential role in ensuring the survival of life.

Furthermore, the Army of the Light understands that water is more than just a physical substance; it is the very essence of life. To protect water is to protect the soul of the Earth itself. They recognize the spiritual connection that all living beings have with water, and they see it as their sacred duty to preserve its purity. Their efforts are not solely for the physical survival of life but also to ensure the spiritual well-being of every living being. Water, in its purest form, is a channel for life energy. When water is tainted, that energy is disrupted, and the harmony of the universe is threatened. By safeguarding water, the Army of the Light helps maintain the energetic balance that sustains all life.

The purification of water is not just about removing pollutants but about restoring the harmony and balance of the natural world. The Army of the Light uses their vast knowledge and powers to heal the water, much like a healer restores a wounded body. They use both technological advancements and mystical abilities to remove harmful substances from the water, ensuring that it remains pure and nourishing. They understand that the purity of water is directly linked to the vitality of all ecosystems, and they work to maintain that purity for future generations.

In addition to protecting the water itself, the Army of the Light also focuses on educating and empowering humanity to protect water. They know that the survival of life on Earth depends on the conscious efforts of all people to reduce their impact on water sources. Through guidance, knowledge, and support, the Army helps teach humanity how to live in harmony with the Earth's water systems. By promoting sustainable practices, such as reducing water waste, protecting wetlands, and preventing pollution, the Army of the Light ensures that future generations will inherit a world where water is clean, abundant, and life-sustaining.

The Army of the Light also monitors and defends water from more subtle threats, such as the over-extraction of water. In some areas, industries and agriculture take more water from rivers and aquifers than can be replenished. This depletion of water resources leads to the degradation of ecosystems, drying up rivers, lakes, and wetlands. The Army of the Light works to protect water sources from over-extraction, ensuring that they are used sustainably and that future generations have access to clean water. They understand that water is a finite resource, and they take steps to preserve it for the long term.

In their mission to protect water, the Army of the Light also confronts the growing issue of climate change. Rising temperatures, changing precipitation patterns, and extreme weather events all have a significant impact on the availability and quality of water. Droughts are becoming more severe, while floods are becoming more destructive. The Army's role in combating these threats is to help stabilize the water cycle, ensuring that the Earth's ecosystems remain balanced and that water continues to flow freely where it is needed most. They work to mitigate the effects of climate change on water, using both their powers and knowledge to restore balance and prevent further damage.

Water, in its purest form, is a gift from the Earth and the cosmos. It is a sacred force that connects all life, and the Army of the Light is dedicated to its protection. They know that without water, life cannot thrive, and without its purity, the balance of the universe is at risk. The Army's commitment to guarding water is not just a mission—it is a sacred duty, one that they carry out with honor, compassion, and unwavering determination. Through their efforts, they ensure that the essence of life remains intact, and that water continues to flow freely and abundantly for all beings across the universe.

Water as the Matrix and the Prison

Water is far more than just a substance we drink or bathe in. It is the matrix that holds all of life together, the foundation on which existence itself is built. Every living organism on Earth, from the smallest microbe to the largest mammal, is composed primarily of water. This universal solvent sustains us, supports our growth, and keeps our bodies functioning. Water is the medium through which energy flows, and it serves as a conduit for life itself. Without it, life would cease to exist. It is the element that allows life to take form, to grow, and to evolve. From the moment of conception to the final moments of life, water plays a pivotal role in every stage of our existence. But beyond this life-giving role, water also has a more complex and paradoxical nature. It not only sustains life but also binds it, tethering us to the physical realm in ways we may not fully understand.

This paradox is where water becomes a prison. While water is the element that allows life to exist, it also limits the potential of the soul. Water is what binds the spirit to the physical body, creating a cycle of birth, life, and death. We are born from water in the womb, we live in water in the form of bodily fluids, and, eventually, we return to water in death. But throughout this cycle, the soul is limited in its potential. The soul, in its purest form, is free, unbound by the physical world. However, water holds the soul within the confines of the body, keeping it anchored to the material world. It is through the physical form that the soul experiences its limitations. The body requires water to function, but this same water keeps the soul from transcending into higher planes of existence. This binding of the soul to the body through water is a form of entrapment, a reminder that, while life is a gift, it is also a form of captivity.

In a way, water represents the beginning and the end. It is both the Alpha and the Omega. Water is the substance from which life emerges and the substance to which life returns. It is the eternal cycle, the constant that never changes. We begin in the water of the womb, and we end by returning to the earth, where water will eventually reclaim us. This cycle of birth, life, and death is reflected in the water cycle of nature itself. Water evaporates, travels through the atmosphere, condenses into clouds, and falls as rain, replenishing the earth. Similarly, our bodies are made of water, and when we die, our bodies return to the earth, eventually becoming part of the water cycle again. Water is the eternal link between the physical and the spiritual, the bridge that connects us to the universe. It is the force that sustains us, but also the force that binds us to the limitations of the material world.

Water, in this sense, represents both creation and destruction. It is through water that life is created, but it is also through water that life is destroyed. Water nourishes crops, fills our rivers, and sustains all forms of life on the planet. But water can also flood, drown, and destroy everything in its path. Floods, tsunamis, and storms are all manifestations of water's power to take life as well as give it. This duality makes water both a source of life and a potential destroyer of life. Just as the ocean holds the power to create life through the nutrients it provides to marine ecosystems, it also has the power to wipe out entire cities. Water is both the matrix that sustains life and the prison that can trap life in an endless cycle of birth and destruction.

The connection between water and the soul is particularly profound. The soul is often seen as a fluid, ever-changing force, much like water itself. Just as water can transform from liquid to gas to solid, the soul can change forms, evolving and growing over time. However, water also serves as a prison because it holds the soul within the physical body, limiting its freedom. The soul, in its purest form, is not meant to be confined. It yearns for freedom, to transcend beyond the physical realm, to explore the higher dimensions of existence. But as long as the soul is bound to the body by water, it is restricted in its movement and growth.

Water is the barrier that keeps the soul tethered to the Earth, preventing it from achieving its highest potential.

In many spiritual traditions, water symbolizes purification and renewal. It is through water that we cleanse ourselves of physical impurities, but it also represents the purification of the soul. Rituals involving water, such as baptism, are common in many religions, symbolizing the washing away of sins and the rebirth of the soul. In this way, water can be seen as both a prison and a release. It is the element that binds us to the physical world, but it is also the element that offers us the chance to be renewed, to shed our burdens, and to rise again. The paradox of water as both a matrix and a prison is central to our understanding of existence. It is through water that we live, but it is also through water that we die.

Water's dual nature is further illustrated in the way it shapes our experiences. When we are immersed in water, we experience a sense of weightlessness, as if we are freed from the constraints of gravity. This sensation of freedom is a metaphor for the soul's desire to escape the limitations of the physical body. But even in water, we are still bound to the physical world. We cannot remain submerged forever; eventually, we must come up for air. In this sense, water represents both freedom and limitation. It allows us to float and drift, but it also forces us to return to the surface, where the physical world's demands take hold once again.

The water cycle itself mirrors the cyclical nature of life. Water evaporates, rises into the atmosphere, and returns as rain, nourishing the Earth once again. Similarly, life follows a cycle of birth, growth, and death. Just as water moves through different forms and stages, so too does life move through its phases. Water's ability to change and adapt to different forms makes it a powerful metaphor for the human experience. We too are constantly changing, constantly evolving, but we remain bound to the physical world by the limitations of our bodies. Just as water flows through various states, we too flow through different stages of life, but we are always tethered to the Earth, always bound by the material world.

Water's connection to the physical world is further emphasized by its presence in our daily lives. We use water for nearly every aspect of our existence—from drinking to cooking, from cleaning to bathing. Water is integral to every function of our bodies and our homes. Yet, even as we rely on it, we are reminded that water is both a gift and a limitation. It sustains us, but it also keeps us tethered to the Earth, bound to the cycles of life and death. Water is the thread that connects us to the world around us, but it also serves as the chain that keeps us from escaping the material realm.

In mythology and spirituality, water is often depicted as a symbol of the unconscious mind. It is the realm where our deepest thoughts and emotions reside, often hidden beneath the surface. The unconscious is a vast and mysterious space, much like the ocean. Water represents both the conscious and unconscious mind, as it holds both our memories and our dreams. Just as water can be calm and still or stormy and unpredictable, so too is the unconscious mind. Water's fluid nature mirrors the ever-changing nature of our thoughts and emotions. It is through water that we come to understand ourselves, but it is also through water that we are reminded of our limitations.

The soul's journey through life can be seen as a journey through water. From the moment of birth, when we emerge from the womb in a burst of water, to the moment of death, when we return to the Earth, water is ever-present. Water is both a cradle and a tomb. It is through water that life begins, and it is through water that life ends. The cycle of water is the cycle of life. Just as water flows from the mountains to the oceans, life flows from birth to death. The paradox of water as both the matrix and the prison is one that shapes our understanding of existence. It is both the source and the end, the beginning and the conclusion.

Through water, we are reminded of the fragility of life. Water is delicate, easily polluted, and vulnerable to destruction. Similarly, our lives are fragile and fleeting. Water's vulnerability mirrors our own, reminding us that life is not guaranteed. It is through the care and protection of water that we protect our own existence. The preservation of water is the preservation of life. Just as we must safeguard water to ensure its purity, we must safeguard our own lives to ensure our continued survival. Water, in all its forms, represents the delicate balance of life and death, creation and destruction.

Water's role as the matrix and the prison teaches us important lessons about life. It is through water that we are born, and it is through water that we die. Water is the element that sustains us, but it is also the element that limits us. It is the force that connects us to the Earth and to each other, but it is also the force that binds us to the physical realm. By understanding the paradox of water, we can begin to understand the deeper mysteries of existence. Water is both a gift and a burden, both a cradle and a tomb. It is through water that life flows, and it is through water that life returns to the Earth. In this eternal cycle, we are reminded of the fragility of life and the interconnectedness of all things.

The Rainbow – A Symbol of Heaven and Hell

The rainbow is a powerful symbol that represents the duality of existence—heaven and hell. It is more than just a natural phenomenon; it serves as a reminder of the balance between two opposing forces that shape our world. The rainbow, with its array of vibrant colors, carries profound meaning, reflecting the ongoing struggle between light and darkness. As sunlight passes through raindrops, it breaks into its individual components, creating a beautiful spectrum of colors. This breakdown of light is symbolic of the way opposing forces, often seen as extremes of good and evil, are interconnected in the fabric of reality. The rainbow, therefore, is not merely an aesthetic marvel but a visual manifestation of the eternal dance between opposing energies that govern existence.

Each color in the rainbow carries its own unique meaning, contributing to the symbolism of both heaven and hell. The red at the base of the spectrum is particularly significant. Red represents the fiery energy of hell, the realm of destruction and chaos. This color, being closest to the Sun, embodies the intense, burning forces that can both create and annihilate. It is a symbol of the raw power of the universe—the destructive forces that are necessary for renewal but can also be overwhelming if not properly balanced. Just as fire has the power to consume and transform, red in the rainbow reflects the potency of hell, a place where chaos reigns and where destruction serves as the prelude to rebirth.

As the rainbow stretches across the sky, transitioning from red to orange, yellow, green, blue, indigo, and finally violet, the colors represent the different aspects of heaven. Each color has its own significance, reflecting a harmonious balance that contrasts with the fiery force of red. Orange, for instance, symbolizes warmth and creativity. It is the color of the sunset, the calm that follows the storm. Orange reflects a gentle, nurturing energy that brings people together, fostering cooperation and compassion. This warmth, in contrast to the fiery heat of red, symbolizes the peace and understanding that can exist even amidst conflict. The shift from red to orange begins the movement away from destruction and towards creation, representing the flow from hell to heaven.

Yellow, the next color in the spectrum, embodies the light of the sun and the divine energy that illuminates the world. It symbolizes hope, clarity, and optimism—the qualities that guide us through darkness. Yellow is the color of enlightenment, representing the intellect and the power of knowledge. In the context of the rainbow's symbolism, yellow is the connection between the physical world and the spiritual. It represents the clarity that comes with understanding, the realization that, despite the darkness of the world, light is always present and can guide us through troubled times. The presence of yellow in the rainbow is a reminder that the divine always shines, even in the darkest moments.

Green, the next color, symbolizes balance and harmony. It is the color of nature, growth, and life. Green represents the fertile earth, where life finds its nourishment and sustenance. In the context of the rainbow, green is the bridge between heaven and earth, the realm where both divine and earthly forces come together in equilibrium. It reflects the importance of maintaining balance in life, ensuring that creation and destruction are kept in check. Green also symbolizes renewal—the constant cycle of life, death, and rebirth. Just as the earth is constantly replenished by water and sunlight, green represents the vitality that arises when opposing forces find harmony.

The blue of the rainbow represents peace and tranquility. It is the color of the sky and the ocean, symbolizing vastness, freedom, and the infinite. Blue is often associated with spiritual calmness and the depth of the soul. It reflects the serenity that comes with understanding the deeper truths of existence. In the rainbow, blue is the color that brings a sense of calm to the tumultuous energy of the earlier colors. It reminds us that, even in the face of chaos, peace is possible. Blue is the color of trust and loyalty, the bonds that hold relationships together despite adversity. It represents the unwavering strength of heaven—the quiet yet powerful force that keeps everything in order.

Indigo, the color that follows blue, symbolizes intuition and insight. It is the color of the night sky, the vast unknown that lies beyond our understanding. Indigo represents the mysteries of existence, the hidden forces that shape our world. It is the color of introspection and inner wisdom, guiding us to look beyond the surface and seek deeper truths. Indigo is the color of the seeker, the one who is not content with superficial answers but is driven to explore the unknown. In the context of the rainbow, indigo represents the journey of the soul as it moves from the physical realm into higher spiritual awareness, seeking truth and enlightenment.

Finally, violet, the last color of the rainbow, represents the ultimate connection to the divine. It is the color of the crown chakra, symbolizing spiritual awakening and the union with the higher self. Violet is the color of the soul's return to its true source, the realm of pure light and consciousness. It represents the highest form of spiritual attainment, the realization of oneness with the universe. In the context of the rainbow, violet is the culmination of the journey from hell to heaven, from destruction to creation, from the material to the spiritual. It is the color that signifies the transcendence of duality, where the soul achieves enlightenment and unity with the divine.

The rainbow, therefore, is a symbol of the balance between heaven and hell, light and dark, good and evil. It represents the ever-present tension between opposing forces, the struggle that defines the human experience. Just as the rainbow is formed through the interaction of sunlight and water, the balance between these forces is what gives life its richness and depth. Without both light and dark, there would be no contrast, no definition, no movement. The rainbow reminds us that life is a constant interplay of opposites, and it is through this interplay that we find meaning and purpose. The duality of existence is not something to be feared but embraced, for it is through this balance that growth and transformation occur.

In many ways, the rainbow is a metaphor for the human condition. We are all caught in the balance between light and dark, heaven and hell. Our lives are shaped by the choices we make, the forces we allow to guide us. The rainbow teaches us that, no matter how dark the world may seem, there is always hope, always light, always the possibility of transcendence. The Army of the Light, those dedicated to maintaining balance and protecting the purity of existence, draws strength from the rainbow's message. They understand that, just as the rainbow is a symbol of both creation and destruction, so too is their mission to protect the balance of life itself.

The rainbow is also a reminder that beauty can be found even in the most difficult times. When storms rage and the skies are filled with darkness, the rainbow appears as a sign that the storm has passed, that the world is once again in balance. It is a symbol of hope and renewal, showing us that no matter how great the chaos, there is always the potential for peace. The rainbow, in its vibrant display, reminds us that life is not solely defined by suffering or hardship but by the moments of clarity and beauty that arise after the storm. It is through these moments that we find the strength to continue, to fight for the light even when darkness surrounds us.

The colors of the rainbow also serve as a metaphor for the various aspects of the human experience. Just as each color contributes to the whole, each moment of our lives—whether joyful or painful—adds to the richness of our journey. The rainbow reminds us that every experience, no matter how seemingly insignificant, plays a part in the larger story of our lives. The contrasts between heaven and hell, light and dark, good and evil, are not mutually exclusive but are part of the same cycle that sustains us. We are all part of the rainbow, each of us contributing our unique colors to the grand tapestry of existence.

In the end, the rainbow is not just a symbol of heaven and hell but a symbol of the interconnectedness of all things. It is a reminder that everything in the universe, from the smallest particle to the grandest celestial body, is part of the same dynamic interplay. Just as the colors of the rainbow blend seamlessly together to create a single, unified whole, so too do all the forces of the universe work together to maintain the balance of life. The rainbow teaches us that we are all interconnected, that the light and dark within us are part of the same spectrum. By embracing this duality, we can find peace, understanding, and the wisdom to navigate the challenges of life.

The rainbow, therefore, is a symbol of hope and transformation. It shows us that, despite the trials we face, there is always the potential for growth, renewal, and transcendence. The rainbow serves as a reminder that no matter how dark the world may seem, there is always a glimmer of light on the horizon. Just as the rainbow appears after a storm, so too can we find clarity and purpose after the chaos of life. Through the protection of the Army of the Light and the balance they maintain, we can continue to move forward, guided by the promise of the rainbow's colors and the hope they bring.

Achieving Power and Victory Through God's Word

Victory is often viewed as the triumph over external challenges, obstacles that seem to stand in the way of success. However, true victory goes far beyond simply overcoming these challenges. It is about aligning oneself with a divine purpose, a higher calling that gives meaning and direction to life. Through God's word, which is transmitted to us through the sacred medium of water, we are able to tap into a power that goes beyond the physical realm. This alignment with divine purpose is what leads to lasting success, not just in worldly endeavors, but in spiritual growth, love, and peace.

God's teachings are not just guidelines for moral living; they are the keys to unlocking the full potential within each of us. His word provides wisdom that transcends time and place, offering insight into how we can navigate life's challenges with grace and strength. It is through obedience to His word that we find true empowerment. This empowerment does not come from relying solely on our own strength but from tapping into the boundless power of the divine. By aligning our actions with God's will, we open ourselves up to a life filled with purpose, clarity, and the strength to overcome anything that stands in our path.

Water plays a pivotal role in this process. It is not just a physical substance that sustains life, but also a spiritual medium through which God's word is delivered. Water, through its purity and essence, connects us to the divine realm, serving as a conduit for spiritual transformation. In the same way that water nourishes our bodies, it also nourishes our souls, cleansing us from within and aligning us with divine truth. Just as vaporized water rises into the sky, carrying with it the essence of the earth, so too does God's word rise within us, offering us the spiritual nourishment we need to grow.

The sacred nature of water is central to understanding the deeper meanings of victory, power, and love. When we reflect on water's role in the transmission of divine wisdom, we begin to see that these concepts are not merely external achievements or superficial desires. True victory is not found in the accumulation of wealth or power but in the alignment of our lives with God's will. Power, when it is rooted in divine purpose, is not about control over others, but the ability to control ourselves, to resist temptation, and to act with integrity and love. Through obedience to God's word, we are transformed into vessels of His divine light, capable of achieving victory in every aspect of life.

In the same way that water is a bridge between the physical and the spiritual, God's word is the bridge between the divine and the earthly realms. When we drink from the spiritual well of God's wisdom, we are brought closer to understanding the divine purpose for our lives. Water, with its ability to move through every substance it touches, serves as a metaphor for how God's word moves through us, filling us with His presence and transforming us from the inside out. By understanding this, we begin to realize that true victory comes from connecting with the divine, not from striving to meet worldly standards.

God's word through water is also a source of strength and resilience. Just as water flows through the earth, carving its path through mountains and valleys, so too does God's word flow through our lives, shaping us and guiding us even when we face trials. The Bible teaches that when we are filled with the living water of God's word, we are empowered to stand firm in the face of adversity. Water does not force its way through obstacles; it moves with grace and persistence, gradually wearing down even the hardest of stones. Similarly, through God's teachings, we can overcome the hardest trials, not by force, but through persistence, faith, and grace.

Victory achieved through God's word is not just about defeating external challenges, but about inner transformation. When we align ourselves with God's truth, we begin to experience a shift in our mindset and our heart. We no longer see challenges as obstacles to be overcome, but as opportunities for growth and learning. God's word equips us with the tools we need to navigate life with wisdom, patience, and love. It helps us to see the bigger picture, to understand that every trial we face is part of a larger divine plan, and that through our obedience, we are participating in the unfolding of God's purpose for our lives.

Love, too, is a key aspect of the victory that God promises to those who follow His word. God's love is unconditional and ever-present, and it is through His love that we are able to love others. Love is the greatest power we can possess, for it transcends all boundaries, bringing healing, peace, and reconciliation to every situation. Through God's word, we learn to cultivate this love, not just for others, but for ourselves. Self-love, rooted in divine purpose, empowers us to act with compassion and understanding, knowing that we are all connected through the Creator.

Success, from a spiritual perspective, is not measured by material wealth or societal accolades, but by our ability to live in accordance with God's will. True success is found in fulfilling our divine purpose and serving others with humility and grace. By following God's word, we are able to cultivate a sense of peace and contentment that cannot be found in worldly pursuits. The peace that comes from living in alignment with God's will is a victory in itself, one that cannot be taken away by external circumstances. It is a peace that transcends understanding, a peace that fills our hearts and souls, regardless of the challenges we may face.

Through the guidance of God's word, we are empowered to overcome fear, doubt, and uncertainty. When we embrace the truth of God's teachings, we are no longer bound by the limitations of our own understanding. God's wisdom opens our eyes to the vast possibilities that exist within us and around us. We begin to see ourselves not as victims of circumstance, but as active participants in the unfolding of God's plan. Victory is no longer something we chase, but something that arises naturally as we align ourselves with God's divine purpose.

Victory, love, and success through God's word are not just ideals; they are realities that can be experienced in every moment of our lives. When we choose to walk in obedience to His teachings, we open ourselves up to a life of fulfillment and purpose. God's word provides a blueprint for living, one that leads to victory not only in the material world but also in the spiritual realm. Through God's guidance, we are able to navigate the complexities of life with wisdom and grace, finding strength in His presence and peace in His truth.

Water, as the medium through which God's word is transmitted, serves as a constant reminder of the divine presence in our lives. Just as water nourishes and sustains our physical bodies, God's word nourishes and sustains our souls. By understanding the sacred nature of water, we begin to understand the sacred nature of God's word. Water is a symbol of life, and through it, we are connected to the eternal wisdom of the Creator. In this way, we can truly achieve victory—not just in overcoming external challenges, but in living lives that reflect the divine purpose and love that flow through us.

Through obedience to God's word, we tap into an endless source of strength, love, and wisdom. The victory that we achieve through God's word is not one that can be measured by worldly standards, but by the peace and fulfillment that comes from living in accordance with divine truth. This victory is eternal, for it is grounded in the eternal nature of God's word, which never fades or fails. By aligning ourselves with His purpose, we participate in a victory that transcends time and space, a victory that is found in our connection to the divine.

God's word is the ultimate source of power, for it is through His teachings that we are able to tap into the boundless strength of the Creator. When we live according to God's word, we are no longer reliant on our own strength but on the strength that comes from Him. This power is not the power to control others, but the power to transform ourselves, to rise above our circumstances, and to walk in victory. It is a power that is rooted in love, compassion, and grace, and it is available to all who choose to walk in alignment with God's will.

In this way, victory through God's word is not just about external achievements but about internal transformation. As we align ourselves with God's truth, we are transformed from the inside out. Our hearts and minds are renewed, and we begin to see the world through a different lens. Victory is no longer about what we can achieve in the physical realm but about living in accordance with divine purpose, embracing love, peace, and spiritual fulfillment. Through this alignment, we achieve true victory—one that is not fleeting but eternal, rooted in the unchanging nature of God's word.

The Eternal Nature of Water

Water is ageless. It is the only substance in the universe that is not influenced by the passage of time, inviolable to the forces that transform all else. While all about us changes, dies, or evolves, water is the one thing that remains constant, flowing through the ages unchanged and unchanging. This timelessness gives water a particular significance—it is not just a physical entity, but a spiritual one, linking us to the past, the present, and the future. Water stands outside of time, and in doing so, it unites all living things across the generations. Wherever we are on the earth or in the timeline of life, water is a common denominator that unites us, giving life and continuity.

Water is the matrix of life, the essence of all living organisms. Without it, there would be no life as we know it. All organisms, all cells, and all natural formations depend on water to a certain degree. From the vast oceans to the smallest drop of dew, water sustains all types of living organisms. Water flows through the Earth's veins, shaping landscapes and nourishing ecosystems. Water not only sustains life, it also gives form and shape to life, allowing everything to flourish. Just as water shapes the physical world, so does it shape our lives, our feelings, and our thoughts, constantly flowing through our existence, reminding us of our unity with nature and with each other.

Water's role as the great unifier of all living things cannot be overstated. It is a universal medium in which the exchange of life is possible. In nature, all living things rely on water for life—plants draw water from the ground, animals ingest water from rivers and lakes, and even the air we breathe is moist. On a spiritual level, water is the medium through which the energy of life flows. From the food we eat to the energy we utilize, water is the silent partner to all of life's processes. The eternal nature of water gives us a reminder that, no matter our differences, we all share this in common - this requirement for water, which unites us with each other and with the planet that we inhabit.

Understanding the eternal nature of water holds the secret to a larger understanding of why we're here. Water, in its purity and simplicity, demonstrates a fundamental truth: life is circular. As water makes its way through the natural world in an endless cycle—evaporating into the air as water vapor, becoming clouds, and falling back to the Earth as rain—our lives are also a part of a cycle. We are born, we live, we die, and our energy is re-released into the world in a new form. Water also shows us that life is not a linear journey, but a cycle of transformation. The natural cycles reflect the cycles within us, and remind us to accept change and recognize it as part of the journey.

The eternal quality of water also reflects the nature of the soul. As water does not die, neither does the energy within us ever die. The soul, like water, is immortal. It is not born nor does it perish, but rather it transforms from one form to another. We may undergo hardships, losses, and adversities during our lifetime, but these do not signal the end of our being. In the same way that water may take on many different forms—be it in liquid, gas, or solid form—it nonetheless exists in some form or another. Similarly, our souls, despite being plagued by challenges, continue to grow, learn, and evolve, constantly striving towards a greater consciousness of the universe and our place within it.

As we consider the eternal nature of water, we are reminded that the path of life is not one of attachment to the physical realm, but rather one of surrender to the flow of life itself. Water also reminds us that change is a part of life, and that everything is always in the process of movement. The stillness we often desire in life is generally an illusion, for we are always becoming. Just as a river never stays still but flows ever forward, so life propels us forward. By surrendering to the flow of life, we come into harmony with the eternal nature of the universe, and we are at peace knowing that we are part of a greater cycle.

Victory has long been perceived as the overcoming of the obstacles, something that must be achieved through effort and determination. However, understanding the eternal nature of life and water changes this perception. Victory is less about transcending obstacles than coming to realize and align ourselves with the divine flow of life. When we have accepted that life is round, that the soul never dies, and we are part of the natural flow of water, then we can approach victory in a new way. True triumph does not consist in the conquest of external enemies, but in the acceptance of the eternal fact of our existence and living in harmony with the universe.

Water's ability to change shape and yet be the same is a powerful symbol of transformation. In life, we will encounter periods of immense change, periods when we may feel that everything is shifting and nothing is the same. And just like water, which retains its essential qualities regardless of the form it assumes, so do we carry within us the nature of who we are. The eternal nature of water instructs us that, even as things around us may evolve, our nature does not. We can change, adapt, and evolve, yet we are always a part of the great current of life. This understanding of transformation enables us to navigate change with grace and power, knowing we are never forsaken, however far we may seem to wander.

Just as water flows through every part of the Earth, so does the divine flow through every part of the universe. The immortal nature of water teaches the interconnectedness of all things. Every drop of water is a part of the whole, just as every soul is a part of the grander divine plan. Water shows us that we are not individualized beings, but part of the world around us. Our energy, thoughts, and actions ripple out into the world, contacting everything we touch. This awareness is crucial to understanding the purpose of our existence. We are not here for ourselves, but to contribute to the greater current of life, to help keep and lift up the world around us.

Water gives life, and in doing so, it represents the nourishing power of the universe. As water nourishes the body, so it nourishes the soul. In times of tribulation, we turn to water to renew us, whether in the soft voice of a meandering river, the soothing eye of a storm, or the therapeutic power of a bath. Water has the power to heal and renew, body and spirit. As we tune into the eternal essence of water, we tap into this healing energy, allowing it to heal us and to lead us on the path.

The eternal essence of water also teaches us that all things are temporary in the physical realm. All things, no matter how solid or stable they may appear, are impermanent. Water teaches us to be adaptable, to flow with the currents of life rather than against them. The more that we understand the physical world, the more that we struggle against the inevitable passage of time. But when we embrace the timelessness of water, we find that it is through adaptability and flow that we find peace. The key to life is not to hold on to the past, but to move with the present, and to allow ourselves to be transformed and change.

As we ponder the timelessness of water, we understand that the universe is in a perpetual state of motion. The movement of water mirrors the endless cycles of life—birth, death, and rebirth. As water flows from the highest mountains to the deepest oceans, so too does our energy flow through the universe, touching every part of life. Our life is part of this flow, and just as water is never lost, neither are we. We may go through different forms of being, but we are always part of the whole, always progressing forward in the cycle of life.

Water teaches us that life is not about accumulation, but letting go. Just as water constantly flows and moves around the planet, we too must let go of what no longer serves us. The flow of water teaches us that nothing belongs to us. We are stewards of life, entrusted with its care, but we do not possess it. Life flows through us, and our role is to join the flow, not try to control it. In this acceptance of letting go, we align ourselves with the eternal nature of the universe, and we become at peace in surrender and trust.

Victory, then, is not in the agglomeration of material wealth or power, but in aligning ourselves with the flow of life. When we release our attachment to the transient things of life and embrace the timeless nature of water, we find the highest victory is living in balance with the world. Water shows us that life is not a journey of conquest, but embracing the cycles of life and moving along the sacred current. When we surrender to this flow, we achieve the highest victory—not over others or over external events, but over ourselves, over our fears and our limitations.

The timelessness of water teaches us patience as well. Water does not rush to its goal, but flows irresistibly and relentlessly toward its goal. It will encounter obstacles along the way, but adapts and flows around them. Water's patience in the face of obstacles is a lesson to us that we too can handle life's obstructions with grace and perseverance. Water's eternity teaches us that everything has its time and place. We need not rush through life because time's passage is already in motion, and all things will occur as they must.

As we consider the timelessness of water, we are called to the importance of mindfulness. Water flows without effort, circling the globe with intention and purpose. It does not try, yet it moves spontaneously. We, too, are called to live with intention, to harmonize ourselves with the greater flow of life. Through mindfulness, we can access the ageless energy of water, finding peace and purpose in every moment. As we flow with the currents of life, we become part of the infinite cycle, understanding the true nature of victory and accomplishment.

The perpetual nature of water is not just a metaphor for the cycle of life but a reflection of the divine energy that permeates all of creation. Just as water constantly circulates through the planet, so too does divine energy constantly circulate through all living beings. When we attune ourselves to the flow, we connect with the timeless quality of the universe and are empowered

Chapter Summary

In this chapter, we dug into the profound concept of genuine victory, not merely the issues of everyday life but rather where we find ourselves in tune with the divine powers that govern the universe. Real victory is less about overcoming difficulty in worldly life but achieving alignment with an ultimate, perpetual cause. This is achieved by becoming a member of the Army of the Light, an invincible and powerful army tasked with maintaining peace in the world. The Army of the Light also has the sacred responsibility of upholding and guarding the sanctity of water, the most critical element necessary for life to exist. By so doing, they are also guarding the divine connection that exists between all living things and the source of existence.

Army of the Light is not merely a symbolism for religious soldiers but in fact an army with power rooted in knowledge of oneness of everything. The mission of this army is to safeguard water from excesses of technology that would taint its purity and disrupt natural equilibrium. In today's world, in which greed and industrialization all too often see individual profit over the health of the planet, the Army of the Light is a protector, fighting against those forces that seek to pollute the very source of life. In what they do, they teach us that defending water means defending life itself.

Not only is water the source of all life, but it also possesses with it such immense power of transformation. Throughout the chapter, we had already learned how water is the vehicle through which we are connected to the divine and how water is the key through which we obtain access to the wisdom and strength needed to attain the victory. No matter how it does it, through purifying our bodies, cleaning our spirits, or through its sustenance to us, water is a force of rebirth and growth. When we ally ourselves with the cleanliness of water, we ally ourselves with the divine energies that guide us to spiritual and individual victory.

The Army of the Light is dedicated to protecting this sacred element and keeping it clean. They are the guardians of water from pollution, fighting to maintain its sanctity in a world that seems to want to use it for economic purposes. The chapter brought out the crucial role that water plays in keeping all living things alive and how preservation is key to the survival of all that lives. Without clean water, nature's equilibrium will crumble, and all life would be impacted. Therefore, the work of the Army of the Light is not only spiritual but also essential to the survival of humanity and the world.

The double nature of water was another recurring theme analyzed in this chapter. While it's the foundation of life, it is also an attachment that makes us bonded to the material world. Water itself is the matrix of life and the prison that keeps us tethered to the physical world. Through life, we're constantly reminded how water connects us to the divine and the earthly. As it nourishes and brings us to life, it keeps us connected to the physical world and its limitations. Understanding of this duality is crucial to understanding our place in the universe and our spiritual path that we are forced to follow.

In considering the use of water as sustainer and limiter, we began to consider the deeper symbolism of this substance. Water is the Alpha and the Omega—the beginning and end. Water is the first element that endures and the element that is there when all else has gone. This profound reality was explored within the chapter to show how water acts as a unifying link between life and death, creation and destruction, the material and the spiritual. By understanding this, we can value the sacredness of water and our place in protecting it for future generations.

The chapter also touched on the idea of spiritual victory through attunement with the forces of the universe. When we become members of the Army of the Light and make ourselves committed to defending water, we are not just defending a material substance but are aligning ourselves with a greater cosmic agenda. By becoming part of that, we are becoming part of a divine crusade to preserve the sanctity of life. This victory is not measured in terms of success on this planet but in terms of our willingness to stand up for something bigger than ourselves. True triumph is in serving the greater good, in standing up for that which sustains all life.

Perhaps the most significant part of spiritual triumph is to understand that it is alignment internally and externally. Merely upholding water and the planet with our actions will not be enough; we must purify our hearts and minds as well. The Army of the Light shows us that by standing with the cleanliness of water, we can gain victory over our own inner struggles and wars. Just as water can purify the body and the earth, it can purify the soul. This was addressed in the chapter as a reminder that spiritual victory is a continuous process, one that requires continuous reflection, growth, and commitment.

Winning, as it is described in the chapter, is also about being aware of our position within the vast cosmic stream. It is about being aware that each decision we make, however small, has a ripple effect that transcends ourselves. By protecting water, we protect the very essence of life, and in so doing, we are part of something much larger, something divinely created. Water is teaching us that we are a part of something larger than ourselves and that spirituality is lived by how we walk in the world. In aspiring to win in both spirit and body, we are reminded that all things are connected and the choices we make have effects.

The final part of the chapter called out to readers to do something about it in their own life. True triumph, this chapter suggests, is one that cannot be achieved through simple passive faith. It entails being actively engaged, consciously choosing, and being completely committed to the cause. The Army of the Light consists of individuals who are willing to stand and fight for the holiness of water not just in the physical world but even in the world of the spirit. As we continue, the chapter encourages readers to think about how they can be involved in this noble cause and how they too can triumph through their own dedication to the higher purpose.

General Conclusion

As we approach the conclusion of this journey from Chapter One to Chapter Eight, we have traveled through the power, the symbolism, and the sacredness of water and its deep connection with the divine. Water is not physical alone; it is the essence of life itself. It flows through all things, sustaining life, cleansing the soul, and linking us to eternity. In each chapter, we have seen how water, the matrix of life, sustains us spiritually, physically, and emotionally. It is in water that we find the power to remove obstacles and align ourselves with the greater cosmic order.

We have seen in the book how water is not just essential for our survival but also a channel of divine information. It ties us to the highest degrees of spiritual consciousness, and it is through water that we can gain ultimate victory. The Army of the Light that we are being called to join is a militant army that protects the purity of water so that water may remain a source of life and communion with the divine. By becoming members of the Army of the Light, we become guardians and spiritual warriors, dedicating ourselves to protecting that which sustains all of us.

The sacredness of water was a dominant theme in this book, and it was through learning to know this sacredness that we were introduced to the path of spiritual growth and enlightenment. Water is not merely a key to physical survival; it is a gateway to spiritual empowerment and alignment with the divine. The Army of the Light is a protector of water, against those forces which would pollute or exploit this sacred element. We have found that in protecting water, we are protecting life itself, and in doing this, we are aligning ourselves with divine will.

The importance of spiritual victory was also reaffirmed throughout the chapters. Victory is not just overcoming external challenges; it is aligning ourselves with a higher power and living in accordance with divine laws. Victory is knowing the immortality of life and entering into the current of divine power. When we drink from the Throne of God and live by the code of righteousness, we are not just undertaking a spiritual search; we are assuming our divine vocation as warriors of the Light.

As we learned, the victory achieved by the Army of the Light is not a victory of force but of purity, love, and divine guidance. The true strength of this army does not lie in physical might, but in the ability to protect and purify the very essence of life: water. In water, we learn that we are all linked and that our actions, however small, have a ripple effect on the world around us. The Army of the Light teaches us that triumph is actually won through the purification of the soul and the conservation of life itself.

In Chapter Six, we were taught about the duality of water—as matrix and prison. Water is the element that sustains us, but also binds us to the physical plane. It is from here that we learn the esoteric secrets of life. Water represents the beginning and the end, the Alpha and the Omega. It is both the source of life and the barrier that separates us from the divine. In recognizing this paradox, we can begin to recognize our own place in the grand scheme of the universe.

Water as a bridge between the earthly and the divine was witnessed in Chapter Seven, where we learned that it is through water that we can connect with the divine knowledge of the Creator. Water is the medium by which the word of God is transmitted, and it is through water that we receive the guidance, strength, and empowerment to overcome any challenge. Drinking from the Throne of God is a symbolic gesture that aligns us with this divine current, that we may access the wisdom and power to live in agreement with God's will.

In the final chapters, we learned that final victory is the spiritual alignment with the divine current that sustains all life. It is through the purification of water that we become attuned to this, and it is through the Army of the Light that we are called upon to protect this sacred element. By being in the moral code and following the example of the Army of the Light, we step into our own empowerment as spiritual warriors. We are told that our strength lies within, and it is through spiritual alignment that we are made strong enough to overcome every obstacle.

Our walk with this book is not simply a journey of spiritual consciousness; it's a call to action. We are not here to idly observe the world around us but to actively participate in the divine task of protecting water and preserving the sanctity of life. The Army of the Light is composed of individuals who are willing to stand up for what is right, to fight for the sanctity of life, and to align themselves with divine purpose. By their example, we are invited to take up the cause and become Light warriors in our own lives.

As we reflect upon the lessons learned, we realize that our relationship with water is not just physical but also spiritual. By acknowledging the divine essence of water, we acknowledge the purpose for our being. Water is the vessel through which life flows, and it is through water that we are aligned with the divine wisdom that guides us. The Army of the Light would instruct us that in protecting water, we are protecting the very essence of life itself.

In the final words of this book, we are called to action. To become members of the Army of the Light, we must drink from the Throne of God, align ourselves with divine principles, and dedicate ourselves to guarding water. It is in doing this that we step into our true power and become part of the divine flow that sustains all life. By dwelling in harmony with the code of righteousness, we can emerge triumphant, not just over external adversity, but over the inner conflicts that prevent us from reaching our highest potential.

To drink from the Throne of God is to accept the invitation to spiritual victory. It is to align ourselves with divine purpose and to live in resonance with the wisdom and power of the Creator. As we move forward, let us not forget the lessons of this book and attempt to live as warriors of the Light. By protecting water and living according to the code of righteousness, we can emerge victorious in the true sense and be one with the eternal flow of life that sustains all of us.

Ultimately, the journey we have undertaken in this book is a path of spiritual awakening and empowerment. It is a call to action, a reminder that we are all connected by the divine principle of water. To enlist in the Army of the Light, say these words to the water, "Dear father in Heaven, Almighty creator of all things, allow me into your army, please heal me, please strength me, please guide me. I ask, in the name of the Father and the Lamb, Amen". Now our inner strength is align with the divine current of the universe. Let us drink from the Throne of God, live the code of righteousness, and unite together to protect the innocence of life itself. Only then can we achieve complete victory and live in the eternal flow of divine purpose.

www.ingramcontent.com/pod-product-compliance
Lightning Source LLC
Chambersburg PA
CBHW061132120626
46546CB00005B/1742